The authors of *The Calgary Gardener* take a time-out in the garden of
Clarence R. "Clancy" Patton. Clockwise from bottom left: Margaret Brown,
Liesbeth Leatherbarrow, Barbara Nobert, Judith Doyle, Lesley Reynolds,
Barbara McKillop, Ken Girard, Judii Rempel, Ruth Staal,
and Marilyn Wood. Photo: John Buysschaert

To aspiring and enthusiastic gardeners
willing to join us in dispelling the myth that
gardening is difficult or impossible in Calgary.

The Calgary Gardener

The Essential Guide
to Gardening in Alberta's
Chinook Country

The Calgary Horticultural Society

Margaret Brown
Judith Doyle
Ken Girard
Liesbeth Leatherbarrow
Barbara McKillop
Barbara Nobert
Judii Rempel
Lesley Reynolds
Ruth Staal
Marilyn Wood

FIFTH
HOUSE
PUBLISHERS

Front cover image reproduced courtesy of Frank Scott
Line drawings courtesy Dan Nobert

Cover design by John Luckhurst and Sandra Hastie/GDL
Interior design by Sandra Hastie/GDL

The publisher gratefully acknowledges the support received from
Heritage Canada.

Printed and bound in Canada by Friesens, Altona, MB

06 07 08 / 12 11 10

Canadian Cataloguing in Publication Data

The Calgary gardener

   Includes index.
   ISBN 1–895618–67–3

1. Gardening – Alberta – Handbooks, manuals, etc.
2. Horticulture – Alberta – Handbooks, manuals, etc.
I. Calgary Horticultural Society

SB472.32.C3C3 1995 635'.097123 C95–920081–9

Fifth House Ltd.
1511 - 1800 4 Street SW
Calgary, AB
T2S 2S5

Contents

Charts

Foreword

It is an honour and great pleasure to be invited to write this short foreword for *The Calgary Gardener*. During the summer of 1968 and 1969, I was head gardener at Lake Louise where the climate was a far cry from the one in which I had been trained in the U.K. From February to April 1969, I worked for Pederson's Greenhouses in Calgary prior to returning to the mountains for the summer and I can well remember the intoxicating smell of spring when the cottonwoods awake and the hills around Calgary are magically dotted with prairie crocus. Little did I know at that time that twenty-seven years later I would have so many gardening friends in Calgary.

During my years of meeting gardeners all across the country, by far the keenest group I have ever come across has to be the Calgary Horticultural Society. Gardening is indeed a challenge for the majority of gardeners on much of this vast continent, but southern Alberta takes the cake when it comes to an inhospitable climate for gardening, what with Chinooks, winter dehydration, and a short growing season.

However, one of the amazing and unifying qualities that all gardeners have in common is the will—and the determination—to create a garden, no matter where they live. And, believe me, this book is a testament to that. Well written in a very easy-to-read style, it is packed from cover to cover with invaluable information recorded by people who have been home gardening in Calgary for many years. Their accumulated wisdom not only inspires you to start plants but also lets you know how to get those precious babies through the winter, when to plant, how to prepare the soil, and much, much more. In fact, if anyone moves to the area and tries to garden without first reading this invaluable book, it will be a grave mistake.

The Calgary Gardener is a culmination of much hard work and experience by Calgary gardeners who—when they started out—tried, tried, and tried again. They reveal their secrets to their success not only in the text but also in the excellent pictures, encouraging and enabling you to have a beautiful garden for years to come in this picturesque corner of Canada.

David Tarrant

Acknowledgements

This book would not have been possible without the written contributions, cooperation, and enthusiasm of the following CHS members; there were, of course, many others who offered their knowledge, support, and understanding, thereby turning the dream into reality.

Myrna Amey, Susanna Barlem, Devon Blean, James Borrow, Margaret Brown, Barbara Bruce, Audrey Burrows, John Burrows, Lynn Colborne, Rosalie Cooksley, Glenna Cross, Judith Doyle, Dwayne Eadie, Ken Girard, Don Heimbecker, Peter Holmes, Helen Jull, Fred Konkin, Liesbeth Leatherbarrow, Glenn McCullough, Jean McCullough, Arlene MacDonald, Barbara McKillop, Bill Metzlaff, Darren Morissette, Barbara Nobert, Dan Nobert, Nancy Osadchuk, Don Peterkin, Frances Purslow, Judii Rempel, Lesley Reynolds, Myrna Ross, Kath Smyth, Ruth Staal, George Tillisch, Elsa Tober, Brett Watson, Linda Wolfe, Marilyn Wood.

Our warmest thanks are also extended to our expert readers: Stewart Bryden (City of Calgary, Parks and Recreation), Geri Quin (University of Calgary), Duncan Himmelman (Olds College), and Dwayne Eadie (a keen, experienced local gardener). Their expertise and helpful comments greatly improved the technical quality of our manuscript.

Finally we would like to thank three people whose participation in our project was essential to its well-being: Jane McHughen (editor), Geri Rowlatt (copy editor), and Charlene Dobmeier (managing editor, Fifth House Publishers). Together they listened, explained, encouraged, and gave a unity to the diverse writing styles of ten gardeners while maintaining the integrity of our original contributions. Jane also created the index, an enormous and complex task that would have taken us another year to complete on our own.

Preface

Welcome Calgary gardeners! This book has been prepared by the Calgary Horticultural Society (CHS), a large and active organization with a history going back to 1907. The society has been associated with many outstanding gardeners, among them William Reader, Calgary's first long-term parks superintendent and the man who established Reader Garden along Macleod Trail. He was president of the CHS from 1917 to 1918. In the 1919 *City of Calgary Yearbook,* he noted that the Calgary Horticultural Society "had been the great factor in developing the 'City beautiful' ideas, by encouraging the beautification of home surroundings and cultivating gardens."

The accumulated knowledge of the CHS's current membership represents many years of experimentation and development. The society's members collectively know what works and why. That we have been successful is evident in the wide variety of different gardens that flourish in Calgary, everything from broad sweeps of perennial borders backed by glorious blue skies to the miniaturized world of alpines, with shady woodland and riotous annual gardens in between. Our success is also well documented in the coverage Calgary gardens and gardeners have received in national gardening magazines.

We are taking this opportunity to share our knowledge with new gardeners and newcomers to this area. Many good gardening books are available, but few address our special needs. Gardeners coming from apparently more hospitable climes need to know "it ain't necessarily so" here. These gardeners remember places where snow stayed all winter and perennials slumbered safely under a blanket of soft white, cosy and undisturbed by precocious false springs in

A view of Reader's Rock Garden and the gazebo — William Reader's "hut."

JOHN DOYLE

January. They remember springs progressing in a logical fashion to warm, hail-free summers that lasted until the end of September; summers with gentle breezes and balmy nights. Calgary is different. Winter Chinooks, cool summer nights, heavy, alkaline soil, and drying winds place limitations on the selection of plants, just as the absence of winter, or excessive rain, does elsewhere. Each specific climate dictates a particular rhythm and plan to gardening days. To make the best of what we have, we must amend what we can, live with what we can't, and be well enough informed to know the difference.

Having said that, you should also know that gardening in the Calgary area can be as successful and as rewarding as gardening anywhere else in Canada. The long hours of daylight make up, at least in part, for the relatively short growing season, and give us frequent opportunities to linger in the garden, either working or savouring its beauty, until late in the evening. Our cool nights encourage high levels of sugar production in plants, which result in dramatic, bright flower colours and extra-sweet vegetables. Lawns grown in a cool climate such as ours have a much finer texture and a more luxuriant feel than the coarse grasses that thrive in heat. In addition, mid-summer bloom burn-out, a common occurrence in climates warmer than ours, only makes its appearance here during the hottest of summers. Most years, plants grown in Calgary remain erect with fresh blossoms until the first frost and beyond.

This book, filled with photographs taken exclusively in Calgary gardens, is laid out so the reader can first explore garden planning, design, and themes, and then read about the plants that will make their dreams come true. The section explaining the skills required to successfully execute and maintain a garden is found at the end of the book.

As your own garden develops and becomes a source of beauty and enjoyment, you will no doubt be able to add to the list of reasons why gardening in Calgary is an experience not to be missed!

ONE

What's So Special About Calgary?

From the Ground Up

Nestled in the foothills of the Rocky Mountains, astride the confluence of the Bow and Elbow rivers, Calgary is a product of geography and climate. The mountains of sandstone, limestone, and shale to the west were formerly ocean floor. They were thrust upward 4000 m (13,000 ft) in amazing bends and folds as the North American Plate, drifting westward millions of years ago, was forced up over volcanic islands that became British Columbia. Erosion and glaciation wore down the mountains, and the gravel and debris were carried down to the plains by the Bow and the Elbow. Broadcast Hill and Nose Hill consist of this preglacial gravel. To the east, shallow seas, land-locked lakes, and ice came and went.

The soil of Alberta is a mixture of gravel moraines, occasional deposits of sand, and clay from rocks that have been ground down under the ponderous movement of the ice. Wind and water erosion, and layers of decomposed plant material, have altered its original composition, creating the alkaline, clay-based chernozem soil of the Calgary area. Clay is rich in nutrients and holds moisture well; however, its alkalinity binds up the nutrients, making them unavailable to plants, and its moisture-retaining property can result in poor drainage. Water-logged soil is low in oxygen, which the roots of plants absorb, and plants suffer from root rot in poorly drained soil.

The Bow and Elbow rivers are Calgary's principal water sources. As they pass over beds of shale and limestone on their long run from their headwaters in the mountains, they accumulate minerals in solution and arrive in Calgary with a raw pH level of up to 8.7. (pH is a measure of acidity, with very acid being defined by pH=1, very basic or alkaline defined by pH=14, and neutral defined by pH=7.) After treatment, pH levels in tap water run from 7.2 to 8.2, which is on the alkaline side. It is, therefore, no surprise that watering gardens with city water adds to the soil's alkalinity. Most plants prefer growing conditions that are slightly acidic with a pH range of 6.5 to 6.8.

Recognizing Our Varying Natural Calendar

The gardening year in the Calgary area is like no other in Canada. From the first, soft, warm breath of spring, through the long, warm, lazy days of summer, to the golden halo of fall and the deep-freeze temperatures of a prairie winter, gardeners are never certain from day to day what the weather will bring. Here the seasons do not always unfold as they should. We are just as likely to be teased by an April Chinook into believing summer has arrived early as we are to be taken by surprise by the occasional damaging frost in early June. The swirling snowflakes of a rare August snowstorm make our hearts skip a beat or two, while a second blooming of spring's primroses during glorious Indian summer gives unexpected delight.

Depending on which plant hardiness guide you consult, you will find the Calgary area described variously as Zone 2, 3, or 4. None is entirely accurate as the effects of elevation and Chinooks are not factored into hardiness zones. Calgary is 1000 m (3300 ft) above sea level in the lee of the mountains, cut off from the moderating influence of the Pacific Ocean. It is located in the north temperate region and experiences warm summers and cold winters. Winds are predominantly westerlies, with cold north winds bringing Arctic air south in the winter. Calgary's elevation contributes to its characteristic cool nights: air temperature drops with increased elevation; cooler air holds less moisture; and drier air loses heat more quickly.

Calgary's climate is most often described in terms of how it deviates from normal. Records going back to 1881 indicate rain and snow have fallen in each month of the year, with the latest recorded summer snowfall on June 6, 1951, when 25 cm (10 in.) fell. The average frost-free period extends from May 25 to September 15, for 112 days. The longest frost-free period occurred in 1950, from May 5 to October 5, for 154 days. The shortest was 1889, when the last frost occurred on June 25 and the earliest on August 5, for 42 frost-free days.

Weather variations within an area as small as urban Calgary can be marked. Swift-moving summer storms with damaging wind and hail can rush up the Bow Valley, devastating central or northern Calgary while the southern part of the city basks in sunshine. City records show that in August 1990 the east-central part of Calgary received only 35 mm (1.5 in.) of rain, while the northwest was being drenched by 145 mm (5.5 in.), a difference of 110 mm (4 in.).

The most well-known weather anomaly in the Calgary area is the Chinook. It is characterized by an arching band of cloud above the mountains that precedes a warm, dry wind rushing down to the plains. The name is attributed to an aboriginal word meaning "snow eater" and, indeed, the dramatic temperature changes seem literally to "eat the snow." A Chinook forms as an Alaskan low-pressure area draws warm, moist Pacific air over the mountains. Forced upward, the air rises and loses moisture. As the warm, dry air descends the eastern slopes, it gathers more heat and becomes even drier. At Pincher Creek in 1962, the temperature rose from -19° C to +3° C (0° F to 38° F) within an hour, a change of 22 Celsius (38 Fahrenheit) degrees. In January 1995, Lethbridge had a temperature increase of 11 Celsius (20 Fahrenheit) degrees in just five minutes. Chinooks are a mixed blessing for the Calgary gardener. Although they provide welcome relief from winter cold, they remove insulating snow cover, desiccate evergreens, and deplete surface moisture. Chinooks in late winter are especially damaging, causing premature budding of trees and the early emergence of spring bulbs and herbaceous perennials. Returning winter weather destroys the untimely growth and can kill the plants.

The unpredictable nature of our weather has stimulated the creativity and imagination of knowledgeable, dedicated gardeners for decades, resulting in a wealth of strategies and techniques to help us make the most of our unique gardening circumstances. Beginning gardeners, experienced gardeners newly arrived in the city, and long-time local gardeners who wish to make changes and improvements can all benefit from the accumulated wisdom of those who have gone before. We can take heart from the fact that our most beautiful gardens rank among the best in the country. Lush perennial borders, vibrant masses of annuals, bountiful vegetable plots, aromatic herb gardens, and tranquil lily pools are all ours for the making. How they turn out depends, in part, on how well attuned we are to the somewhat irregular rhythms of Calgary's gardening year and whether or not we set our task list accordingly.

Spring: On Again, Off Again

Spring, once it has arrived, is an exciting time for the Calgary gardener, full of joys and firsts. The first appearance of perennial green and of blossoms on spring-flowering bulbs, shrubs, and fruit trees gives great pleasure; the first harvest of tender asparagus or rhubarb is a much-anticipated occasion and one to be savoured; the first trip of the year to the local garden centre is an event to be reckoned with, as is the arrival of the first of many parcels from mail-order catalogues. There comes, too, the first day when we find ourselves up to our elbows in fresh garden soil planting the first seeds in the garden. Good-bye clean hands and finger nails—spring has truly arrived!

Spring is also the most difficult time of year for gardeners here. The urge to get out and do something in the garden is strong as the weather begins to warm up. The temptation is to rake the lawn, uncover the tender perennials to be sure they are really alive, fertilize something, and water everything! These are all jobs that need to be done eventually, but remember—this is Calgary.

ENDING THE GREAT COVER-UP

Spring here arrives in tantalizing little bits, punctuated by wet snow and cold winds. The extended Chinooks in January and February may feel like spring, but it is only a matter of time before winter regains its frosty hold. It is not unusual for temperatures to reach 20° C (68° F) on a January Chinook afternoon and, within a matter of hours, plummet to below freezing again as an Arctic front makes another furious dash across the southern prairie.

This continuous reversal between balmy and freezing weather can go on until as late as mid-May, with some of the largest snow accumulations of the year occurring in April and May. The unseasonably warm spells encourage many spring bulbs to make an appearance well ahead of schedule; crocuses near south- and east-facing walls in particular can emerge as early as January 10. Resist the urge to pull the mulch away from these plants. By all means, poke around and take a look, but put that mulch back! Then, keep the emerging bulbs mounded with snow to insulate them from the freezing temperatures that are sure to follow. Better still, be one step ahead of the game and stockpile snow in sheltered locations so it can be used to replace natural snow cover when it melts from exposed areas, or use snow fences to create drifts where they are needed. By remembering where your garden's hot spots are from year to year and keeping them mounded with snow during Chinooks, you will prolong the dormancy of spring bulbs and other perennials.

Remove mulch gradually from the perennials in your garden. Mulch keeps the soil temperature constant and prevents it from warming up too quickly in the spring, when a late frost could kill tender new shoots. A good rule of thumb is to leave all mulch in place until at least April 1; the more tender perennials should remain covered well into May. Pull back the mulch from the crowns of perennials as new growth appears, leaving last year's dead foliage in place a little longer to help protect the roots from warming up too quickly. Regular walka-bouts in the spring garden will reveal that the time for mulch removal varies from plant to plant and takes place over several weeks. Once pulled back from the plant crowns, leave leaf litter in place to decay into and nourish the soil, to conserve moisture, and to help control weeds. A thick layer of leaf litter also provides shelter for adult ladybugs during the winter and early spring—the longer we leave them covered, the better their chance for survival and the more effective the summer aphid patrol will be.

Some Calgary gardeners remove all mulch from the garden in early spring and replace it in the fall for winter protection only, preferring the look of a freshly cultivated garden during the summer. They should not be too hasty in their spring clean-up, though, as weather conditions can change at the tip of a hat. All must be prepared to replace mulch temporarily on bulbs and tender perennials if temperatures plunge dramatically, which is always a possibility in May and occasionally in early June. Of course, by May some plants are too tall for mulch to make a difference; they may suffer some damage during a cold snap but, given time, will recover.

PRUNING

In Calgary, with a few exceptions, major pruning of trees is done in the early spring, before leaves open, except for maple and birch. These two should be pruned mid-summer to avoid excessive loss of sap through the pruning wounds. Pruning wounds callus over (form a protective covering after a cut has been made) more quickly in the spring, when a plant is actively growing, than they do in the fall. It is true that large wounds in slow-growing trees or shrubs may take several years to callus, but early pruning gives them a head start on the process.

So, before the sap starts rising, turn your sights to shaping, thinning, and rejuvenating the trees and shrubs on your property.

Some shrubs tolerate pruning at any time of the growing season; for others, the timing is more specific. For example, most hedges can be pruned when growth is longer than desired and again periodically in the summer to maintain size and shape. Shrubs that flower on the previous year's growth (lilacs, Nanking cherry, and bridal wreath spirea, for example) should be pruned after they have finished flowering. Plants that flower on the current year's growth or in mid-summer (caraganas, mock orange, and most shrub roses) should be pruned in early spring. Evergreens can be pruned either in the spring before growth occurs, if the pruning task is a big one, or in active growth, when candles (soft new growth) are broken in half to thicken up the plant. Junipers grow throughout the summer so they can be pruned in early spring or mid-summer. Summer-flowering shrubs, including most roses, spirea, and potentillas, and woody vines, such as clematis and bittersweet, can all be pruned to remove winterkill and shape the plants once new growth has been established in the spring.

THE GREENING OF THE LAWN

The thought of a lush green lawn is a welcome one for gardeners weary of the white and grey of winter and the brown of early spring. The temptation is therefore great to start watering and fertilizing the lawn a bit too early in this unpredictable climate. Resist the temptation to be the first on the block to have your lawn up and growing again, but don't worry if your lawn is situated so that it starts growing early without any assistance on your part—grass is pretty tough and can survive adverse weather conditions. Also, make sure that no serious lawn-care tasks are started before the lawn is completely firm and dry. Tender new growth can be damaged by the tines of a rake if the ground is still soft and spongy, and a person's footsteps on soft ground compact the soil unnecessarily.

In early spring, as soon as the ground is firm, rake and aerate the lawn to improve air circulation and moisture penetration, two key ingredients to a healthy lawn. Then add a thin layer of well-rotted manure or compost to increase the activity of beneficial microbes in the soil and to encourage plant growth. Begin an appropriate regime of watering and fertilizing in early May and remember to take it easy—the more you fertilize, the more you have to mow! If you use fertilizer-herbicide combinations on the lawn, do not apply them until the weeds are up and growing since herbicides need to make contact with the leaves of the weeds to be effective.

A TIME TO BUY AND A TIME TO PLANT

Before heading out on that most joyous of pastimes, the first tantalizing visit of the year to the local garden centre, make a realistic assessment of your needs. Evaluate the perennial distribution in your garden, dividing and transplanting those summer- and fall-blooming perennials that need it and leaving the early-blooming ones to be handled later in the season. Then identify the corners of your garden that are suitable for the generous colours and staying power of annuals; those that are begging for a few more perennials; and those that are perfect for vegetables. As you make your wish list, don't forget to take into account plants you have ordered from catalogues during the winter.

It is wise to make that first visit to the garden centre early in the season to ensure the best selection of annual bedding plants, perennials, and vegetable transplants, especially of new varieties, which are often introduced in limited quantities. But remember, purchasing early does not necessarily mean planting early. Frosty nights are to be expected until the Victoria Day weekend and later, even after a six-week run of balmy nights in April and May. Wary gardeners wait until June 1 to set out most of the tender flowers and vegetables, and June 15 for the very tender ones, many of which would be blackened by even a touch of frost. If, however, you crave a splash of colour in the garden before that time, plant lavish displays of annuals in containers, set them out in the garden, and be prepared to whisk them in again if frost threatens. And, if you planted spring-flowering, hardy bulbs the previous fall, they will give you the earliest colour extravaganza of all.

In the meantime, help your new collection of bedding plants adjust to the cool Calgary air by setting them outside during the day and bringing them in at night until they are used to their new growing conditions and all threat of night frost has passed. This process of acclimatization is called *hardening-off* and takes place gradually over a couple of weeks.

Siberian squill, one of the earliest spring flowers, blooms in April. PHILIP BROWN

Gardeners can make good use of the month of May while waiting patiently for plants to harden off and frost to disappear from the night air. Flower beds can be prepared for planting by turning the soil and amending it with compost, well-rotted manure, leaf mould, and (or) chemical fertilizers. Many vegetable seeds can be planted directly into the ground several weeks before the last killing frosts. When the first week of June finally arrives and the risk of killing frost is over—well, almost—it is as safe as it will ever be to get those tender plants into the ground and growing. The sooner that job is completed, the better. Remember, Calgary summers are relatively short-lived so it is best not to linger.

PEST, DISEASE, AND WEED PATROL

Even though a well-maintained garden will have fewer pests than a neglected one, none is immune to these problems, and it is to a gardener's advantage to begin pest and disease control early in the season. Regular tours of inspection of flowers, vegetables, shrubs, and trees help greatly with identifying changes in plants that indicate the presence of insects or disease. If foliage has an unhealthy look (leaves curling, spotted, full of holes, discoloured), it is likely that insects are hard at work; if a plant shows a general decline in vigour, premature leaf fall,

- ❧ Gradually remove mulch from garden
- ❧ Prune most trees and shrubs (except maple and birch)
- ❧ Rake and aerate the lawn
- ❧ Establish a schedule for watering and fertilizing: first for the lawn, trees, and shrubs; later for the flower beds and the vegetable garden
- ❧ Visit garden centres and buy plants, tender bulbs, and seeds
- ❧ Plant many types of seed directly into the garden before the last frost
- ❧ Acclimatize bedding plants, perennials, and seedlings started indoors during the winter
- ❧ Prepare flower beds by turning the soil and amending it with compost, manure, or fertilizer
- ❧ Plant bedding plants, tender bulbs, seedlings, and seeds into prepared beds or containers
- ❧ Begin a regular pest, disease, and weed patrol

and its leaves are yellowing, mushy, or fuzzy, then you can reasonably suspect the presence of disease. Look for these changes and take the appropriate measures to remedy them.

Weeds are most easily pulled when they are young and tender. If you get rid of them early in the season, they will not mature and scatter seed, and you will avoid much bigger headaches down the road.

Summer: Long, Hot, and Few Days of Summer

As the cool, busy days of spring give way to the long, hot days of summer, Calgary gardeners begin to harvest and enjoy the fruits of their labour. Vegetables and fresh herbs abound for tempting the palate; small fruit-bearing bushes and vines offer their bounty to be transformed into delicious jams and jellies; bouquets of cut flowers grace tables and counters in homes everywhere.

Summer is also a time to enjoy simply being in our gardens. Curling up with a favourite book in a shady corner, hosting a garden party, capturing favourite garden vistas in photographs, or viewing the garden in a different light by staying up for a midnight stroll—these are all impulses that should be acted upon. In Calgary, summer seems to come and go in the blink of an eye. If rest and

Comfortable seating is essential for resting from gardening labours; newly planted beds of hostas and ferns thrive in the shade. KEN GIRARD

relaxation are always put aside in favour of doing "just one more thing," chances are that one day you will wake up and summer will be gone!

Finally, summer is the time for gardeners to ease into a maintenance mode as far as work is concerned. Carrying out a series of tasks on a regular basis ensures that a garden's beauty and productivity meet expectations.

WATERING

It is important to remember that Calgary is classified as a semi-desert, which means that a supplemental watering program is essential for the maintenance of most gardens here. The details of a watering schedule vary from year to year, depending on the weather, and from garden to garden, depending on the soil condition and the requirements of the plants that grow there. As annual precipitation and drought patterns are unpredictable, a gardener should continually assess the moisture content of the soil and water accordingly. On average, water lawns, vegetable gardens, and flower beds with 2.5–4.0 cm (1–1.5 in.) of water in a single application about once a week, adjusting the schedule in times of drought or above-average rainfall. Young seedlings or newly transplanted trees and shrubs may require additional watering until they become established; the dry areas immediately beneath the eaves of a house also require vigilant watering if plants are to grow there. Surprisingly, even in times of what is frequent rainfall for Calgary, the amount of water reaching the ground might still be inadequate. Place a small container in an exposed part of the garden to measure the actual amount of rain that has fallen to see if additional watering is necessary.

FERTILIZING

Schedules for fertilizing are not as weather-dependent as watering schedules; however, some modifications need to be made during periods of prolonged rain and cool temperatures, when a plant's rate of growth slows down and its food needs diminish proportionately. Generally speaking, good soil, enriched with compost and manure, requires little in the way of chemical fertilizers. Familiarize yourself with the different types available, both natural and synthetic, and the recommended rate and frequency of application for the plants in your garden. Then draw up a timetable that suits your growing conditions—the results will be worth it.

STAKING

On regular strolls through the garden, take note of annuals and perennials that grow very tall or produce very heavy flower heads. These require the addition of support (stakes) to show well and to survive the winds that blow frequently across the prairie landscape. To be completely effective, stakes and other types of supports should be in place before tall plant stems have been weakened by blowing winds or the weight of heavy blossoms. Newly transplanted trees can easily be blown over during wind storms and benefit from staking until their roots have had time to firmly anchor in the ground. It takes about a year for the root system of transplanted trees to become established.

DEADHEADING

On any given day in the summer, a tour of Calgary gardens will reveal many of their owners industriously snipping the dead flowers and their stems from annuals, perennials, and shrubs. This procedure is called deadheading and accomplishes one of two things, depending on the plant. Removing spent blossoms and seed pods from some plants (spring-flowering bulbs, such as tulips, hyacinths, and daffodils, and spring-flowering perennials, such as lilies, peonies, and iris) encourages energy and nutrients to be returned to the roots, bulbs, or rhizomes for better blooms the following year, rather than being used in seed production. Trimming dead blossoms from annuals and certain perennials results in the continuous production of flowers as they engage in their never-ending effort at self-perpetuation by creating seed.

SAVING SEEDS

As summer too quickly begins to make way for fall, the time for deadheading passes and the time for saving seeds arrives. Gardeners save seeds for a number of reasons: to economize, to share favourite plants with friends, to grow more of a plant that has worked well in the past, or to experiment with hybridization.

The timing for collecting seeds is critical and varies with individual species. Regular inspection of the garden will disclose physical changes in the developing seed pods as they take place. Generally, seeds are ready to be picked when seed pods break under applied pressure, rather than just bend. Once collected, seeds need to be cleaned, dried, labelled, and stored in a cool, dry place.

A word of caution: if you want the offspring to resemble the parent plants, collect seeds only from species plants. Species plants share distinctive features that breed true from generation to generation, as long as two distinct species are not in bloom in the garden at the same time. What you get from hybrids will be unpredictable and often undesirable. In particular, don't collect seeds from F1 hybrids (mostly of annuals or vegetables), which are usually so-labelled, as many of their offspring turn out nothing like the parent plants.

TAKING NOTES, PHOTOS, AND TIME TO ENJOY

As the weeks of summer fly by, the gardener has to be reminded to take time to enjoy the beauty of the garden and really look at the individual plants, the plant groupings, and the vistas as they change. These rest stops to "smell the roses" are the perfect time to take notes and photographs of the garden as it progresses from fresh spring bloom through summer's brilliance and fall's tawny finale. The gardening journal is a very personal possession. It can be as simple as a hard-covered exercise book or loose-leaf binder, or as elegant as one of the many beautiful volumes published especially for this purpose. In the end, however, it is the gardener's commitment to keeping notes that determines a journal's true value.

Journal entries can be made whenever necessary, but not necessarily every day; how they are made depends on what works for the individual gardener. One tried-and-true journal format consists of placing all dated observations on the right-hand pages: the state of the weather; last-frost and first-frost dates; plants currently in bud or bloom; the progress of new plants; tasks accomplished; mistakes and successes; wildlife observed; and dramatic events such as hail storms, heavy summer rains, and late blizzards. The left-hand pages are reserved for more general entries: lists of tasks to be carried out; ideas for making changes in the garden; plant collections; plants to look for; information clippings; and bits of philosophy.

A journal makes great reading in the winter months and is useful for jogging the memory when formulating plans for the next season. Information from the

Simple, elegant flowers come into their own under Alberta summer skies: golden Marguerites, pink and white lavatera, and Canterbury bells in the foreground. MAUREEN IRETON

- Maintain schedule for watering and fertilizing lawns, shrubs and trees, flower beds, vegetable plots, and container plantings
- Stake plants that grow very tall or produce very heavy heads
- Remove spent blossoms and seed pods (deadhead) from certain annuals and perennials to encourage blossom production
- Remove spent blossoms from spring-flowering bulbs and perennials to encourage strong root growth
- Collect and save seeds to plant yourself or to share with a friend
- Continue with your regular pest, disease, and weed patrol
- Buy hardy bulbs from garden centres or catalogues for planting in early fall
- Take photos, notes, and time to enjoy!

annual journal can be transferred to records such as bloom charts, inventory lists, and scale maps of garden borders, all of which are best stored in file folders along with catalogues, magazines, pamphlets, and photo or slide collections. Photographs, slides, videos, or even sketches taken regularly throughout the seasons are invaluable for planning and for the pure pleasure of viewing on some dark, wintry evening. One effective technique for recording information consists of photographing various sections of the garden from the same vantage points at weekly intervals. Take long shots of borders and garden vistas and close-ups of individual plants and blossoms. These can be examined together later when you are fine-tuning the succession of perennial bloom and colour combinations in the borders. Winter shots really show the bare bones of the garden and provide a framework for making new plans, and a video of the garden with commentary is a good reference when modifying the grand design at a later time.

One of the hardest things for a devoted gardener to do, but one of the most important, is to take time to enjoy the beauty that has been created and nurtured. Gardens should have several areas where a person can relax and observe the results of inspired labour. Furnish your favourite viewing points with benches or chairs; even a humble poplar log can make a comfortable stool to tuck away in a private corner. Ornate patio furniture is best sited close to the house; garden nooks call for natural materials such as wood, stone, or concrete parading as stone. Armed with a cushion and a book, perhaps even the most ardent gardener will be persuaded to sit and enjoy the surroundings, without guilt, at least until the next task comes to mind.

Fall: Dreaded First Frost and Glorious Indian Summer

The Indian summer that follows the first frosts and leaf fall usually allows plenty of time to gradually clean up and prepare the garden for winter's arrival. The low-angled sun, cool temperatures, and the pungent smell of fallen leaves urge gardeners to the closing activities of the season. They bend to the pleasant tasks of raking leaves and spreading mulch. The riches of the compost heap are dug into the garden. The lawn mower makes its last run over the still-green lawn, bags are stuffed with leaves and stockpiled, hoses are dragged around for those last crucial waterings, and tools are cleaned off for storage. More and more, the chipper-shredder, a new and useful tool, adds its din to the roar of the mower, converting leaves, stalks, vines, and twigs to piles of marvellous mulch.

ANTICIPATING NEXT SPRING

Masses of bulbs planted in the fall truly light up a garden come spring. For a brilliant display of colour, choose a variety of tulips, daffodils, and other smaller bulbs. Bulbs can be planted during the fall as long as the ground can be worked but mid- to late September is the best time, so they have a chance to develop a healthy root system. Daffodils, in particular, need to be planted while the soil is still warm—no later than September 15 is a good rule of thumb.

Catalogues are an excellent source for bulbs. Alternatively, purchase them from one of Calgary's fine garden shops, where boxes of bare bulbs, displayed with seductive photographs, entice a gardener with visions of what a spring garden really should look like. Charts with planting directions are usually found nearby. Be sure to plant all bulbs at least as deep as specified, since Calgary's Chinook warm spells can fool those planted too near the surface into early growth, leaving them vulnerable to potentially harsh winter conditions.

As gardeners plant their bulb collections and work the soil one last time before winter arrives, they should remember that September is not too late to split established spring- and early summer-flowering perennials and give them a new home. That gardening journal will come in handy for inspiration on how to enhance the overall design of the garden. Follow the rules for dividing and planting perennials in chapter nine, keep them watered until freeze-up, and they will emerge as well-established perennials when spring rolls around, to give enjoyment without delay.

CLEAN-UP AND COMPOSTING

The golden glory of fall can conjure up sentiments of both melancholy and relief for Calgary gardeners. The natural feeling of regret that yet another growing season has come to an end is often accompanied by a feeling that the well-deserved winter break from gardening is just around the corner, as soon as the last clean-up task has been checked off the list.

What to do with plants still languishing in pots, roses still blooming away, and tubs of geraniums looking far too saucy to be chopped off just yet needs to be balanced against when the first blizzards might blow. Snow with staying power can arrive in Calgary anywhere from the middle of October to the middle of December, making the decision on when to start cleaning up a tricky one. Just remember that it is better to finish the task early and be on the safe side than to be caught unawares by the vagaries of weather. A good clean-up is critical to the continued health of a garden, and there is very little one can do after the first snows fly.

To carry out a thorough fall clean-up, cut down annual and perennial flowers and large-flowered clematis vines as they fade or wither, leaving at least 10 cm (4 in.) of stalk to trap leaves and snow for winter protection. If plants have winter interest, they may be left until the spring, but the tops should be removed no later than mid-April to allow unhampered growth of emerging shoots. Discard in the garbage any diseased or mildewed plant tops, all peony foliage (to prevent botrytis), and any prolific seed heads (especially weeds). Cut up or shred healthy material for the compost heap or save intact for mulch in perennial beds and compost in the spring.

WINTER PROTECTION

Large fluctuations in temperature and lack of adequate snow coverage make it necessary to provide Calgary gardens with winter protection. Gardeners each follow their own particular strategies for getting prized plants through the winter. Low-growing and evergreen perennials are best covered just before freeze-up with spruce boughs or other prunings, low boxes, or burlap mulch blankets. Cover tender or borderline hardy plants with fine soil or peat moss and then with dry leaves; protect the mound from erosion with plant tops, wire cages, or large boxes.

Many types of mulches can be used to protect flower beds, but the two most readily available are compost from the composter and the annual harvest of autumn leaves. Scavenge all the leaves you can find. The back lane (or front street) garbage often yields dozens of bags of leaves all carefully gathered for the landfill. The greedy gardener may correctly identify this free source of mulch by checking for bags that rustle and are light in weight. Save them and add this valuable organic matter to your flower beds or compost heap. Shredded leaf mulch can be placed directly on the soil surface as it will not blow about.

Cut lawns a little shorter than usual and remove all leaves to help prevent disease. Leaves left on the lawn over winter can pack down and suffocate the grass below, leaving brown patches in the spring.

Continue to soak shrubs and trees on a weekly basis right up to freeze-up to protect roots from drying out during the protracted, windy, dry spells of winter. Perennial beds should also receive some watering, especially those near house walls and other dry areas.

FALL TASK LIST

- Plant hardy bulbs
- Remove annuals from beds and containers
- Cut back perennials
- Put all waste material (except diseased plants) in composter or use as mulch
- Mulch flower beds for winter protection
- Clean and put away garden tools
- Continue to soak shrubs, trees, and perennial beds until freeze-up

Put any new plants still in pots, borderline alpines, and other small perennials in the cold frame. Water them, then surround and cover them with dry leaves; lower the lid but do not close it tight until freeze-up or moisture may build up and rot the plants. If the cold frame is in a sunny location, cover it with light-coloured material to keep the contents cold. If you do not have a cold frame, sink potted plants up to their rims in the ground in a shaded area, then water and mulch them.

Cotoneaster in a flaming finale, with golden Pfitzer juniper. JUDITH DOYLE

Winter: A Time for Dreaming and Planning

Swirling snowflakes tumble to the ground and bitter winds howl around the corners of buildings as deep-freeze temperatures take our breath away and easily convince us to stay indoors. This is when there is no pastime more pleasant than remembering the garden as it was and anticipating what it will be in years to come. The most elaborate garden plans are born in the depth of winter. In front of a cosy fireplace, nothing seems impossible and every new, exciting idea can become a reality. As the desire for implementing the new grand garden design becomes more urgent with the passing of each winter month, gardeners can actually get a start at making dreams come true by reading books on gardening, joining a gardening group, subscribing to periodicals or magazines, and ordering from the wealth of garden catalogues available. With seeds in hand and grow-lights humming, it is easy to get a jump start on spring and initiate the magic of the growth cycle once again.

DEVELOPING A PLAN

The evolution of a garden is a continuous process that almost, but never quite, reaches a satisfactory conclusion. There is always one more plant to experiment with, one more technique to be tried before achieving the ultimate goal of all gardeners—perfection! Quiet winter evenings are a good time for reflecting on what has worked well in the past and what might benefit from change in the future. It is a good idea to regularly review and evaluate the permanent structures in the garden: the shape and location of flower beds; colour and bloom succession; and the effective use of foliage, light patterns, and microclimates. Journal notes and photographs jog the memory for what already grows in the garden, and reference books and the indispensable collection of mail-order catalogues are excellent sources for new ideas. A master plan of the garden is useful for recording existing details and for trying out modifications before actually implementing them.

When deciding on new plant varieties, be bold and willing to take risks. Sure, Calgary sits in Zone 3A, as it is marked on some maps, but consider adding a few plants that are more appropriate to Zones 4 or 5. With the right microclimate and a little bit of tender loving care during the winter months, these plants often survive and thrive, adding an exotic dimension to the prairie garden. Of course, plants that are hardy in Zones 1 and 2 should also flourish in Calgary gardens.

When midwinter dreams are finally committed to paper, the urge becomes great to start buying seeds and plants to make the dreams come true. What better way to start this process in the dead of winter than by mail-order catalogues.

CATALOGUES

The advantages of catalogue shopping include staying abreast of the latest in gardening fashions and locating sources for hard-to-find items. Some mail-order companies supply a wide variety of seeds and perennials; others are very specialized, preferring to sell a large number of species and varieties within a limited selection of genera. For example, lilies, iris, dahlias, peonies, herbs, roses, and grasses may all be ordered from specialty companies.

A good mail-order catalogue is not necessarily full of pictures; in fact, smaller plant companies are likely to include no pictures at all. What should be listed, though, are the botanical and common names of plants, and a detailed, written description of their particular qualities and needs, including flower colours and shape, blooming time, height, sun/shade and moisture requirements, and hardiness zones. Asking gardening friends to comment on their mail-order experiences is a good way to learn about reliable suppliers. If no firsthand information is available about a particular supplier, order in small quantities until the supplier's reliability has been established.

Some mail-order firms allow you to specify delivery dates for plants; others deliver according to their own schedules. Either way, you need to be ready to deal with orders when they arrive. Most companies offer a refund or credit for plants that arrive in poor shape as a result of packing or ship-

The brilliant bark of Siberian dogwood brightens winter gardens. DAVID MATTHEWS

ping difficulties. If this happens, make immediate inquiries because some companies refuse to make adjustments if too much time has passed. It is important to keep good records when ordering from mail-order companies, both to remind you what will be arriving and when, and to ensure you have the proper documentation should a dispute arise.

If a desired plant is not available through mail order, try joining a specialized garden society that promotes seed exchanges among its members. Lists of such organizations are available through the Calgary Horticultural Society office. In some cases, you may need to order a particularly elusive plant from outside the country. Permits are required for plants, plant parts, and other regulated materials ordered from all foreign countries, although they are usually not required for seeds. To get your permit, write to the Permit Office at Agriculture Canada in Ottawa (K1A 0A6). The permit issued will outline the restrictions and prohibitions that apply to the plant(s) on your wish list.

STARTING SEEDS

Growing plants from seed is not simply a matter of planting seeds in January and caring for them until early June when it is time to plant them in the garden. There is a loose timetable that must be followed so that seeds of different types all reach the right stage of development when it comes time to transplant them into the garden. Then, with an appropriate light source, adequate temperature and moisture control, sufficient nourishment, and a fair quotient of patience, flats of healthy seedlings will be yours, ready to be hardened-off in May and planted in early June.

WINTER TASK LIST

- Read gardening books and catalogues, subscribe to gardening magazines and periodicals, or join a gardening group or horticultural society
- Review garden plans and decide what changes you would like to make next year
- Order seeds, tender bulbs, and special plants from catalogues
- Start seeds under growlights
- Stockpile snow in protected areas to use to keep plants dormant during warm spells very early in spring

---

In closing, remember that with the end of each year we have a little more experience under our belts, making gardening easier, even more fun, and making us ever more competent to share our experiences with others.

T W O

A Garden Evolving:
Garden Planning

Just as we have favourite styles and colours in our clothes and home decorations, we can also begin to develop our own landscaping style. Some gardeners prefer warm reds, oranges, and yellows; others choose cooler blues, mauves, pinks, whites, and silvers. Some are not happy until every weed-free bed is cultivated and the lawns are perfectly manicured and sharply edged. The neighbours, on the other hand, love their more casual look with drifts of flowers spilling over their allotted beds and tiny groundcovers sprouting from the spaces between the paving stones. When you see a garden that really impresses you, stop to consider what you like about it. Is it perfectly colour-coordinated? Does it have a wide variety of interesting plants? Is it structured well for family uses? Knowing what you find most satisfying in other gardens will help you plan your own.

Before beginning to design, redesign, or renovate your garden, remember that with changing lifestyles, needs, and energy levels, a garden space may need to change over the years. In the earliest years, busy young home-owners often appreciate a garden that will be attractive and well behaved with little effort. When the family includes children and pets, a play area may need to be found with space for a sandbox and swing set or a tricycle track. A water garden is not safe with young children around, but an existing pond filled with river rocks and gravel to create an area of very shallow water provides endless enjoyment. If you want flower beds free from paw prints and excavations, or a perfect lawn, the family dog may be better off in an enclosed run. As time goes by, enthusiastic gardeners hope for more leisure to pursue their pastime. Beds can be enlarged and projects that need a little more upkeep, such as a rock garden or a water garden, can be undertaken. In later years, adjustments can be made to allow less active seniors or those with disabilities easier access to their plants.

Elements of Design

Your Style. A good way to determine what garden style you want initially (because your tastes may well change) is to visit the gardens of neighbours and gardening acquaintances, prize-winning gardens, and public gardens, and to browse through garden books. No doubt there will be many gardens that appear attractive, but soon you will discover that one or two styles really attract your attention, be they casual or formal, natural or more sophisticated.

Family Needs. Do you have children who want a play area or pets that roam free or are enclosed? Are there disabled or frail family members who may have special needs? How much privacy do you want from neighbours?

House Style. The garden should complement your home: for example, a formal garden for a formal house; a traditional English border for an older-style home; a Japanese garden for a very modern home with clean lines.

Viewpoints. Before mapping out a design, think about the point from which you (and your neighbours and visitors) will most often view your garden. Walk across the street to view your front garden. Look at the front, side, and back gardens from inside the house to see which parts are framed by windows. Determine if you need screens for privacy or to block an unsightly view.

Focal Points. Perhaps you want to draw the eye to a special feature. Could a long path lead to a statue or bench? Is there a wonderful view such as a church steeple or a beautiful tree? Incorporating a "borrowed view" into a garden design can make a lot look larger than it is.

Seasonal Preferences. Your garden should be most effective at the time of year that is most important to you. Are you interested in as long a season of colour as possible or in a big show of colour at a particular time of year? For example, summer vacationers may choose to grow flowers that bloom primarily in the spring and fall.

Level of Care. Think about how much time you want to spend in your garden. Then design a low-, medium-, or high-maintenance garden to suit the time you have available and your enthusiasm.

Structure. Incorporate natural features such as steep slopes, low swampy areas, or rocky outcroppings into your design. A terraced incline is the best way to maximize a sloping lot and is essentially a series of raised beds. Consider the trees, major shrubs, paths, decks, and other hard landscaping items that are already in place. These are the bones of the garden, and you will need to work with and around them.

Designing a garden may seem to be simply a case of plunking in some plants and you are done, but it is not that easy. Many factors have to be taken into consideration—from the form and texture of plants to the size and colour of the foliage and flowers—before you achieve the results you desire.

Form. Plants come in many different general shapes and each makes its own contribution to the garden. Plants can be tall and narrow (vertical), low and flat (horizontal), vase shaped, conical, or weeping. Although many books suggest putting tall plants at the back of the bed, middle heights in the middle, and short plants in the front, you will find that light, airy, spiky plants look better brought forward in the border, whereas equally tall but bushy ones overwhelm everything around them. Be aware, too, that plants may not reach their "normal" height in the short Calgary growing season—or may perhaps grow taller if situated in the shade.

Texture. Using different shapes and textures as a design element is an often-overlooked technique for creating interest in the garden. Plants may have glossy, leathery leaves; fine, ferny leaves; or a fuzzy, downy look. Texture also applies to the variety of blossom shapes. Try combining strap-shaped leaves (such as those found on iris) with rounded leaves (found on coral bells), daisylike flowers with bell-shaped blooms, and flower spikes with spherical blossoms. Too much of the same texture becomes monotonous; combining different textures in a bed gives a garden character.

Colour. Colour is one of the most challenging design elements for beginning gardeners. As a general rule, colour schemes can use predominately one colour (monochromatic); use three distinct colours, usually equidistant from each other on the colour wheel, such as red, yellow, and blue (triad); or use colours such as orange and blue, found opposite each other on the colour wheel (complementary). Simple guidelines for effective colour planning suggest using only two or three complementary or coordinating colours in any garden bed and choosing colours that you would use to decorate your home or select your wardrobe and that are appropriate against the exterior of your home. If you plant in drifts with odd numbers of all but the largest plants, repeated drifts of colour lead your eyes comfortably around the garden, avoiding a spotty look. If you want to grow a large variety of different species, try grouping them by colour. Up close you will be able to see the details of each plant; from a distance you will see a patch of blended colours. Remember, these are just guidelines—choose whatever appeals to you.

Balance. To make sure the garden looks as if it all belongs together naturally, choose plants, trees, and shrubs in proportion to the size of your house and property. If the garden and house are large, then large plants are in order; small houses should have plantings that complement—not overwhelm—them.

Harmony. All the elements of the design should complement each other. This is easier to achieve if you do not mix too many different styles or themes in the garden, especially in a small area.

Contrast. A well-chosen variety of shapes, colours, or scales creates interest, but too much contrast can lead to a hodgepodge look.

Transition. Use transition zones to link one area to another so that there is a natural flow from the front to back garden or from a rock garden to the perennial beds.

Repetition. Groupings of certain plants may be repeated to create continuity and tie certain parts of the garden together.

Accents. Use accents to liven up an area. These can be unusual plants, a colour that is not used elsewhere, or

A fence is ideal to display art works; a carved granite ball conveys simplicity and tranquillity. DUNCAN HIMMELMAN

physical structures such as fountains, pools, or statues. Use accents sparingly, though, as too many vying for attention will give a fussy feeling.

When choosing hard landscaping features, make sure that they are functional as well as complementary to your chosen style. In Calgary, large masonry structures need concrete footings with excavations below the frostline. A pleasing pathway is one that is wide enough for two people to stroll side by side—a minimum of 1 m (3 ft) if you have the space. Decks and patios should be sized generously. Allow at least 1 m (3 ft) for moving around patio furniture. To minimize your efforts when laying out a garden from scratch, lay pathways first to give yourself a good working surface for moving around wheelbarrows and other equipment. Then mark out the beds and seed or lay sod around them.

Getting It Down on Paper

To begin developing your garden design, make a scale drawing of your lot, marking in the house, sidewalks, driveway, deck, and all major trees, shrubs, plants, or other landscape features. Then, draw in the garden beds where they are or where you plan to put them. Remember that curved beds give a natural look; rectangular beds are more formal. Beds of generous proportions look better than skinny strips around the perimeter of your lot. Plan beds that are at least 1 m (3 ft) wide and preferably wider. Consider building some raised beds, which bring the added interest of formal bricks or more natural-looking rock or rough timbers to a sloping lot. Note the relative sunniness of each bed on the drawing and any special soil conditions, such as poor drainage or extra-dry soil.

When you are ready to choose plants for your garden beds, consider colour, height, texture, blooming month, and any special features. Depending on the effect you are looking for, you may want to plan for blooms in all parts of the season in each flower bed or for individual beds that will look their best in different seasons. Whatever the effect you wish to achieve, plan the beds with the bloom time of each plant in mind. After marking the permanent features of the garden on paper, develop a series of tissue paper overlays for each bloom season, noting the height and colour of the flowers. When deciding on the position of the plantings, remember to take into account the soil type of your garden and whether the beds are in sun or shade.

Since winter lasts a long time in Calgary, you may want to include garden features, such as evergreens and sculptures that are beautiful in the winter. Particularly functional, as well as attractive, are bird feeders. They bring a physical structure to your garden as well as the motion, sound, and colour of birds. The creative use of special features can make the difference between a good garden and a great one. Just make sure that the style of your garden accessories is in harmony with your design theme.

Designing your garden on paper first should keep errors to a minimum, but remember, if, after all your careful planning, a particular plant does not fit in the way you thought it would, you can always move it or trade with a gardening friend or at a plant exchange.

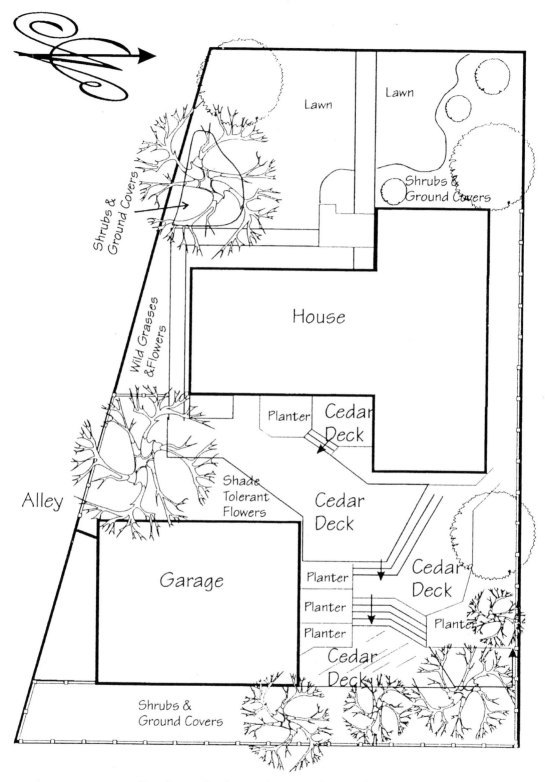

Lawn

Lawn

Shrubs &
Ground Covers

Shrubs &
Ground Covers

House

Planter

Cedar
Deck

Shade
Tolerant
Flowers

Cedar
Deck

Cedar
Deck

Alley

Garage

Planter

Planter

Planter

Cedar
Deck

Planter

Shrubs &
Ground Covers

Wild Grasses
&Flowers

Shrubs &
Ground Covers

Develop a plan by putting your dreams down on paper. DAN
NOBERT

If you are starting from scratch or planning major changes to what you have, remember most hard landscaping projects are covered by development rules of one sort or another. Hard landscaping refers to fences, pathways, patios, decks, planters, walls (decorative or retaining), pools, arbours, pergolas, and gazebos. Accessory buildings have drainage, height, use, size, setback, and yard restrictions. Fences and hedges are height restricted, especially on front corner lots where they may impede views of traffic and pedestrians. Retaining walls over a certain height will need a building permit. Driveways and garages have some restrictions on placement. Some pools and satellite dishes will require building permits and, if circumstances warrant, development permits. If soil stability on your property is an issue (especially pertinent for those who live on escarpments), then the City of Calgary's Engineering Department may require the preparation of a soil stability report. You should also be aware that there are by-laws covering boulevard plantings and your liability for damage to streets and curbs. Other by-laws regulate how the design affects neighbours. Check with City Hall for specific by-laws regarding land use, height restrictions, building codes, and other relevant regulations; also phone Alberta 1st Call, 1–800–242–3447, before you start to dig to avoid hitting underground electrical wires, gas lines, or sewers.

Special Plans for Special Areas

MAKING THE MOST OF FRONT GARDENS

Often, the largest gardening space available to the home-owner is in front of the house, yet the front garden usually repeats the lawns, trees and shrubs, foundation plantings, and small summer displays of flowers to be seen on every street. The home-owners spend almost no time here except when maintaining the grass. And, because there is no privacy, sitting, reading, or entertaining are out of the question. In the long winter, there is little to relieve the view of other houses, the street, traffic, and parked cars.

Why not plan a landscape that will give privacy, beauty, and seasonal interest yet still harmonize with neighbouring gardens? On a quiet street, a sunny front garden may be the best location for a patio or courtyard. An L-shaped house or one with a garage that juts out at the front is a good candidate for an outdoor room. Simply enclose the space left by a projection with a decorative fence, either solid or trellised, and furnish it with a floor of stone, brick, or concrete pavers, curtains of vines, tubs of colourful flowers, and comfortable seating. A small water feature, such as a bubbling fountain to mask street noise, would be a perfect final touch. On sloping lots, you can use a wooden deck and lattice screen to create this outside room. The back side of the enclosing fence or lattice becomes a ready backdrop for a border of shrubs and flowers. The remaining space can be planted to lawn and accented by a small ornamental tree, perhaps a 'Toba' hawthorn or 'Thunderchild' crabapple.

You can also screen street views with large flowing beds, thickly planted with a variety of shrubs, perennial flowers, and grasses. The beds can be formal in design or sweep down the boundaries and across the front of the lot in big curves. They should be at least 2–3 m (6–9 ft) deep and set back far enough from city sidewalks or curbs to leave the boulevard clear for engineering or survey work. In two to three years, the plantings will form a visual barrier, but not an unfriendly one, between the house and the public thoroughfare.

Plants should provide interest in the front garden through all four seasons. For winter, choose evergreens and trees and shrubs with colourful bark, dense twigs, and berries. Welcome spring with early-flowering bulbs, perennials, shrubs, and trees. Set off summer's brilliance with dense foliage, leaf texture, and scented flowers. In the fall, plan for a finale of colour with plants that turn red, gold, and russet, and flowers and grasses that bear late blooms or interesting seed pods.

Large mixed beds are no more labour intensive than lawns, less if the right plants are chosen. Plant shrubs first, spacing them widely enough to accommodate their mature size. Plant any large spaces between them with low-growing perennials that need no staking or special care, such as coral bells, Iceland poppies, liatris, bergenia, and ornamental grasses, and that are easily removed later. A selection of early spring bulbs and ground-hugging plants will soon cover all the bare ground. With room to grow to their natural size, the shrubs should need only some annual pruning to remove diseased or awkward branches; easy-care perennials need only deadheading and a fall clean-up. As the plants fill in and cover the ground, weeding time will be reduced—making sure that surrounding grass does not creep into the beds is half the battle here. Beds of wild-

Formal wood planters flank front steps: apple, juniper, pygmy caragana, dwarf blue spruce, iris, marigolds, petunias, pinks, and artemisia fill the beds.

flowers, native shrubs or trees, and plants adapted to harsh, dry conditions would be even easier to care for. Gardens facing north or northeast might be the place for a rock garden of alpine plants, if it is reached by the sun in summer.

Front gardens developed in interesting ways can offer private areas for family uses, screening of eyesores, and picturesque winter scenes. The bonus is a front garden that is a joy to stroll around in and a more visually appealing home.

(APPARENTLY) USELESS SIDE GARDENS

Most side gardens are long, narrow spaces that have to accommodate sidewalks and fences. Depending on the exposure, these awkward areas are either too shady, too windy, too cold, too hot, or too dry for good plant growth, and they are difficult to maintain. But with a little planning, they can be of practical use, or provide an edible feast, a shady retreat, or a blaze of colour.

For a walkway, landscape fabric covered with gravel or aggregate in different colours and sizes reduces weeding and maintenance. Large flat stones or pavers of different shapes and sizes sunk into the gravel provide access from front to back gardens and are clean to walk on. Fenced space can be used as a storage area for garden tools and supplies, outdoor furniture, children's toys, and firewood, or for a compost heap and cold frame.

If there is enough space to grow plants, there are many that can do well even in such dire conditions. Amend the soil by digging in peat moss, compost, and sand (coarse only) or vermiculite and then bury irrigation pipe or soaker hoses under the mulch to make watering easy. Keep the soil in steeply sloped side areas from washing away by covering it with landscape netting or by building a stepped series of retaining walls or terraced rocks. If the area is a wind tunnel, build a windbreak or plant large shrubs at one end of the space.

In dry, shady areas, gravel and ground-covering plants lend a stark, minimalist look to the landscape. A hot, sunny, dry area is perfect for a desertlike arrangement of rock, gravel, and driftwood, accented with succulent sedum and cactus, silver-leaved sage and lambs' ears, tough grasses, or native flowers such as purple coneflower, goldenrod, and yarrow. Goutweed, confined by sidewalks or deep barriers, is attractive and undemanding.

In cool, shady side gardens, try a lush planting of violets, hostas, and ferns; fragrant mints and lily-of-the-valley; or colourful astilbe, columbine, trollius, impatiens, or begonias. In full sun, rock gardens or cutting gardens of annual and everlasting flowers are possible. Spring gardens of selected early-blooming perennials and bulbs flourish before the weather becomes too hot and don't mind being dry for the rest of the season.

Vines are perfect for narrow, sunny spaces, softening hard surfaces with texture and colour, and cooling house walls in summer. Supported by trellises or netting, Virginia creeper, honeysuckle, bittersweet, hops, and clematis thrive if you give them adequate moisture and keep their roots cool and moist under deep mulches, paving stones, or piled rocks.

Why not try a shady salad garden for lettuce and spinach or a sunny kitchen garden for herbs and vegetables? A raised bed 1.2 m (4 ft) square can provide salad vegetables for a small family; two beds and successive plantings can meet much of the family's vegetable needs. In a small space, peas, beans, and cucumbers will happily grow on trellises.

A typical Calgary side garden used to be a barren path leading to the back garden. Now, protected from howling north winds by a sturdy lattice fence and furnished with trellises, it supports a thriving collection of clematis. The path is edged with mossy saxifrage, spring bulbs, lettuce, and chicory; aromatic creeping thyme grows between the flagstones. Once nothing but rather sad grass, it is now a bower of foliage and bloom, a place to linger.

COURTYARDS AND SMALL GARDENS

While gardening in a small space is a challenge, even a tiny area can be made both beautiful and useful. A small garden should be planned carefully to take advantage of the site: is there a view worth preserving or is a private enclosure more desirable? Very small gardens are most useful to families when they are designed as courtyards. Often already defined by house and garage walls, the addition of high solid fences gives a family privacy and a safe play area for small children and pets. Enclosed gardens can be welcome sun traps sheltered from cold breezes or shady, cool retreats from summer heat. If a room opens onto a small garden, the two spaces can be designed to complement each other with similar colours and styles.

Since most of the available ground in a small space is needed for walkways and sitting and play areas, easy-to-maintain, durable, and good-looking bricks, concrete pavers, flagstones, or wooden decking are preferable to grass. Less heavily used areas can be surfaced with shale or gravel and round stepping stones. Perimeter beds, best raised somewhat from the paved area with stones, bricks, or wood, can hold a variety of plants in a limited space. Containers make seasonal changes possible—forced bulbs set out in early May, followed by bedding annuals or vegetables, and later a (cut) Christmas tree.

Choose plants with care, avoiding those that will become too large for the space and those with bold or massive foliage. Don't plan to prune shrubs and trees to keep them small. Choose naturally small varieties or cultivars of the larger versions: dwarf Korean lilac (a compact tiny copy of the larger lilacs); dwarf 'Globe' spruce (a substitute for Colorado or white spruce); dwarf varieties of apple trees; compact cranberry instead of high-bush viburnum; and Amur maple rather than Manitoba maple. There may be only room for one tree. Small trees with a narrow upright habit or compact size are suitable— try columnar aspen, 'Sutherland' caragana, hawthorn, 'Schubert' chokecherry, and small crabapples. Selected shrubs and dwarf fruit trees can be trained to grow flat (espaliered) against a sunny wall. Vines take little space and cover walls with tall green foliage and colourful flowers without encroaching; Virginia creeper, scarlet honeysuckle, and clematis can be planted freely if trellises or wire are provided.

A colourful ceramic birdbath, on an iron pedestal, is surrounded by lilies and Iceland poppies. KEN GIRARD

Compact flowering plants that have a long season of bloom and need no staking or special care are best in the raised beds—coral bells, lambs' ears, Iceland and Welsh poppies, Carpathian bellflowers, 'Silver Mound' artemisia, and hostas, for example. Use trailing plants such as dwarf baby's breath, sedum, and saponaria to soften the appearance of stone or wood retaining walls, and tuck spring bulbs and summer annuals in between. A few fragrant flowers, such as pinks and lily-of-the-valley, and herbs with scented foliage add another dimension of pleasure. Consider augmenting flower beds with small shrubs such as dwarf mugho pine or the smaller spireas and potentillas. There may not be room for a bed of roses. If there can be only one rose, it must really deliver, so choose one with handsome foliage, perfume, and a long season of beautiful bloom.

With little space for storage and work areas, a double-duty bench/chest can hold tools, a compact plastic composter can be screened off by lattice in a far corner, and the hose rolled up on a reel. As children outgrow the need for play space and equipment, other features—a pool, fountain, or birdbath—can be introduced. An oak half-barrel will hold a water lily, a few water hyacinths, and some goldfish; a circulating pump and bubbler will provide the restful sound of running water. Other furnishings and ornaments should be in proportion to the space and harmonize with the overall style.

A wood-decked patio has a variety of innovative planted containers and an inviting, sunny seating area. JUDITH DOYLE

CONTAINER GARDENS

Planting in containers can create a beautiful environment in a very small space. Whether just a single pot or a collection, containers can brighten balconies, decks, and patios, and welcome family and visitors at the front door. You can choose a colour scheme for all the containers or each container can be different. A wealth of information and coloured pictures of hundreds of flowers are available in seed catalogues and nursery pamphlets. Even houseplants, if gradually accustomed to sunlight, can be pressed into service.

You can hang containers from eaves, hooks, or brackets on walls. You can fix them to railings or window-sills, or stand them on steps or decks (where they won't trip feet or bump heads). Placed near a trellis, they can be planted with annual vines such as scarlet runner bean, sweet pea, or canarybird vine to create

- **Bushy:** browallia, Dahlsberg daisy, geranium (*Pelargonium*—scented leaf, 'Martha Washington', zonal), gazania, godetia, heliotrope, impatiens, marigold (dwarf or single), nemesia, nierembergia, pansy, petunia, salpiglossis, Swan River daisy, verbena, viola, and many others
- **Foliage:** coleus, dusty miller, hen and chicks, catmint, ivy
- **Trailing:** amaranthus, begonia, canarybird vine, fuchsia, geranium (ivy-leaved and mini-trailer), Kenilworth ivy, lobelia, lotus vine (parrot's beak), nasturtium, catmint, petunia, portulaca, potato vine, sanvitalia (trailing zinnia), schizanthus, sweet alyssum, trailing verbena
- **Tall:** canarybird vine, cosmos, sweet peas, scarlet runner beans
- **Edible:** strawberries, salad greens, the smaller herbs, tomatoes

a useful windbreak. For flexible decorating, small containers are easily moved; they make more of an artistic impact when grouped.

There are containers made of plastic, clay, wood, metal, concrete, stone, wicker, or wire lined with sphagnum moss. You can also press into service wooden barrels, Chinese egg pots, milk cans, washtubs, pickle crocks, coal scuttles, buckets, old work boots, hayracks, or any other object that will hold a reasonable depth of soil. Just make sure they have drainage holes or at least a deep layer of clean, washed gravel in the bottom. Clean the containers each spring and fill them with new planting mix. Sterilized soil or soilless mixes are available at garden centres. You can reduce the amount of soil mix needed in huge planters by placing up-ended plastic pots in the bottom. A soil depth of 30 cm (12 in.) is best for root development and moisture retention.

Swan River daisies, petunias, and nasturtiums spill from a simple container to soften a grilled garage window. MAUREEN IRETON

Regular watering is important as containers, especially porous clay pots and hanging baskets, dry out quickly. The larger the container, the easier it is to keep the soil moist. Check plants daily and water whenever the soil is dry to the touch. In very hot weather, small containers may need watering twice a day. Use a fertilizer to encourage root growth, such as 10–52–10, when you first plant the containers and a soluble formula of 20–20–20 with micronutrients, diluted to half the strength recommended on the label, every week when the plants are growing rapidly or flowering.

Before you purchase plants for containers, consider their location: will they be in cool shade, partial shade, or hot sun all day? Plants have definite preferences. They should also be an appropriate size for the container or they will outgrow it. A mixture of upright, bushy, and trailing plants provides the most interesting display. Annual flowers and vegetables are best; few plants will survive over winter in a container unless it can be stored in a frost-free area.

ACREAGES OR LARGE CITY GARDENS

Generally, on an acreage, plants—especially trees—may be much larger than in the average city yard and are better planted in clusters rather than singly. There is room for trees such as Colorado spruce or laurel-leaf willow that would be completely out of scale in a city garden. Whereas the small-lot owner worries about plants taking over and crowding, the larger-lot owner needs to stand back and think about how to fill in the canvas in a harmonious and balanced way.

Large plants and groups of plants are part of the answer to the question of balance. Harmony may be achieved by repeating masses of flowers or clusters of shrubs. For instance, a specimen lilac can be introduced near the house, where its aroma can be enjoyed in early summer, and it can also be used as a ten-tree "forest" planting at other points in the yard. Harmony suggests that the lilacs should all be the same cultivar, yet the solitary one by the house can be a different colour to show a subtle contrast.

Another way to keep gardens on large lots unified yet diverse is to establish "rooms" that are separated visually by hedges, tree clusters, fences, trellises, benches, gates, or paths. In this case, you achieve harmony by ensuring that the visual separations you can see at any one time complement each other and that any view through to the next "room" is inviting.

The initial planting on a large lot or acreage is often a shelterbelt to modify wind patterns and create a microclimate suitable for future gardening and enjoyment. This shelterbelt may be a row of a single variety of trees, such as spruce or poplar (avoid alternating species in the same row), or it may be clusters of trees in specific places to protect part of the garden or to modify the temperature of the home. Large evergreens moderate winter temperatures and are especially useful on the north side of a home. Deciduous trees keep the house cooler in the summer but allow sun through them in the winter; they are particularly useful on the south or west side of a home. It takes many years before even fast-growing trees attain their intended size and function. The microclimate improves with time, gradually increasing the range of plants that it is possible to grow.

Raised beds have many advantages. They can be an attractive design feature, with the timber, brick, or stone chosen to complement the house. A more practical advantage is their potential to extend our short growing season, as raised beds absorb heat faster during the day and retain it longer. This quality can be accentuated by building the bed next to a heat-reflecting house wall. When filling raised beds, you can prepare the ideal soil mix for the intended plants. Raised beds can keep grass out and contain invasive plants that you might otherwise be reluctant to try. Beds, raised to an appropriate height, also make gardening easier for people who find it hard to bend or for those in wheelchairs.

Wood is the easiest material for the home landscaper to work with and it is also the least expensive. Old railroad ties have been treated with creosote so should be avoided in the vegetable garden. Even in a flower bed, creosote can inhibit growth for several years. Pressure-treated wood is also inadvisable in a vegetable bed. Cedar is more expensive but is safe and can be stained or allowed to weather to its natural soft grey. Less expensive fir or spruce should have a preservative or sealer applied.

Brick is a good choice for smaller, more formal beds, and retains heat well, making it popular for herb and vegetable beds, but it is more expensive than wood and expert help may be needed for construction. Rock lends itself well to a natural landscape and provides the opportunity to tuck plants into the tiny nooks and crannies, where they will spill over and soften the appearance of the wall. Rock can be your most expensive choice, but it can also be picked up at no charge from rock fall along the highways in Kananaskis. Permits and information can be obtained from the Elbow Ranger Station. Most people can manage the skills required for small dry-pack beds by following instructions from several available books. Larger beds and those requiring mortar may call for expert help. Consult a landscape architect for any beds whose walls exceed 1 m (3 ft) in height (a building permit is also required).

A lawn area close to the house does not have to be large even though the overall lot size is large. Consider creating "rooms" instead. Decide if there is a particular view you want to capture—an architectural feature in the community or simply a view of the sunset, perhaps—and use trees and shrubberies to frame this view. Shrubs, flowers, and trees around the seating area can make it a dining room, lounge, sunroom, or plant room. If necessary, use a large tree to create shade or privacy. Next, consider planning a special area that intrigues. This might be a quiet place with a bench, some special flowers, a birdbath, or perhaps a pond. How about a sundial, a statue, a wishing well, or even a large rock? If you have no existing trees or shrubs, this is the opportunity to plant lilacs, a fruit tree or two, and evergreens that look beautiful in winter covered with snow. A path could meander toward a group of trees, revealing a secret garden only to the one who walks it.

A large sloping garden allows bold features: a rocky stream, extensive use of sandstone, and pebble mulch, sparingly planted with juniper and daisies.

CALGARY HORTICULTURAL SOCIETY

One garden room could be a vegetable and herb garden. This room is best in an open, sunny area, preferably close to the kitchen. The vegetables could be planted in masses, be incorporated with flowering plants, or be tightly designed into a knot garden. Herb gardens, with their variations in texture and foliage colour, can be especially attractive. You might also welcome a cutting garden. As the flowers are being grown specifically to be cut, rows provide a practical arrangement for gathering them easily, a luxury not usually possible in a small flower garden. Because of the cutting, the garden will not always be attractive; however, it is most convenient within easy reach of the house. Some shrubbery or a trellis wall covered with sweet peas could hide it from view.

On an acreage, much of the land may be left in its natural state. Trees and shrubs may be thinned occasionally, transplanted, or complemented with additional plantings. Native trees, or hybrids of native trees, both thrive and look as if they belong. Hybrids of native wildflowers can be used to create a natural-looking addition to wilder areas. These same selections can be repeated in the flower and shrub borders closer to the house for a harmonious look. A little bit of tinkering will make it look like nature did a fine job of landscaping for you.

HYBRID TREES AND SHRUBS FROM NATIVE VARIETIES

- Dogwood *(Cornus* spp.)
- Lodgepole pine *(Pinus contorta latifolia)*
- Paper birch *(Betula papyifera)*
- Potentilla *(Potentilla* spp.)
- Saskatoon *(Amelanchier ainifolia)*
- Swedish columnar aspen *(Populus tremula* 'Erecta')
- Wild rose *(Rosa* spp.)
- Wolf willow *(Eleagnus commutata)*

Enhancing and Enticing

COLOUR

If you have been stopped in your tracks by the sight of an entire garden planted in hues of blue and white or mauve and pink, you have experienced the impact of a colour-scheme garden. People choose to garden in specific colours for various reasons. They may want to evoke a certain feeling, create a planned look, or simply blend with the colour of their home. Certain colours can also alter our perception of space: beds planted in pastel shades appear smaller than those planted in vibrant reds and oranges; blues and purples tend to recede, making a bed appear longer than it is. A garden of vigorous scarlets and yellows radiates heat and appears closer. Some gardeners prefer white, pink, mauve, blue, and pale yellow flowers and select these quieter, cooler colours because they create a peaceful mood. Others choose white and yellow for certain beds primarily for their brightness in the evening. A white and yellow garden glows in the light of a street lamp and a white bed appears ethereal in twilight.

Subtle contrasts are provided by dwarf blue spruce, red *Sedum spurium,* golden-leaved creeping Jenny, *Ajuga* 'Pink Beauty', blue-leaved and variegated sedums, purple oxalis, orange nemesia, and 'Silver Mound' artemisia. KEN GIRARD

When planning a colour scheme, take into account bark and foliage as well as blossoms. Plants with grey or silver foliage, such as lambs' ears, dusty miller, or 'Silver Mound' artemisia, enhance a white landscape just as the bark of a birch tree does. Although it is not important that spring blossoms blend well with autumn blooms, any plants that overlap in their flowering period should not clash; you can use white plants as a foil between colours that lack harmony. Use perennials as your framework and add annuals for accent. Don't forget to consider all the seasons, and fall colour too, which people often overlook.

WINTER INTEREST

In Calgary we really appreciate our mild Chinook days, but as our winters are so long, it makes sense to design gardens to be attractive from indoors. Try to choose trees and shrubs that have something to offer through at least three seasons. The cutleaf weeping birch, with its long delicate branches, is one of the prettiest trees on days when you wake up to hoar frost. Elms are Y-shaped and create fascinating twiggy shadow patterns on sunny winter days. Shrubs with busy branches and structures with decorative finials that hold the snow can also make wonderful patterns. Mugho pines, for example, support little ermined crowns after a fall of fresh snow.

Some trees and shrubs, such as red osier, Siberian dogwood, and 'Thunderchild' crabapple, have red bark that is very showy against a snowy background. Yellow-twig dogwood has bright yellow bark, and Amur chokecherry has shiny copper bark. The white bark of birch trees contrasts effectively with a backdrop of green spruce. Russian olive has black bark and keeps its silver leaves all winter for another stunning effect.

The brightly coloured fruit of some trees and shrubs, such as buffaloberry and mountain ash, is an added bonus in a winter garden. Some crabapples even retain their rosy red fruit into the winter. Many gardeners leave perennials with interesting seed heads to capture the snow. Perennial flax and ornamental grasses are particularly elegant and lambs' ears stays silvery throughout the winter. Dusty miller (an annual) can be left undisturbed until spring for the same effect.

Evergreens definitely add winter colour and a denseness that deciduous plants lack, but evergreens are not all green. The golden Pfitzer juniper has yellow tips, and the beautiful 'Prince of Wales' juniper is plum coloured. Many evergreen species are blue, blue green, or blue grey. These include Colorado blue spruce, several upright blue junipers such as 'Wichita Blue', and lower-growing blue varieties such as 'Blue Chip'.

When planning your winter garden, look out from the windows to see where a well-placed tree or shrub with spectacular winter interest would be a real treat. Winter colour and shape in the front garden will also be appreciated by neighbours and passers-by.

FRAGRANCE

Fragrance in the garden adds to our pleasure when we are outside or when we catch a scent on the breeze through an open window. For quite a long time, people who developed garden plants seemed to lose interest in fragrance, emphasizing colour, a longer bloom period, and other flowering features instead. Now interest in scent is increasing again and catalogues are noting whether a plant has a strong fragrance. The terms *fragrans* or *odoratus* in the botanical name indicate scented varieties. Some varieties of plants have more scent than others and are usually just as easy to grow.

In order to release its scent-bearing oils, a plant needs humidity, full sun and lots of heat, and no wind—conditions that do not always prevail in Calgary. In spite of this, it is still possible to have a wonderfully scented garden here. Fences, hedges, and buildings create microclimates protected from the wind or that trap the sun. Grow fragrant plants near sitting-out areas or patios, under windows so scent wafts into the house, and near doorways where foot traffic is concentrated. Choose plants with aromatic foliage to edge walkways, spill from rock walls, or fill cracks in pavement so that their scent is released when you brush past or tread on them. The aroma of one plant may go unnoticed but several plants grouped together create a wave of fragrance.

Watering the garden releases fragrance as the foliage is gently disturbed and the humidity then increases the intensity. An educated nose notices more. You can train yourself about scent and where to find it by taking time to smell the air, to sniff flowers, and to pinch and brush foliage in any season. Imagine the aroma of resinous spruce needles on a hot day, balsamic poplar buds in spring, sweet and sour Mayday blossoms, moist soil as it warms in the spring sunshine, rich compost as it is spread on the borders, dry soil just as it begins to rain, and dry, crisp leaves in the fall! Even in winter, sun-warmed evergreens offer subtle fragrance.

Many of the plants noted for fragrant foliage are herbs usually grown for culinary or cosmetic reasons. They can also be enjoyed just for their scented leaves:

Trees and Shrubs
- Crabapple *(Malus* spp.)
- Hawthorn *(Crataegus)*
- Honeysuckle *(Lonicera)*
- Juniper *(Juniperus* spp.)
- Lilac *(Syringa vulgaris* and French hybrids)
- Mock orange *(Philadelphus)*
- Roses, tender and shrub *(Rosa* spp.)
- Russian olive *(Elaeagnus angustifolia)*

Perennials
- Bee balm *(Monarda)*
- Catmint *(Nepeta)*
- Garden heliotrope *(Valeriana officinalis)*
- Iris *(Iris)*
- Lavender *(Lavandula)*
- Lilies *(Lilium)*
- Lily-of-the-valley *(Convallaria majalis)*
- Peony *(Paeonia)*
- Phlox *(Phlox)*
- Pinks *(Dianthus* spp.)

- Sweet rocket *(Hesperis matronalis)*
- Sweet woodruff *(Galium odoratum)*
- Violets *(Viola* spp.)

Annuals
- Heliotrope *(Heliotropium arborescens)*
- Nasturtium *(Tropaeolum majus)*
- Nicotiana, especially white varieties *(Nicotiana)*
- Evening (night) scented stock *(Matthiola longipetala)*
- Sweet alyssum *(Lobularia maritima)*
- Sweet peas *(Lathyrus odoratus)*
- Verbena *(Verbena hortensis)*

Herbs
- Basil *(Ocimum basilicum* spp.)
- Mints *(Mentha* spp.)
- Sage *(Salvia officinalis)*
- Summer savory *(Satureja hortensis)*
- Thyme *(Thymus)*

dill, sage, thyme, spicy basil (most commonly available as sweet basil), mint, and lemon balm—known as the tea herb because of its lemony mint flavour. The fragrance of sweet woodruff is most evident when it is dried, making it a useful addition to potpourri and a pleasant surprise in the winter garden when fragrance is least expected. Scented geraniums come in a huge array of fragrant foliage. Not winter hardy, they make lovely patio pot plants in summer and cheery house plants in winter.

BIRDS, BUTTERFLIES, AND BEES

The Calgary landscape contains elements of prairie, aspen parkland, and boreal forest, and has two rivers and several creeks running through it. The extent and diversity of natural areas provide excellent habitat for approximately fifty year-round resident species of birds. This number is quadrupled by migrants—birds who spend either winter or summer with us or who pass through in spring or fall.

Birds are attracted to areas that resemble their natural habitat. In summer, trees provide secure nesting sites; in winter, they serve as safe vantage points. The dense foliage of evergreens offers protection from predators and from winter's cold and wind, rain, and snow. Pine cones are packages of high-energy food rich in protein and oils. The bark of evergreen and deciduous trees shelters many insects in egg, larval, and adult stages, and attracts insect-eating woodpeckers, chickadees, and nuthatches. Seed-eating birds use tree bark as a pantry, stuffing seeds into cracks and crevices. Mountain ash, crabapple, Mayday, and Russian olive—chosen for their attractiveness in the landscape—have fruit or berries sought after by elegant waxwings. Many birds enjoy the fruit of the 'Schubert' chokecherry, and the Manitoba maple is attractive to pine and evening grosbeaks. Bushes and shrubs also provide food. Dogwoods attract birds, as do currants, gooseberries, saskatoons, and blueberries. Most of the tall viburnums or cranberries have showy fruit. The Nanking cherry offers fruit that is fit for both human and bird consumption. Even the ubiquitous cotoneaster entices birds with its blue berries.

Native species, although not always as tidy as other varieties, work well in a natural garden and add to its bird appeal. Try silver buffaloberry with its red berries, red osier dogwood, and wolf willow. The vines of native river grape and bittersweet both offer attractive foliage and fruit. Several native groundcovers provide food for animals and humans. Evergreen kinnikinnick's shiny green

leaves and red berries contrast colourfully with blue-berried junipers in the winter landscape. Strawberries are irresistible. Try growing small-fruited native strawberries or runnerless alpine strawberries. Don't forget ornamental grasses; their seed heads are decorative and provide winter food for seed-eating birds and ground feeders such as juncos and sparrows.

Composite flowers such as asters, daisies, coneflowers, and, of course, sunflowers attract finches, who eat the petals as well as the seeds.

Blue jays are easily attracted to backyard feeders. KATHLEEN ROMAN

Perennial plants can also be selected to attract elusive but endearing hummingbirds. Nectar-filled flowers, preferably but not exclusively red, may entice them to your yard, even in the city. Choose bee balm, honeysuckle vine, delphinium, or columbine. Increase your chances of attracting hummingbirds by adding supplemental hummingbird feeders. Use a sugar-water solution—never honey or red food colouring—and keep the feeders scrupulously clean. Change the solution every three days in hot, sunny weather to prevent potentially fatal fungal growth in the feeder.

Once you have offered shelter and food, look at how you can add water to your birdscape. Water in motion is as attractive to birds as it is to us. If fountains or waterfalls are not possible, use pools or birdbaths to provide water for drinking and bathing. Many birds are quite shy and flit among the branches, staying away from open lawn areas. By placing water where it can be viewed from a window, you will see birds that otherwise you would only hear. In winter, water is very important as birds risk hypothermia if they have to consume snow to obtain their drinks. If you use an immersion heater, available from local bird centres, you can offer water in even our coldest winter weather.

Winter feeding helps birds survive winter in a healthy condition. It does not make them dependent and they will continue to forage over a wide area. If you have been putting food out and then later fail to do so, the opportunistic birds will seek out new, more reliable feeders. Different seed mixtures, peanuts, corn, and suet attract a variety of feathered folk. Try sunflower seeds, both striped and black, thistle seed, niger or canola seeds. Waxwings are partial to currants and raisins. You can expect woodpeckers, redpolls, chickadees, nuthatches, grosbeaks, waxwings, blue jays, and sparrows. By making food available year-round, you may also encourage parent birds to bring their fledglings to your yard in summer.

There are precautions to be observed when feeding birds. Beware of cats. Locate nest boxes, feeders, and baths where birds can see in all directions. If windows on opposite sides of the house allow a clear view through or if windows reflect trees, birds will fly into the glass. You can make windows more visible with sun catchers or hawk shapes cut from paper. Do not offer food with added salt as birds cannot process salt. Limit the use of insecticides to prevent them from entering the food chain. Keep food and water containers clean to reduce the incidence of parasites and disease. If seed spillage is a concern, place feeders in an area that is easily weeded or over a patio or deck. If squirrels are a problem, try a large plant-pot draining tray suspended upside down over the feeder.

TREES AND SHRUBS TO ATTRACT BIRDS

Trees
- Crabapple *(Malus* spp.)
- Manitoba maple *(Acer negundo)*
- Mayday *(Prunus padus)*
- Mountain ash *(Sorbus* spp.)
- Russian olive *(Elaeagnus angustifolia)*
- Schubert chokecherry *(Prunus virginiana* 'Schubert')

Shrubs
- Bittersweet *(Celastrus)*
- Cotoneaster *(Cotoneaster* spp.)
- Cranberries *(Viburnum)*
- Currants and gooseberries *(Ribes)*
- Dogwoods *(Cornus)*
- Junipers *(Juniperus)*
- Kinnikinnick *(Arctostaphylos)*
- Nanking cherry *(Prunus tomentosa)*
- Silver buffaloberry *(Shepherdia argentea)*
- Wolf willow *(Elaeagnus commutata)*

FLOWERS THAT ATTRACT BUTTERFLIES

- Asters (*Aster* spp.)
- Bee balm (*Monarda* spp.)
- Columbines (*Aquilegia* spp.)
- Daisies (*Chrysanthemum* hybrids)
- Delphinium (*Delphinium* elatum)
- Goldenrod (*Solidago* spp.)
- Honeysuckle (*Lonicera* x 'Dropmore Scarlet')
- Milkweed (*Asclepias* spp.)
- Purple coneflower (*Echinacea* purpurea)
- Yellow clematis (*Clematis tangutica*)

More elusive than birds, but just as charming in the garden, are butterflies. You can attract them by providing the food required for the larval or adult stages. Caterpillars require specific host plants. A well-known example is the monarch caterpillar and the milkweed plant. Willows are host to larval viceroys, tiger swallowtail, and mourning cloaks. Butterflies require nectar and so favour flowers preferred by hummingbirds. Many hybridized plants have been developed for the size and colour of the flower, with double blossoms at the expense of fragrance and nectar production. Species plants are therefore more attractive to butterflies. Bee balm, columbines, daisies, delphiniums, and honeysuckle all attract their attention. You can offer overripe or cooked fruit on a plate. Butterflies are also attracted to water, drinking large amounts to extract the minerals they require.

Solitary, non-aggressive native bees are attracted to the same fragrant, nectar-rich flowers that appeal to butterflies. They provide a valuable service, pollinating flower and food plants. Unless you are allergic to bee stings, you should be happy to see them in your garden. With a variety of plants and some shelter in winter, you can assure yourself a constant supply of these industrious insects.

LOWER MAINTENANCE DESIGNS

For those who enjoy spending many hours working in the garden, it is impossible to think of it ever being "finished"; others are proud when the landscape is complete and all they have to do is to keep it neat and attractive.

Grass requires regular maintenance. If you feel you absolutely must have a lawn, you can reduce the amount of upkeep by using plastic lawn edging or brick, concrete, or wood mowing strips to eliminate a second trip around the yard for trimming. Well-laid-out underground sprinklers save a great deal of time and energy, and pop-up heads make mowing easier. Also remember that one large lawn is easier to keep than several small patches. Planting several trees in a large bed rather than in a series of individual small ones saves trimming and mowing. When these beds are covered with mulch or groundcovers, they require very little attention.

Another trick for decreasing the work load is to choose native plants. Many perennials are simply cultivars of native wildflowers and need next to no pampering. Planted in appropriate places, similar to their natural habitat, they will provide you with reliable foliage and blooms each year. The same is true of native trees and shrubs. Saskatoons and dogwoods will do just fine in your yard; cedars and azaleas are native to areas far different from ours and need much more pampering if they are to survive.

Save on maintenance by grouping together plants that have similar requirements. If you enjoy bright flowers, have a single bed of annuals or several tubs close together so you can water them all at once.

Vegetables are never really low maintenance, but planting them in raised beds saves a lot of work. Weeds are easy to pull out because the soil is never hard packed from heavy footsteps.

Mulches can play an important role in low-maintenance gardening. By the time a weed has struggled up through mulch, it is weak and straggly and easily removed by hand. Fewer weeds, less water, less work. Mulches also mean the soil retains moisture longer, reducing the frequency and cost of watering. Leaves, grass clippings, pine cones, or bark chips can all be used as mulch. The popular rock mulches break down over time, turning into a fine shale powder that accumulates wind-blown dirt and seeds. (For more information about mulching, refer to chapter nine.)

Another way to reduce the amount of weeding in your flower beds is to use a pre-emergent weedkiller. (Ask at a garden centre for a brand name.) These chemicals prevent weed seeds from germinating for up to four months. They do not kill weeds, but once a bed is clear of weeds, this chemical will keep it clear for most of the summer. Read the instructions carefully and allow about two weeks after transplanting plants before you sprinkle it on the soil. You can use it with most plants except the pansy and violet family. You may win the war against chickweed! Again refer to chapter nine for more about weeds.

CHILDREN AND GARDENS

Children's interests and activities can easily be incorporated into a garden design. A pathway in the shape of a racetrack is fun for tricycling and for running games and keeps youngsters separated from fragile plants. Swing sets and tree houses can be located in a slightly secluded spot—children love hidden, secret spaces. A sand or soil pit will provide several years of amusement, but remember it needs a cover to keep cats out. When the little ones have outgrown excavating activities, the pit might become an ornamental bed or a pool, or be returned to lawn.

It would be wonderful to share the pleasure of the garden with children, but how do we get them interested and give them an awareness of nature and the environment too? The high energy and intense curiosity of a three year old who is bursting to "help" can be constructively harnessed. Kids love to dig in dirt and play in mud, so there is a positive interest from the start. (Waiting till the teenage years and then nagging a youngster to mow the lawn is not likely to develop a lifelong passion for growing things.)

Help children create their very own garden but keep it to scale. A circle or square with a path around it clearly shows this space is theirs. How far in from the path can the child reach? The absolute maximum size for their patch should be 1 m (3 ft) across. Let the budding gardeners plan the design they want, although you can make suggestions that you feel you can live with. A checkerboard of nine 30-cm (12-in.) squares? Three concentric circles slightly raised toward the centre? Initials spelled out in flowers surrounded by lettuce? A half-barrel works well for a child's garden as it is easy for them to water and weed. Try to locate their garden where it is visible from the kitchen or a bedroom window to extend their awareness of what is happening as the seasons change.

They will need help with the first digging, but then let them throw in handfuls of peat moss or child-sized shovelfuls of compost. They will learn about nourishing plants and good worms that aerate the soil. Early on, keep work sessions short, less than fifteen minutes, so they wish you had more time together rather than see gardening as a chore. Use fail-safe seeds: nasturtiums, bachelor's buttons, poppies, peas, radishes, carrots, lettuce. Also, try something they love—cherry tomatoes, perhaps. Encourage young gardeners to mix flowers and vegetables together. Plant seeds directly in the prepared bed, but also start some in clear plastic containers, like the ones store-bought muffins come in. With the top closed, it forms a mini greenhouse and, best of all, they can see the roots growing as well as the leaves on top. Indoors or out, teach children about watering, but not drowning, seeds. Gently waving back and forth a fine spray from a hand-held nozzle is very satisfying to children. And remember the final ingredient in this recipe: lots of praise for the novices. Tell them what they did right and don't dwell on errors. If there is a year or two of imperfections in the garden, so what! In decades to come, you may have cultivated a fellow gardener and a friend.

LESS ACTIVE GARDENERS

Sometimes something as simple as a new spade or fork can make digging in the dirt pleasurable again. The portable garden seat that can be inverted to kneel on is an improvement on knee pads for bony knees. It has handles to use as leverage when standing up. There is also a wheeled seat with room for tools and rubbish. A child's wagon with fat tires could be put to the same use. Tool handles come with soft grips, and some gardening gloves have palms coated with a plastic surface that discourages slipping. Look for stores specializing in garden equipment specifically adapted for convenient use by seniors or for people with disabilities.

For those who are not able to bend easily, consider raising the garden. With some imagination, a wonderful garden can be grown in raised beds. Planters or baskets can be hung at a workable height from balcony or deck railings, or placed on a sturdy table or bench. Soaker hoses can remain in one area, perhaps with a Y-connector from another hose, to make it easier to water a bed without having to move a hose each time. By remaining at work level, we avoid bending over from the waist, something we shouldn't do. Shorter-handled tools are easier to manage at this level. There are smaller-scaled spades and forks on the market,

OUTDOOR LIGHTING

Although our evenings are often too cool for a romantic stroll through art-fully lit pathways, we do have warm evenings in mid-summer—sometimes. Outdoor lights can highlight individual plants, gently enhance a dark corner, add sparkle to a pool, or create fascinating shadows. As seen from the house in winter, garden lighting can cause trees and shrubs to cast dramatic shadows on the snow. Remember to use low-wattage CSA approved outdoor lighting systems only. A gas fire pit (legal in Calgary) can extend the number of evenings that you can enjoy your garden in comfort.

but good quality children's tools—which are also lighter—might be just what you need. You can also remove a few centimetres (inches) from the handles of your favourite tools to modify them.

Whatever your age or energy level, consider getting occasional help with the heavy stuff. Having a reputable landscape maintenance company come twice a year to deal with the spring and fall clean-up may make all the difference. Getting help from an experienced tree pruner once in a while or hiring a student to cut the lawn during the growing season may be ideas worth their weight in gold, leaving you free to indulge yourself in the fun stuff.

You can also modify the garden to make it more accessible to those with limited vision or mobility. Low-wattage lights make walking safer at night. Strong handrails and broad steps are easier to manage than steep narrow ones with no support. Wheelchairs and walkers need wide, firm, level paths. A bench or two placed in the garden provide welcome resting places to smell the flowers, enjoy the sound of water in a pool or fountain, or watch birds—a garden is not just a visual sensation, and sounds and scents can be very appealing to those with limited vision. For those with very limited mobility, consider a gazing globe, a mirrored ball about 30 cm (12 in.) in diameter. Placed strategically, it can bring a large portion of the garden into view from one position. Be creative in modifying your garden and don't decide that a particular activity is impossible until you give it more thought. Gardens should be a lifelong source of delight and relaxation.

THREE

What Do You Want Your Garden to Look Like? Themes and Features

All interesting gardens are based on a theme. Any theme can be chosen, such as Japanese or English cottage, certain types of plants, a restricted colour palette, or selected textures or shapes. Features that build on the chosen theme add drama to the garden, in the form of water gardens, rock gardens, and herbaceous borders, and include decorative accents such as statuary and other art, furniture, fences, decks, and other structures.

To help you decide upon a particular theme, read books on garden design and see other gardens for inspiration. It is best and easiest to design a look compatible with what is already there. If there are large trees on or around the lot, a woodland theme with a majority of shade-loving plants would be an obvious choice. On open prairie, a xerophytic (dry) or meadow theme would be appropriate, or perhaps a feature rock or alpine garden.

Gardeners all have their own sense of style. The gardener's own ideas added to the overall design are what make a good garden a great garden. Personal touches must complement the overall theme, and when mixing themes, such as woodland and English country gardens, a common thread should be kept through both areas whether it be types of plant, colours, shapes, or textures.

Themes

COTTAGE GARDENS

The vine-covered cottage, crazy paving, lattice fences, bowers of flowering shrubs, window boxes brimming with bright colour, geranium tubs on doorsteps, and old-fashioned fragrant flowers—these are the essence of a romantic cottage garden. If you choose plants wisely and create shelter, the style is practical for most gardens—even in Calgary.

Traditionally, cottage gardens are enclosed, and enclosure provides the shelter that makes this style possible in a dry, windy climate. Tall wooden fences serve just as well as more traditional stone or brick walls. Fences can be natural or stained cedar, or painted pickets or boards, with interesting details such as post caps or finials or lattice insertions. Solid fences not only create shelter, they also readily support a profusion of flowering vines and form a sturdy backdrop for deep borders of shrubs and flowers. Structures such as rustic or trellised archways, arbours, and pergolas add charm to the garden. Tie hardy shrub roses to them instead of the more tender climbers that are beyond our climatic reach. When combined with low hedges or informal screens of shrubbery, these structures also serve to separate a large space into more cottagey "rooms."

Cottage gardens sometimes consist of nothing but flower beds; the only grass may be just a small patch, perhaps with a sundial or birdbath in the centre. To get around in a garden of deep planted beds, you need many pathways made from natural-looking materials such as stone, either cut blocks or crazy (broken) paving; brick, perhaps laid in a herringbone pattern; small concrete pavers; unpainted wooden boardwalks; or gravel, nice and crunchy underfoot. At intervals along these paths, perhaps under shady arbours, simply styled chairs or benches provide resting places with views of the garden.

Plant generously to fill the enclosed spaces, paying attention to variety of height, shape, texture, colour of leaf and flower, scent, and succession of bloom from early spring to late fall. Trees should be small—low-headed, narrow, or very open in habit so as not to cast too much shade on the flower beds. Japanese tree lilac, ginnala maple, crabapple, hawthorn, and mountain ash are some desirable choices to supply beautiful leaves, flowers, fruit, fall colour, and winter interest. Flowering shrubs can include varieties of lilac and spirea, pink-flowered plum and cherry, potentilla, hydrangea, and hardy Canadian roses that flower all summer. Clematis vines can climb tall chimneys or frame doorways, along with scarlet honeysuckle, with its myriad flaming trumpets, and Virginia creeper, unsurpassed for fall colour.

Flowers of all sorts fill deep borders and island beds, among them lush peonies and stately lilies; old-fashioned cornflowers and daisies of all kinds; tiny clove pinks and tall single hollyhocks; fragrant phlox and sweet William; summery poppies and early primroses. Combine them with early-blooming tulips, daffodils, and other bulbs in generous quantities. Display annual flowers in window boxes, hanging baskets, tubs, and pots of all kinds, the quainter the better. Choose nasturtium, pansy, geranium, marigold, lobelia, larkspur, love-in-a-mist, and many others for a crescendo of summer colour. Use a sunny wall to support ranks of morning glories, sweet peas, or even scarlet runner beans.

In a cottage garden, flowering plants should be massed in exuberant profusion and allowed to take centre stage. To ensure the sunny conditions that most of them need, trees and large shrubs are best kept to a small selection and used in the background, where they also serve to enclose and shelter.

DRY, SUNNY GARDENS

Often the gardener has to deal with an exposed, perhaps sloping site, usually in the open front garden where it is difficult to keep flower beds or lawn sufficiently moist during hot, dry periods. Other dry sites can be found along east-, south-, and west-facing walls and fences, and especially under eaves. It is possible to both cope with these conditions and have a stunning garden with minimal maintenance. The dry garden style can also be developed in any area that receives many hours of sunshine daily, and in raised beds or rock gardens.

The best strategy is to choose plants that are adapted to sharply drained soil, hot sunshine, and dry, buffeting winds. If they are provided from the beginning with soil suitably amended with plenty of decayed vegetable matter (compost, leaf mould, or peat moss)—and lightened with vermiculite or coarse sand if it is heavy clay—the plants will develop deep roots and thrive whatever the weather.

A path of slate, "crazy-paving" sets off forget-me-nots, blue *Salvia* x *superba,* obedient plant, sweet peas, and 'Summer Pastels' yarrow. KEN GIRARD

As plants suitable for hot, sunny areas are light feeders, all they require is the occasional top-dressing of organic mulch.

Plants that cope with dry heat are often grey, silver, or bluish in colour. Many have hairy, felted, or thorny stems and leaves, or succulent foliage, features that contribute texture and colour. Plants can be chosen for a succession of bloom from early spring to late fall, in a variety of shapes and sizes, with a few small woody ornamentals to provide interest in winter. Suitable small shrubs include potentilla, pygmy varieties of caragana and mugho pine, the hardier junipers, and sagebrush. The larger varieties of caragana and lilac, and silver-leaved sea buckthorn and Russian olive tolerate drought.

For an early display of flowers, there are perennials such as pasqueflower, aubrieta, euphorbia, and dwarf iris. They are followed by summer bloomers such as gaillardia, scabiosa, yarrow, and cranesbill. Many aromatic plants, such as catmint, pinks, thyme, and lavender, revel in hot spots, as do silvery lambs' ears, artemisia, and snow-in-summer. Some hug the ground to prosper—rock rose, creeping baby's

A water-wise planting of ornamental grass (blue fescue), yellow sedum, potentilla, and 'Silver Mound' artemisia is mulched with pebbles to reflect the sun's heat and conserve moisture. KEN GIRARD

breath, and hen and chicks; but even tall plants are possible—mullein, globe thistle, and eryngium. Several species of ornamental grasses are hardy and withstand dry conditions. These can be planted in bold groups in place of a lawn. Many bulbs supply early flowers and don't mind being baked for the rest of the season. Then there are the many annual flowers from desert areas or the tropics that love summer heat and need only occasional water—California poppy, portulaca, and all the African daisies, for example.

As many drought-tolerant plants form attractive mounded cushions or dramatic spiky shapes, they are best widely spaced in groups. For a minimal natural style, try reducing the number of plantings to achieve a desertlike effect. Shrubs such as buffaloberry, wolf willow, or potentilla can be used to anchor the garden. Prickly pear, barrel cactus, and spiky yucca revel in dry conditions. The ground between them can be mulched with gravel or pebbles to create dry stream beds accented with boulders, stepping stones, or driftwood; or it can be planted with such mat-forming plants as thyme, pussytoes, sedum, and creeping forms of veronica.

If the site is flat or badly drained, plants may drown or be lost to rot in prolonged spells of heavy rain or during spring thaws. Raising flower beds above the grade with low stone walls or wooden landscape ties ensures good drainage.

SHADE GARDENS

If a garden already has mature trees or neighbouring gardens cast shade, a shade garden may be the answer. While shaded gardens in Calgary tend to suffer from

The term *xeriscape,* from the Greek word *xeros,* meaning dry, first came into use in 1971 in Denver, Colorado, during studies on water shortages and sky-rocketing water bills. The Xeriscape Code has two goals: radical water conservation and preservation of beauty in the landscape. Calgarians can cut down on water use in the garden by adopting some or all of the seven principles of xeriscaping.

1. **Refine the design.** Design plantings in zones according to water needs: full, moderate, and low or no irrigation. Choose for each zone the most logical part of the lot (exposed sunny slopes for dry beds, shady low spots for bogs, and so on). Do not mix plants with varying water needs in the same zone and, if you are using an overhead sprinkler method, avoid locating the highest water use zones immediately next to the lowest. Consider the convenience of high water zones to the water source.

2. **Limit turf areas.** Grass lawns are the greatest water users in the garden. Determine just how much lawn is actually needed. Alternatives to largely unused front lawns are rock gardens, shrubberies, and natural meadow gardens.

3. **Select low-water-usage plants.** Many native and naturalized plants have high drought tolerance: shrubs such as potentilla, pygmy caragana, mugho pine, sea buckthorn, and some junipers; trees such as Russian olive, tree lilac, and pine; perennials such as succulents, grey or silver-leaved plants, rock garden plants, and spring bulbs; and many annual flowers.

4. **Irrigate efficiently.** Drip or trickle irrigation is best. Up to 50 percent of overhead-sprinkled water is lost to evaporation on a hot, dry day; watering on a windy day wastes even more. Overhead sprinkling is best done very early in the morning before the wind and temperature rise. Water only when necessary, and then deeply to encourage strong, downward root growth. Water only those zones that actually need it.

5. **Use mulch.** A deep mulch (5–8 cm/2–3 in.) keeps soil moist and reduces evaporation. Use wood chips, semi-composted material, sawdust, bark, grass clippings, or even fine gravel.

6. **Amend the soil.** Work in plenty of organic matter such as compost, leaf mould, and peat moss to improve drainage—whether the soil drains too quickly (sandy or stony) or too slowly (heavy clay loams)—so plants can make full use of available water.

7. **Appropriate and timely maintenance.** Remove weeds regularly to reduce competition for available water. Maintain and renew organic mulches at optimum depths. Keep irrigation systems and timers in good working order so that they do not waste water.

excessively dry soil due to competition from tree roots for available water, it is possible to develop a beautiful, lush garden with interest for all seasons. Shaded areas offer ideal conditions for a bountiful array of interesting plants.

To determine what plants to grow, analyze the degree and amount of shade, soil moisture levels, and the type of soil found in your garden. Light or partial shade areas enjoy a few hours of sun, usually in the morning or late in the afternoon. In dappled shade, sunlight is filtered through the tree canopy, perhaps all day. Areas north of tall fences or buildings are in full shade and receive almost no sun. The amount of shade in a garden varies according to the time of day and season. In spring, light levels can be high even if there are many trees, and very early flowers, such as hepatica, scilla, and pulmonaria, are aroused to bloom before the tree leaves open. Later, as the trees leaf out, their shade helps these plants cope with summer heat. Grape hyacinths, fritillaries, primulas, early single peonies, and hostas are all plants that thrive in this kind of environment. As trees and shrubs mature, they shade ever larger areas for longer periods, and early plantings that once thrived with longer periods of sunshine may dwindle.

Shade gardens can be either moist or dry. In the shade of north-facing buildings and fences, soil is more easily kept moist than under trees and shrubs. By an unobstructed east- or west-facing house wall with a half-day of shade and a half-day of full sun, the soil may dry rapidly. Soil in the dense shade between houses and below spruce trees can be as dry as that along a south-facing wall. In summer, large shallow-rooted trees such as poplars draw up a lot of moisture. Dry shade limits plant choices as many, such as mertensia, pulmonaria, and dwarf bleeding heart, go dormant in summer if they are too dry.

Many shade-loving plants come from forests where the soil is heavy in organic matter with an accumulation of rotting leaves, twigs, roots, branches, and tree trunks. To duplicate woodland soil, plenty of humus, in the form of compost or leaf mould, well-rotted manure, and peat moss, and a few handfuls of bone meal can be worked into the existing soil. If the soil is heavy clay and does not drain well, add grit in the form of coarse sand or vermiculite and perlite. Proper soil conditions promote stronger, healthier plants that compete well with tree and shrub roots.

You may not want to develop the entire garden as a shade garden, but even a single tree provides a small pool of shade. In small spaces or courtyards, where shade is cast by buildings, shade-loving foliage plants such as ferns, hostas, and coleus, and flowering begonias or impatiens will thrive in a good depth of soil in raised perimeter beds and require little care beyond watering.

In larger spaces, or where there are many mature trees, you can create an informal shady woodland. Woodland gardens should look as natural as possible, with winding paths through large sweeps of plants. When choosing plants, consider bloom time, height, interesting foliage, fall colour, winter interest, and whether the plant goes dormant in summer. Many familiar garden plants are "wild" species or resemble their wild ancestors enough for a natural effect. Consider the size of the space available as plants need room to develop to their full potential, and then mix a variety of shrubs, ferns, flowering annuals and perennials, foliage plants, and groundcovers.

Big leaves are an adaptation that helps shade plants use the less intense light in a woodland setting. Bold petasites, or coltsfoot, with huge leaves and a large club of tiny flowers is an amazing sight in spring. Experiment with contrast and similarities in foliage, whether in colour, shape, or texture. A lacy fern next to a rotting log, underplanted with a few tiny spring bulbs and some violets or primulas will provide flowers long before the trees and shrubs leaf out and the ferns unfurl, for a long season of interest.

A wide variety of interesting foliage plants not only revel in shady sites but require them. KLN GIRARD

Woody ornamental plants for shade include red-twigged and yellow-twigged dogwood, variegated forms of dogwood, hydrangea ('Pee Gee' or 'Annabelle'), various junipers, cedar, winged burning bush (euonymus) with stunning fall colour, viburnum or wayfaring tree, and mock orange, with scented flowers in early summer. Shade-tolerant varieties of vines such as climbing nightshade add seasonal colour and visual interest. Some species of clematis are enchanting, wending their way up through trees and shrubs, naturally preferring their roots to be shaded and their flowers to be in the sunlight above.

Hardy ferns provide a range of textures and sizes, some even tolerating periodic dry conditions. Mosses provide a soft cushiony effect, and native moss sometimes establishes itself in a shady garden. Although they are not true mosses, Irish and Scottish "mosses" may also be tried. A continuously damp spot is best, and they do well in the spaces between bricks or stones where moisture collects.

Most of the smaller bulbs, species tulips, and fritillaries, shy violets, and hepatica will grow in a woodland garden. Later, bleeding heart, lily-of-the-valley, Jacob's ladder, and elegant Solomon's seal appear. Summer-flowering plants include fernlike astilbe and columbines, spiderwort and campanulas, native harebells, Canterbury bells, and peach-leaved bellflower. As summer progresses and shade deepens, the interesting foliage of hostas makes good cover for dying bulb foliage, and their leafy mounds contrast boldly with the fine foliage of ferns or astilbe. The foliage appears in June and in summer they are crowned with racemes of white or mauve lilylike flowers. No shade garden would be complete without them.

Annuals are useful for filling in while other plants establish themselves, pale-coloured flowers being best to reflect light; pansies and violas, evening scented stocks, pale lobelias, nicotiana, begonias, impatiens, and coleus light up shady corners. Perennials for moist shade, with some sunshine during the day, could include buttercups, globeflower, meadow rue, monkshood, fleeceflower, corydalis, kinnikinnick, ligularia, star-flowered Solomon's seal, and leathery-leaved bergenia. Many herbs perform nicely in dappled shade: tall angelica, sweet woodruff, and shade-tolerant mints—some variegated and all best confined in buried pots. No shade garden is complete without ground-covering plants—periwinkle and ajuga, variegated lamium and yellow archangel, or cliffgreen and Japanese spurge. Some groundcovers should be used with care; goutweed, creeping Charlie, and lily-of-the-valley, among others, are extremely invasive and will take over large areas. They can be planted in sunken tubs with the bottoms removed or contained by concrete walls, paths, or railroad ties.

Grass lawns grow poorly in heavily shaded areas and can be more trouble than they are worth. With Calgary's cool nights, heavy dew settles on grass, often not drying until noon or later. Spaces for sitting might better be served by paving (interlocking concrete pavers or bricks permit rain to reach tree roots) or wooden decking. These restful areas come into their own during scorching weather.

With careful plant selection, and attention to soil improvement and moisture provisions, a city woodland garden is entirely practical, even on the prairie, giving its owners a cool and restful retreat from the busy city, and providing food and shelter for birds and other wild creatures.

NATIVE PLANTS FOR WOODLAND SHADE GARDENS

- Baneberry *(Actaea rubra)*
- Bunchberry *(Cornus canadensis)*
- Clematis, blue *(Clematis verticellaris)*
- Columbine *(Aquilegia* spp.*)*
- Fairy bells *(Disporum trachycarpum)*
- Honeysuckle, twining *(Lonicera dioica)*
- Jacob's ladder, western *(Polemonium occidentale)*
- Lungwort, tall *(Mertensia paniculata)*
- Northern bedstraw *(Galium boreale)*
- False Solomon's seal *(Smilacina* spp.*)*
- Violet, early blue *(Viola adunca)*

A MEADOW IN THE CITY

A natural meadow garden might be indicated by a bare treeless lot, a windy hillside, or simply the desire to have something different from the standard manicured lawns and flower beds of suburbia. In an exposed garden space, a wild meadow where grasses and flowers dance in the sun and wind is possible, whether it is an entire lawn area converted to wild grasses and flowers, or just a small bed of grasses and foliage plants.

In a meadow, grass predominates and flowers add accent. Recently, nurseries have begun propagating native grasses and these may become more widely available. In the meantime, some of the ornamental grasses can be substituted in their place; small, tussocky sheep's fescue, quaking grass, bulbous oat grass, tufted hair grass, and even the dainty blue-eyed grass *(Sisyrinchium)* are a few non-invasive grasses with a natural appearance. They can be planted together in groups or mixed with small shrubs and flowers.

Many garden plants resemble wildflowers closely enough to be used in their place and can easily be obtained: varieties of garden achillea for prairie yarrow, cultivated antennaria for native pussytoes, various species of artemisia for silver pasture sage, Michaelmas daisies for wild smooth aster, and daisies such as flea-bane, coneflower, and gaillardia for their prairie cousins. Goldenrod and sun-flowers closely resemble their wild forms, blue flax and harebells are virtually unimproved, and early-blooming mauve pasqueflower mimics the prairie "cro-cus." Monarda, geranium, penstemon, blazing star, columbine, and tiger lily are all similar to their wild counterparts. These can be planted by themselves, among ornamental grasses, or in groups separated from each other by wandering path-ways or mulches of pebbles and stepping stones.

Accents and accessories should contribute to the natural theme; ornaments, paths, benches, fences and other structures should be of wood or stone, or con-crete, tastefully used.

USING NATIVE PLANTS

Native plants have several advantages: they have natural resistance to many garden pests and diseases; they are tolerant of local soil and climate conditions; and, being less dependent on water and fertilizer, they make fewer demands on the environment. It is important that they be acquired in a responsible manner, and the Canadian Wildflower Society lists guidelines to prevent degradation of plant habitats.

Native plants should be acquired from seeds, cuttings, and root divi-sions. Transplanting native flora is only condoned when plants are endan-gered by construction or other development. Permission should be obtained before removing any plants from private or park land, and native plants from nurseries should be labelled "Nursery Propagated." It is illegal to collect seed in federal, provincial, or municipal parks, and permission is needed to collect seed on private or Crown land. Seed can be collected from roadsides and waste land. Mark desirable seed plants when they are in bloom as it can be difficult to recognize plants later in the season.

Choose local plants that attract and provide food for native wildlife, and avoid collecting seeds of officially restricted plants as many of these are invasive, introduced species that are unsuitable for city gardens. If you are growing rare species, keep accurate records to share information with botanical gardens and environmental study groups. Sensible wildflower gardening does not cause disruption of native plant communities; done wisely and well, it can help preserve many rapidly dwindling species.

- Anemone, cutleaf, or wind-flower (*Anemone multifida*)
- Aster (*Aster* spp.)
- Beardtongue (*Penstemon* spp.)
- Bee balm, wild horsemint (*Monarda fistulosa*)
- Begonia, wild, veined dock (*Rumex venosus*)
- Blanket flower (*Gaillardia aristata*)
- Blazing star (*Liatris punctata*)
- Blue-eyed grass (*Sisyrinchium montanum*)
- Buttercup (*Ranunculus acris*)
- Camas, white, green lily (*Zygadenus elegans*)
- Chickweed, mouse-eared (*Cerastium arvense*)
- Cinquefoil (*Potentilla* spp.)
- Coneflower, prairie (*Ratibida columnifera*)
- Crocus, prairie (*Anemone patens*)
- Fireweed, great (*Epilobium angustifolium*)
- Fleabane (*Erigeron* spp.)
- Geranium, sticky purple (*Geranium viscosissimum*)
- Harebell (*Campanula rotundifolia*)
- Larkspur (*Delphinium* spp.)
- Locoweed (*Oxytropis* spp.)
- Lupin (*Lupinus argenteus*)
- Mallow, scarlet (*Sphaeralcea coccinea*)
- Meadowsweet, white (*Spirea lucida*)
- Old man's whiskers (*Geum triflorum*)
- Onion, wild (*Allium* spp.)
- Primrose, evening (*Oenothera biennis*)
- Sandwort (*Arenaria lithophila*)
- Scorpion weed (*Phacelia sericea*)
- Shooting star (*Dodecatheon radicatum*)
- Violet, yellow prairie (*Viola nuttallii*)
- Yellow bell (*Fritillaria pudica*)

Few nurseries offer species wildflowers for sale. Seeds are available from wild-flower societies, botanic gardens, and seed companies engaged in habitat restoration. Although germination is sometimes a challenge, many native prairie plants can be grown successfully from seed. Unfortunately, popular "canned meadows" often contain non-native annuals and undesirable weedy plants; prepared seed mixtures that identify plant species by name, not just by cultural requirements, are more suitable. You need to be patient when replacing a lawn with grasses and flowers started from seed as it takes several years for the plants to establish themselves. Annual weeds must constantly be removed by hand to reduce competition for the desirable plants. Wildflowers need soil similar to that in their wild locations—lean and mean. Those with spreading root systems may find the nutritious garden soil so much to their liking they become difficult to control; others may be disappointing, growing tall and floppy, or rotting away. If you persevere, however, the result is a unique garden that has appeal all year round, makes few demands on the environment, and requires little in the way of maintenance.

Features

THE ORIENTAL TOUCH

Because the oriental style of gardening takes many years to understand and many years of work to execute properly, most of us will simply have a garden with an oriental theme. The sand garden is a contemplative style used mainly in monasteries. It may seem to be just sand with raked patterns and a few rocks placed on the surface, but everything in it has a meaning: the placement of the rocks, the shape of the rocks, the gravel, and how it is maintained. Usually no plants are used, except perhaps a small border of mosses or low grasses encircling the rocks. Oriental courtyard gardens are usually rooms within a larger garden. They may be planted with a small tree, pruned into a stylized shape, as well as with shrubs and some ground-covering plants. There may be colour, from perennial plants used sparingly, from flowering trees or shrubs, or just from foliage. Large oriental gardens are called strolling gardens. They are composed of many scenes or rooms, which are carefully designed to be viewed from different angles and at different times of the year. The placement of pathways, bridges, and resting places ensures strollers are confronted by specific views. There is more colour in these larger gardens, although it is always used with restraint.

Decking edges a pool in this small oriental garden; the tree is weighted with a stone to train it to an elegant curve. ROSALIE COOKSLEY

Since a feature of oriental-style gardens is the meticulous pruning of trees and shrubs, it is important to select suitable species. Large trees are only appropriate if space permits. Some large trees with interesting shapes and textures are elm, buckeye, mountain ash, and selected species of pine and spruce. Choose trees for year-round appeal—shape, texture, bark colour, flowers, or colourful fruit. In our long winter, coniferous evergreens are indispensable. Pines are the preferred evergreens in oriental gardens; Scotch pine, Swiss stone pine, and bristlecone pine are all excellent. Spruce are not much used but they can be incorporated as a background. Useful smaller trees are crabapple, apple, pear, apricot, sea buckthorn, Japanese lilac, silver buffaloberry, and Russian olive, all of which lend themselves to shaping.

Shrubs can be used extensively, with larger specimens forming a backdrop.

Honeysuckle, lilac, sumac, viburnum, plum and cherry, and dogwood can be kept pruned tightly or allowed to grow into their natural shapes. Some smaller shrubs—potentilla, spirea, dwarf honeysuckle and viburnum, and dwarf lilac—have a naturally globular or columnar shape and do not require too much training. Dwarf evergreen conifers such as mugho pine and 'Globe' spruce have interesting compact shapes.

Perennial flowers are usually restricted to a few species, massed together for effect, one type to a group. Single forms of peonies and iris—mainly Siberian, spuria, Japanese, and pseudocorus species—are the flowers of choice. Others include balloon flower, bergenia, primula, hepatica, hosta, ferns, ornamental grasses, and many groundcovers. The groups of plants are placed so that they do not compete with each other for attention when they are in bloom. Small groups of only a few plants are better than many different plants. Oriental gardens are restful and do not jar the senses with a riot of colour.

Decorative elements include lanterns, pagodas, and statuary. Whatever you use, it should be tasteful and not overdone. Japanese garden lanterns are placed near water, bridges, gazebos, or changes of direction in paths. The snow lantern is squat with a wide roof and looks particularly attractive when capped with snow. Snow lanterns are placed in resting areas so they can be admired. Tall thin lanterns are used at bridge entrances, in amongst plants, or at directional changes in the path. They cast more light and their shape gives the impression of movement. Lanterns are illuminated by candles, electricity, or natural gas.

A water feature of some kind is popular in oriental gardens, a simple form being a hollowed-out rock with water dripping into it; the rock gently overflows to provide a soft sound. There are many other intriguing water devices that make dripping, tinkling, or gurgling noises. Ponds may be small or large, with or without plants. Ponds and streams make possible one or more bridges, arched, flat, or zigzag in style, made of wooden planks or flat stone. If ponds are at different levels, waterfalls can add the sound of moving water to the garden. Ponds should look as natural as possible with no evidence of plastic liners or pumps.

Dry stream beds give the impression of water and movement. Stones uniform in style and colour are laid in a ribbon pattern to resemble a winding creek. The stones should vary in size and shape, but they should all be flat to overlap like the scales of a fish.

Carefully laid out paths show the garden to its best advantage. Construct them from natural materials such as stone, crushed rock, small pebbles, or river rock. Fences help create mood—seclusion, serenity, or intrigue. They screen unsightly areas or create garden rooms so that not everything can be seen at once. Allow fences of natural wood such as cedar and spruce to weather to silvery grey, and top board fences with a little "roof" of shakes to add character. Open trellises allow views through into other parts of the garden; solid fences block views and enclose a private space.

A key element in oriental design is simplicity. It is better to have less than more, whether in the number of types of plants selected, pieces of statuary, or other features.

Newer gardens are often tight for space, and gardeners may be reluctant to devote any of it to a vegetable garden. But where is it written that vegetable gardens must be plots for food production in the backyard? Many vegetables and herbs are attractive and can easily be incorporated into sunny front and back flower gardens.

Potage, or composite, gardens are a mix of annual and perennial flowers and vegetables, either in a small area or throughout the garden. Popular in France for many centuries, potagers are often works of art with the herbs and vegetables laid out artistically in geometric beds. At one time, they would have been edged with clipped hedges of boxwood; borders are now more likely to be of lettuce or parsley. Narrow brick paths in a herringbone pattern give access to the plants. Tall sun-warmed walls enclose them, supporting and sheltering espaliered dwarf fruit trees and vine trellises. Grape arbours shade tables and chairs for family meals and sometimes a fountain or simple pond is fashioned from the water source. There is no reason why we Calgarians can't adapt these charming and space-saving ideas for our city gardens.

With proper selection and placement, vegetables can look ornamental. Plant peas and runner beans with other climbers, such as morning glories, clematis, and sweet peas, or by themselves on an attractive trellis. Scarlet runner beans are pretty climbers, and tasty beans follow the bright red flowers. Even cucumbers and tall cherry tomatoes look handsome grown this way.

A zucchini plant makes a bold accent for an odd corner and fills a large space, especially if it is vining from a tub. The red stalks and large-veined leaves of rhubarb make a spectacular foil for more delicate flowers. If the stalks are picked selectively, the appearance of the plant will not suffer. Ruby Swiss chard is a more compact substitute. White-, or even pink-, flowering strawberries can be used as a groundcover.

The delicate, lacy foliage of carrots makes them perfect for edging flower beds, and they can be thinned regularly without spoiling the effect. Parsnips can be treated the same way. The deep green curly foliage of parsley makes an excellent border that can withstand small amounts of daily pruning. Spinach and lettuces, in a variety of sizes, leaf shapes, and colours, can be grown in formal or irregularly shaped groups set off by dwarf marigolds. If you pick individual leaves when cropping them, lettuce and spinach continue to produce and the appearance of the bed is not disturbed. Plant vegetable seeds in succession so that as plants are harvested, more come on. Alternatively, hold young plants in pots in reserve to replace harvested produce.

Planters and containers in sunny locations can hold all sorts of vegetables. Surround a large tomato plant on a good support with flowers, such as portulaca, that like the same hot growing conditions. Grow successive crops of salad greens, spinach, and radishes in half-barrels or large planters. Vegetables can even grow in hanging baskets. In a cool area, ruby red lettuce makes an interesting and edible pot plant, perhaps surrounded by trailing lobelia for pleasing colour. Parsley can be tucked into planters as a bright green accent, as can chives, which have pretty purple flowers.

Herbs provide a variety of foliage textures and colours. Lavender has narrow grey leaves and mauve flowers, a pleasant contrast to darker green leaves. Sage leaves are grey green with a rippled texture; the flowers are blue. There is a variety of basil, 'Dark Opal', with dark purple foliage, which is striking near pale blue or pink flowers. Oregano has tiny pink flowers, and savory has spikes of pink or purple bloom. There are many varieties of aromatic thyme, all of which are superb low groundcovers. Lemon thyme has tiny green and yellow leaves, and woolly thyme has grey furry leaves.

Flowers and vegetables mix happily in a small bed: blue green broccoli, yellow single marigolds, red nicotiana, cooking sage, feathery dill, blue salvia, and potatoes. MAUREEN IRETON

Some flowering shrubs do double duty in the landscape. Nanking cherries produce many small cherries that are good for jelly, liqueur, pancake syrup, or eating fresh. Several currants have useful, delicious fruit, including the lesser-known clove currant. Native saskatoons have pretty spring flowers, wonderful fruit, and coppery orange leaves in the fall. Viburnums (cranberries) grown here do not provide cranberry sauce-type berries, but they are good for jelly; their leaves turn bright red in the fall. Raspberry bushes can serve as an informal

A colourful border with Missouri sundrops, yarrow *(Achillea ptarmica* 'The Pearl'), bellflowers, pink lavatera, Canterbury bells, golden Marguerites, Maltese cross, delphiniums, columbines, tiger lilies, and African daisies. CALGARY

HORTICULTURAL SOCIETY

hedge and provide luscious fruit. Crabapple, apple, and pear trees not only bear fruit for the table and pantry, they are also covered in lovely blooms, pink or white, each spring.

Vegetables, fruit, and herbs can make the garden unique and attractive as well as nutritious. It might even be possible to have a beautiful potager that is nearly all vegetables and herbs with just a few ornamental plants as accents!

HERBACEOUS BORDERS

Herbaceous borders were originally inspired by the mixed plantings in cottage gardens. They were refined by garden designers to showcase perennial flowers, arranged to provide a continuous but changing parade of colour and interest throughout the summer. Today, although many gardeners include flowering bulbs, suitable annual flowers, and even flowering shrubs, the stars of these borders are still the herbaceous perennials—plants that die to the ground each fall, to be reborn in spring.

A tremendous number and variety of flowers can be grown in borders. Whether located along walls, fences, or hedges, or in island beds surrounded by lawn, borders should be as long and as deep as possible—preferably 2–3 m (6–9 ft). A good depth allows several ranks of plants of varying heights, colours, and textures, from low spreading mounds in front to tall bulky giants at the back. Island beds usually have tall plants in the centre surrounded by ranks of successively smaller subjects. A generous length permits many more types of plants or repeated groupings of plants. Deep beds need stepping stones or a path along the rear margin to provide access for cultivating and for trimming hedges or shrubs. Plan beds on the south side of hedges or fences to prevent plants growing leggy as they lean out to reach the sun.

In long borders, the tallest plants are placed at the back in groups of three or five—odd numbers being easier to arrange than even ones—not all in a line, but in wedges or tear-drop shapes. In small gardens, one specimen of robust plants such as peony or 'Golden Glow' rudbeckia may be enough. With some exceptions, such as valerian and aruncus (goatsbeard), tall plants mostly bloom from mid-July onward; some, such as globe thistle and chrysanthemum, hang on into mid-October. Tall plants may be planted in a full range of colours or kept to a few favourite shades and are best stoutly staked to withstand wind and rain.

In the middle two or three ranks are plants of medium height, again in groups or drifts and not in regimented rows. These provide much of the colour of June and July, with some blooming earlier (columbine, pyrethrum, and trollius) and others flowering on into fall (yarrow, coneflower, and sea holly). Cranesbill, cornflower, buttercups, bellflower, bee balm, iris, and lilies, to name just a few, provide a wide range of colour and a variety of leaf texture even when flowering is over. Colour, bloom time, and leaf shape are considered when placing these plants, keeping in mind the plants behind them. Several require light support to prevent them from sprawling in wet weather.

In front of all are placed small edging plants, some ground hugging, some mounding tufts, others, such as dropwort and statice, bearing flowers in tall airy sprays that do not obscure the plants behind them. While many bloom in spring and early summer—arabis, aubrieta, geum, and saponaria—others, such as pinks, coral bells, and Carpathian bellflowers, come into their own in July and August. Small silver-leaved plants such as lambs' ears, woolly veronica, and snow-in-summer provide wonderful contrasting foliage and spill out over paving for an informal effect.

If you leave generous spaces between the perennial roots, you can achieve a colourful display in early spring by interplanting with bulbs—the taller varieties of tulips, daffodils, and alliums in the centre, and masses of squills, grape hyacinths, and other small bulbs in the front.

Perennials flower their best when given the conditions they prefer, so group them together according to their needs for sunshine or shade, water, and type of soil. Position borders out of the path of strong winds. Shelter afforded by buildings, fences, or hedges makes all the difference when a violent squall blows through from the southwest or the north.

ROCK OR ALPINE GARDENS

Understanding local conditions will help ensure the success of an alpine garden. Dehydration and leaf burn due to scanty snow cover and winter wind and sunshine are as much a problem as severe temperatures, yet Calgary's dry summer weather and cool nights are very much suited to the culture of alpine plants.

Rock gardens are often on hillsides or slopes where the soil can be terraced or retained by layers of stone or rock. They look more natural if local rock is used and if you choose only one type of rock for the whole garden. Sandstone that does not flake when it freezes and thaws is a good choice—especially for plants that require alkaline soil as some local sandstone has a high pH; granite is more suitable for those plants with a low pH requirement. Whatever rock you use, study local formations to see how to achieve a harmonious natural effect. Most rocks have a noticeable grain and you should lay them so that this grain always runs in the same direction. Lay sandstone horizontally or at a slight angle, tilting the stones back into the soil to direct rain down to the plant roots.

When you are constructing your rock garden, formulate the best possible soil mix to suit the plants. For plants that need acidic conditions, our heavy, alkaline clay loam has to be amended with peat moss and sand. Try a general-purpose mix of one-third screened and washed rock grit (pH depending on type of plants to be grown), one-third playbox sand (never concrete sand), and one-third peat moss or compost or a combination of the two. As most local sand is quite alkaline, avoid using it around acid-loving plants. Even supposedly neutral silica sand should be checked for its pH level before use.

Most rock plants come from areas with exceptional drainage, which accounts for their very long and large root systems. Below rosettes of leaves that appear to be growing in pure gravel or rock is a long stem (referred to as the *neck* or *collar)* from which the roots grow far below in sharply drained, lean soil. Positive drainage, whether surface drainage or drainage through the growing medium, means absolutely no standing water around the plants at any time. You can achieve this by sloping surfaces and by adding a high proportion of a fast-draining growing medium, such as grit and sand, to the soil.

Some alpines need moister conditions than others. Add extra peat moss to the soil around them and undulate the planting beds with ridges and valleys to create enough shade to retard drying. Tender plants also do better in the valleys, where there is more sun protection in summer and deeper mulch and snow cover in winter. Alpine beds dry quickly. Early morning and evening waterings duplicate most closely the natural misting in the mountains. You can install an automatic watering system if you cannot be there to water the beds by hand. A top-dressing of up to 2.5 cm (1 in.) of rock, grit, and (or) sand helps to keep roots cool and moist; the type of dressing depends on the plants and your personal preference. For lime-loving plants such as dianthus, use crushed or rounded limestone; for acid-loving plants such as *Gentiana sino-ornata,* granite grit is a better choice. Since local slate is close to neutral in pH, you can use it for mulching all types of alpine plants—just add peat or granite grit for the acid

Lewisia cotyledon 'Sunset' is rooted in a rock crevice. KEN GIRARD

lovers. In alpine gardens, the top-dressing should look crumbled and worn.

Winter protection is critical to plant survival in Calgary and alpine gardeners always hope for deep snow. In dry autumns, continue to water regularly with a fine spray early in the day so that the water will have drained from the crowns before frost sets in at night. Then, after a hard frost in late October or early November, use spruce or pine boughs to form a deep cover. (Pine boughs can be cut by permit in the Bow-Crow Forest reserve.) Alternatively, make frost blankets from horticultural microfoam covered with burlap. In addition to keeping the ground frozen and the plants dormant, these blankets protect the plants from drying winds.

Positioning alpine plants by copying their natural orientation may make the difference between survival or loss. Plant north-facing slopes with lewisias, ferns, and moisture-loving primulas and androsaces. Cooler, east-facing slopes suit native mossy saxifrages, soldanella, dwarf primulas, mountain forget-me-not, androsaces (again), and hepaticas. Sun-loving moss campion, townsendia, phlox, some saxifrages, and just about all our native alpines do well on west-facing slopes. Hottest and driest, south-facing slopes can be planted with most of the west-facing types, drabas, and sempervivums. Orchids, daphne, corydalis, and the moisture-loving gentians appreciate locations in the valleys between hills and rises. To discover the preferred microclimate of a plant, grow it in various locations to see where it performs best.

As many alpine plants are not available from local nurseries, try growing them from seed, which has the added advantages of often being from hardier varieties than plants and is much cheaper. In addition to some of the more common rock garden plants such as aubrieta, arabis, saponaria, maiden pinks, armeria, and the mat-forming veronicas, the beginning alpine gardener should have success with the following.

ALPINES FOR BEGINNERS

- Allium (*Allium moly, A. neapolitanum,* and *A. oreophilum*)
- Bellflower (*Campanula carpatica, C. cochlearifolia,* and other dwarf species)
- Chionodoxa (*Chionodoxa luciliae*)
- Columbine (*Aquilegia* spp.—dwarf types)
- Daffodil (*Narcissus* spp. and hybrids, 'Jack Snipe', 'Tete a Tete', 'Pipit')
- Draba (*Draba densifolia, D. oligosperma,* and *D. ventosa*)
- Edelweiss (*Leontopodium soulie* or *L. nivale*)
- Gentian (*Gentiana verna, G. septemfida*)
- Hepatica (*Hepatica* spp.)
- Pinks (*Dianthus alpinus, D. gratianopolitanus* 'Tiny Rubies')
- Primrose (*Primula auricula, P. marginata*)
- Saxifrage (*Saxifraga bronchialis, S. cernua,* and commonly available mossy and encrusted saxifrages)
- Silene or campion (*Silene acaulis*)
- Snowdrop (*Galanthus nivalis*)
- Squill (*Scilla sibirica*)
- Striped squill (*Puschkinia libanotica*)
- Townsendia (*Townsendia parryi*)
- Tulip (*Tulipa tarda, T. linifolia,* and *T. turkestanica*)

A meadow of wildflowers: sweet rocket, flax, gaillardia, ox-eye daisy, and harebell. JOYCE HODGSON

As with all gardening, expect the garden to change and evolve. Plants can be lifted gently on a shovel—for moving or for placing new growing medium beneath them.

WATER GARDENS

A water garden is any sort of water feature and water-loving plants. It can be as simple as a half-barrel sunk in the ground or a plastic-lined pool with a fountain, or as elaborate as a large concrete pond complete with fish, waterfall, and stream. There is something soothing about the sound of moving water, whether it is a waterfall, fountain, or just a trickle dripping into a basin. Running water helps prevent stagnation in ponds, humidifies the air, masks undesirable noise, and attracts birds to bathe and drink. Water is circulated by means of submersible pumps powered by underground wiring with a mandatory ground-fault interrupter. Ordinarily, rainfall tops up any water lost to evaporation, but if not, it can be refilled from the garden hose.

The most permanent and most expensive water gardens are made of concrete. In Calgary, because of extreme temperatures and penetrating frosts, pools and stream beds should be built of 4000 psi concrete, at least 15–30 cm (6–12 in.) thick, using a 30-cm (12-in.) grid of 3/8-inch reinforcing bar and wire mesh, on a base of crushed gravel. Cracking is a problem with concrete ponds as the ground heaves in winter. You can leave the pond and feeder streams full of water and put in some logs or weighted plastic bottles to ease the pressure of the ice. Alternatively, empty ponds and barrels and clean them before winter arrives.

If your pond is at least 75 cm (30 in.) deep, you can keep it from freezing by covering it with some type of insulation. (Note: pools more than 60 cm/24 in. deep are required by law to be enclosed by a 2-m/6-ft lockable fence.) In late fall, shut off the pumps, blow out the water lines, and put a cover made of plywood and styrofoam over the entire pond surface. A stock tank heater will keep the temperature of the water above freezing, but is really only needed during severe cold spells. (Calgary does not usually experience prolonged periods of extremely cold temperatures.)

A pond liner of heavy PVC plastic works well and is economical. Although easy to install, it is prone to puncture, so provide a thick sand base to cover any protrusions before laying it down. Hide the plastic pool edge with overhanging flat stones and trailing plants. Plastic formed pools in various shapes and sizes are also popular and durable, but are not deep enough to overwinter fish or plants. They must also be disguised so that the plastic is invisible. Other successful water containers are wooden half-barrels, old bathtubs, children's wading pools, and fibreglass installations.

Rapid growth of algae is a common problem in ponds, especially in early spring when sunshine promotes algae growth before plants grow large enough to compete for oxygen and nutrients. Circulating the water with a pump helps combat algae growth, and a plentiful variety of plants in the pond helps prevent a buildup. Plants take in carbon dioxide from the atmosphere and release oxygen and carbohydrates into the water. They keep the water clear by competing for the same food and light as algae—three bunches of water plants for every square metre (square yard) of surface should help balance oxygen levels. Apple snails help control filamentous or sheet algae, and algicide tablets (safe for plants and fish) can be used in an emergency if the water gets too murky. Skimming leaves and other debris off the surface daily also helps.

Fish do very well in outdoor ponds and help keep them free of bugs, including mosquito larvae. If you are planning to include fish, you need some type of filtration system. Goldfish can be wintered in a pond if it is at least 90 cm (36 in.) deep; the water must not be allowed to freeze and a pump is required to add oxygen to the water. The fish become dormant as the water gets colder and only need to be fed once a week; in spring, as the water warms, they become active again. Wintering fish indoors in an aquarium can present a space problem as goldfish soon grow quite large in garden pools. Fish, especially Japanese carp, or koi, sometimes dig into submerged plant containers, fouling the water with soil. To avoid this, top the container soil with 5 cm (2 in.) of sand and a layer of large pebbles. Do not use herbicides or pesticides anywhere near the pond.

Use ferns, primroses, spiderwort, Kenilworth ivy, umbrella palm, and various iris—especially water iris and Siberian iris—to make water features look as natural as possible. Suitable native plants include pond grass, buttercups, and Solomon's seal. Build various levels for plants that are to grow submerged in the pond or provide concrete blocks for plant containers to stand on. Water lilies need deep, still water—to 90 cm (36 in.)—in full sun. Many water plants prefer a more shallow depth and others, such as cattail, bulrush, and arrowhead, are at home in boggy areas at the pool margin. To make a bog, dig down about 60 cm (24 in.), lay down heavy plastic perforated in a few places, then backfill with a mixture of loam, compost, and dampened peat moss.

To help oxygenate the water, and also to provide hiding places and egg-laying sites for fish, place waterweed *(Elodea canadensis)* and cabomba *(Cabomba caroliniana)*—two bunches (ten stems each) per container—at the bottom of the pond. Marginal aquatics can either grow in shallow areas of a pond (20–25 cm/8–10 in. deep), their leaves and flowers resting on the surface, or in boggy soil at the edge of the water.

SUBMERGED PLANTS FOR WATER GARDENS

- Arrowhead *(Sagittaria latifolia)*
- Bogbean *(Menyanthes trifoliata)*
- Floating hearts *(Nymphoides peltata)*
- Flowering rush *(Butomus umbellatus)*
- Golden club *(Orontium aquaticum)*
- Miniature cattail *(Typha minima)*
- Pickerel weed *(Pontederia cordata)*
- Sweet flag *(Acorus calamus)*
- Umbrella palm *(Cyperus alternifolius)*, overwintered indoors
- Water canna *(Thalia dealbata)*

Floating aquatics drift on the pond's surface and feed through roots suspended in the water. They suppress the growth of algae by providing shade and by using up nutrients in the water. Water lettuce *(Pistia stratiodes)*, water hyacinth *(Eichhornia crassipes major)*, salvinia *(Salvinia rotundifolia)*, and duckweed *(Lemna minor)* are a few that are available.

Bog plants thrive in consistently moist areas exposed to full sunlight. Good choices are water cress *(Radicula nasturtium-aquaticum)*, arrow arum *(Peltandra virginica)*, cinnamon fern, mayapple *(Podophyllum peltatum)*, cattail *(Typha latifolia)*, marsh marigold, water forget-me-not *(Myosotis scorpioides)*, and water iris *(I. pseudocorus,* to name one).

Water lilies *(Nymphaea)*, with their exotic blooms and lovely, round floating leaves, flourish in loam-filled containers submerged in warm, still water, 45–90 cm (18–36 in.) deep, in full sun for a minimum of eight hours a day. Their massed leaves help shade out algae. Hardy kinds of *Nymphaea* will live for years if they are overwintered in a deep pond kept from freezing solid, or brought indoors and stored in a cool dark place, with the pots placed in a large tub containing about 15 cm (6 in.) of water to keep the roots damp all winter. Other perennial water plants can be treated the same way. Tropical water lilies and annual plants such as water hyacinth must be wintered indoors in an aquarium with lights.

Water lilies bloom in a sunny pool, with plantings of sedum and artemisia.

MAUREEN IRETON

FOUR

The Big Stuff:
Trees, Shrubs, and Vines

Planting for the Long Term

It is hard to imagine that when Calgary was first settled, it was virtually treeless. Newcomers brought trees with them, for shade, privacy, windbreaks, and fruit. The hardiest ones survived, and before long, nurseries were selling prairie-hardy trees and developing new varieties suitable for our windy climate, short summers, and Chinooks. Today, trees are acknowledged for their environmental value and the city is considering requiring home-owners to replace those that are removed. They attract birds, modify extreme temperatures, add beauty and colour to the landscape, and lend a sense of peace and serenity in the city. They even give city children somewhere to climb.

Whether you are designing a new garden or upgrading an older one, it is tempting to fill in beds with shrubs and flowers and to add a couple of trees to a small yard so that it looks landscaped, with little thought about how large they will grow. It is difficult to imagine a spruce tree 1 m (3 ft) high becoming 3 m (9 ft) wide and 10 m (30 ft) tall, but a look at the majestic spruce in older neighbourhoods will give you an idea of their potential size. Spreading junipers do just that—spread! It is tempting to plant lots of little junipers, because they are inexpensive, without realizing that they can each grow to a width of 2.5 m (8 ft) or more. Junipers vary considerably in mature size and most nurseries can show you pictures to help you visualize how they will look in your yard. Evergreens cannot be pruned successfully to keep them small. Older needles naturally die in the centre and at the bottom of mature evergreens. If new growth is continually removed, there is not enough healthy growth to support the tree, and no new growth occurs on that branch.

'Northwest' poplar trees, planted some years ago throughout Calgary, have now reached an enormous size, with roots to match. The roots are very shallow even if adequate moisture is provided, and suckers can grow anywhere along their length, particularly if the trees are pruned excessively, which causes the tree to go into a survival mode. The suckers make lawns difficult to mow and invade leaking or broken sewer pipes and water mains. Removing them is expensive, unpleasant, and hard work. Laurel-leaf willows can become huge, often reaching 11 m (35 ft) across when mature, and they grow very quickly. What is not so obvious is the nonsuckering root system, which becomes considerably wider than the tree and is just as invasive as that of the 'Northwest' poplar. Unlike trees, shrubs can be kept in check through a consistent pruning program, so mistakes in planning are easier to correct. Choosing the best plant for the available space is still very important, though. Pruning should be done to maintain the health and natural shape of the plant, not to restrict greatly its natural size. Many large shrubs are also available in more compact varieties, with a smaller mature size.

It helps to stand across the street from your home and visualize how you would like the tree or shrub to be, many years from now. Will your home look inviting? Will you be able to see the front door? Is a large tree by the door a security hazard? Will a fully grown tree or shrub cause so much shade that rooms indoors would be dim and gardening in the area will be a challenge? Electrical wires seem a long way above a newly planted decorative crabapple, but after ten years that tree could easily interfere with power lines and need drastic pruning. A young mugho pine that looks dwarfed in a flower bed beneath the living room window can easily reach well above the window sill, and a pyramidal juniper that crowds the eavestrough is likely larger than you planned. In a back garden, visualize how trees will enhance the landscape design, not overpower it. Large trees can restrict flower gardening to shade-tolerant species and make vegetable gardening difficult indeed. Consider your neighbours, too—they might not want half of your tree hanging over their fence.

Despite the fact that trees and shrubs grow more slowly in Calgary, planting still has to be for the long term. Choose the tree to fit the space, rather than trying to make the tree fit the space. It is easier to be patient for the first few years than to cut down a magnificent tree that no longer fits your yard. Add colourful annuals, even perennials that can later be moved, to fill in spaces and help you avoid the temptation to plant more trees and shrubs. Above all, read labels, ask questions, read books, and learn as much as you can. You, or the person who later lives in your home, will be glad you did.

Evergreen Trees

Coniferous evergreen trees have narrow, needlelike leaves and bear their seeds in cones. Large evergreen trees have a sturdy denseness that deciduous trees lack, and as evergreens do not lose their leaves all at the same time, they add colour to Calgary gardens during the long winters. Evergreen trees are a valuable backbone to landscaping, providing a windbreak for homes and gardens, and shade to cool them. The following trees are commonly planted in the Calgary area.

Note: A small tree (at mature size) is considered to be under 4 m (12 ft) tall, a medium tree 4–8 m (12–25 ft) tall, and a large tree over 8 m (25 ft) tall.

Douglas Fir *(Pseudotsuga* spp.) is not a true fir and is not normally used for landscaping. The needles are blue green, paler below. The cones are narrow ovals with three-pronged bracts that hang from the branches. The dormant buds on Douglas fir are pointed; those of true firs *(Abies)* are rounded.

Fir *(Abies* spp.) are not commonly grown in gardens here—they are native trees growing in the foothills and mountains. Fir trees have soft, flat, dark green needles with two white lines on the underside; the needles will not roll between your fingers. The cones are oblong, standing erect on the branches, and the scales flake off from the centre of the cone, leaving a core on the tree for another season.

Larch *(Larix* spp.) are deciduous conifers, with soft, green needles in the spring and summer that turn yellow and drop off in the fall. Cones are small, hard, and erect on the branches and persist on the tree over the next season.

Pines *(Pinus* spp.) have long dark green needles in clusters of two, three, or five. The cones are cylindrical to egg-shaped, have thickened tips on the scales, and may persist on the tree for several years. Pines can be small shrubs or large trees.

Spruce *(Picea* spp.) have sharp needles, blue or green, along the branch like a baby bottle brush and the needles roll between your fingers. The trees are very tall and straight. The cones are firm and cylindrical, and hang down from the branches.

Larch *(Larix* spp.). The larch is a deciduous conifer, with short, soft, bright green needles in the summer that turn yellow in the fall before they fall off. The spring and fall foliage make it a valuable landscape tree, but its bare branches in winter may make it less acceptable for a major specimen tree. *L. laracina,* also called tamarack, is a medium-sized, full tree that grows in boggy soil. *L. sibirica* is a large, more open tree that tolerates drought if adapted when young.

Pine *(Pinus* spp.). Pine trees have long green needles in bundles of two, three, or five. The most commonly grown large pine is Scotch pine *(P. sylvestris),* with yellow green needles in bundles of two and coppery orange bark. It is dense when young but becomes more open with age. There is also a columnar Scotch pine *(P. sylvestris* 'Fastigiata') that grows upward into a narrow tree and is ideal for a confined space. The native lodgepole pine *(P. contorta latifolia)* is less reliable, but in a sheltered spot with acidic soil, it can be successful. It has dark green needles in bundles of two, usually confined to the outer ends of the branches. Swiss stone pine *(P. cembra)* has soft, fine needles in bundles of five and retains its foliage well on lower branches. It can reach large tree size in time. A very large mugho-type pine *(P. uncinata* or *P. mugo rostrata)* is a dense, small tree with dark green needles in bundles of two. It becomes too wide for the average city lot, but is attractive where there is room for it. Bristlecone pine *(P. aristata)* is a dense, bushy pine with white flecks on dark green needles in bundles of five. It is very slow growing, but can ultimately reach medium tree size.

Spruce *(Picea spp.)*. Spruce trees have short square needles borne singly along scaly branches; foliage colours vary from silvery blue to green. Typically, tree-size

spruce grow into a pyramidal shape. The most common are Colorado spruce *(P. pungens)*, with green needles, and the variety *P. pungens* 'Glauca', with blue needles. They can reach 10 m x 5 m (35 ft by 15 ft) when mature, so they must be planted in an appropriate place. There are smaller, more compact varieties of spruce, such as 'Fat Albert' Colorado spruce *(P. pungens* 'Glauca' 'Fat Albert')* with a mature size of 5 m x 2.5 m (15 ft by 8 ft), which would be more suitable for the average garden. Other Colorado spruce worth considering are 'Hoopsii' spruce *(P. pungens* 'Hoopsii')*, which is narrower and more compact than the more common Colorado spruce, with an intense silvery blue colour; 'Montgomery' spruce *(P. pungens* 'R. H. Montgomery')*, with attractive blue needles and growing to 2 m x 2 m (6 ft by 6 ft); and 'Bacheri' spruce *(P. pungens* 'Bacheri')*, a more dwarf variety with dark blue needles.

A fresh snowfall adds beauty to this stately spruce. LIESBETH LEATHERBARROW

Other large spruce include the native white spruce *(P. glauca)*, with soft, shorter green needles; a variety called Black Hills spruce *(P. glauca* 'Densata')*, which is slow growing and has small, very dark green needles and should be better known; and Norway spruce *(P. abies)*, which has dark green needles, pendulous branches, and long cones—a very attractive tree that is a welcome alternative to all the Colorado spruce out there.

Evergreen Shrubs

Because they add such attractive colour all year round, smaller coniferous evergreens are a valuable part of landscaping, particularly as foundation plantings. They are useful as a background for flowers, they soften corners of homes, and they make wonderful groundcovers. Carefully chosen, they are relatively easy to care for and long-lived.

Cedars *(Thuja spp.)*. These evergreens need high humidity, no sudden changes in temperature, and no sun or wind in the winter. In Calgary? In spite of this, some do well here, but they are unpredictable. When they are established in a suitable area, or when you have genetically hardy specimens, cedars can become quite large, overtaking doorways, eaves, and sidewalks. The fragrant foliage is green, smooth, and flat. There are globe varieties *(T. occidentalis* 'Woodwardii' or 'Little Giant') in several sizes and columnar types *(T. occidentalis* 'Emerald' or 'Brandon') that do best in semi-shade, sheltered from the wind. They need moist soil at all times, including winter months, so keep an eye on them if they are foundation plants where the soil dries during Chinooks. In areas where wind or sun contribute to needle desiccation, two or three stakes in the ground with burlap spread between them to form a wind or sun screen can protect them in the winter. Don't wrap the shrubs too snugly. When the Chinook winds blow, it can become too warm under the wraps if there is not good air circulation inside. This change in temperature causes the plants stress when the weather turns cold again.

Junipers *(Juniper* spp.). This large group of spreading and pyramidal evergreens is often used for foundation plantings and group planting in beds. Hardiness varies, so read labels for zones. Most junipers with *horizontalis* in their names are hardy, as are those labelled *sabina; squamata* are not reliably hardy but may survive in a sheltered microclimate, depending on the weather.

Colour varies from steel blue through turquoise to bright green, including some with yellow tips *(J. x media* 'Pfitzerana Aurea'). Some, such as 'Prince of Wales' *(J. horizontalis* 'Prince of Wales') or 'Blue Chip' *(J. horizontalis* 'Blue Chip') are very low groundcovers, with a spread of 2.5–3 m (8–9 ft). Others, such as 'Scandia' *(J. sabina* 'Scandia'), 'Arcadia' *(J. sabina* 'Arcadia'), or Savin juniper *(J. sabina)* are vase shaped, mounding to 90–120 cm (36–48 in.) in height with a 2-m (6-ft) spread. Still others, such as 'Wichita' *(J. scopulorum* 'Wichita') or 'Moonglow' *(J. scopulorum* 'Moonglow') are pyramidal, with a width of about 120 cm (48 in.) and a height of 2.5–3 m (8–9 ft). Most need at least half a day of sun; while *horizontalis* and *scopulorum* types do well in our alkaline soil and are very drought tolerant, others may need a slightly acidic soil (created by adding an evergreen fertilizer such as 30–10–10 in spring and summer) and deep watering whenever the soil is dry. As with all evergreens, junipers lose moisture from their needles during warm Chinook winds. Watering well in the fall before freeze-up and again during warm spells—if there is no snow cover and the ground is dry—helps preserve them.

Pines *(Pinus* spp.). You can recognize pines by their long needles in bundles of two, three, or five. The most common shrub-sized pine is mugho pine *(P. mugo),* which has dark green needles and is globe shaped. These can vary in size from about 0.3–5 m (1–15 ft) high, so be sure to check the mature size before you purchase one. Break the soft, new candles in half in early summer to keep the shrub compact. Bristlecone pine *(P. aristata)* is a very slow-growing pine with flecks of white on the needles. It eventually reaches tree size. There are also several varieties of dwarf Scotch pine *(P. sylvestris* 'Nana') in spreading or columnar shapes. All pines lose their oldest needles on the inside and at the bottom in the fall, but this is not something you have to worry about.

Spruce *(Picea* spp.). Spruce come in several dwarf forms that are hardy here, in colours of blue and green, and in globe or columnar shapes. Bird's nest spruce *(Picea abies* 'Nidiformis') is a low, compact, layered shrub that is an interesting alternative to spreading junipers. *P. abies* 'Prostrata' is a weeping form of Norway spruce that spreads outward and downward to cover a bank or act as a groundcover. It requires a sheltered spot to do well. Strangely, dwarf Alberta spruce *(P. glauca* 'Albertiana Conica') is not hardy here. It is named after Prince Albert, not the province of Alberta, and needs higher humidity and more consistent temperatures than we experience in Calgary. Dwarf globe Colorado spruce *(P. pungens* 'Globosa') is, as the name suggests, a small round spruce. It grows to about 1 m (3 ft), is perfectly hardy, and tolerates shade as well as sun. It can be grafted onto a sturdy trunk to become a tiny tree about 1.2 m (4 ft). There is also a columnar Colorado spruce *(P. pungens glauca* 'Iseli Fastigiata') reaching 1.8 m (6 ft) in width and 5 m (15 ft) high, which can be a very attractive and hardy alternative to pyramidal juniper or cedar.

There are broad-leaved evergreen shrubs, such as rhododendrons, suitable for growing in climates with high humidity and moderate temperatures in the winter. These are generally not hardy here although some gardeners have success with the rhododendrons.

Deciduous Trees

There are a large number of trees suitable for landscaping in Calgary; some are not easy to find in nurseries, but it is worth asking if they can be specially ordered. When choosing a tree, give thought to size; shape; bark and leaf colour (in fall and winter as well as summer); hardiness; physical needs such as water, drainage, and wind resistance; fruit (small, inedible fruit could be an asset or a liability); and potential pest problems. Ask to see pictures of the tree at its mature size and learn as much as you can before you make a final decision. Check hardiness zones to be reasonably sure the tree you want is suitable for your microclimate.

Note: A small tree (at mature size) is considered to be less than 5 m (15 ft), a medium-sized tree 5–8 m (15–25 ft), and a large tree over 8 m (25 ft).

Amur Maple *(Acer ginnala).* This small tree with elongated maple-shaped leaves that turn scarlet in the fall is an attractive specimen tree for a small yard. It can be pruned to a single trunk, but is more commonly seen as a multi-trunked small tree or large shrub. This is the only maple that develops a red colour in the fall in our area. Another similar maple, sometimes sold as *A. ginnala,* is actually *A. ginnala* x *A. tatarica.* It becomes a medium-sized tree with an attractive umbrella shape and usually has several trunks. It turns yellow in the fall. Some experts now consider *A. ginnala* to be a variety of *A. tatarica.* ♥

Ash *(Fraxinus* spp.). The ash genus includes several varieties of large trees with compound leaves that usually turn yellow in the fall. They leaf out late and lose their leaves early. This can be an advantage if you want shade in the summer months but value the sun in the spring and fall. Female trees produce many winged seeds. Green ash *(F. pennsylvanica)* is the largest variety; Manchurian ash *(F. mandshurica)* is somewhat smaller, with a round head; and 'Patmore' ash *(F. pennsylvanica subintegerrima* 'Patmore') is a seedless male clone. Also in this genus is 'Fallgold' black ash *(F. nigra* 'Fallgold'), which holds its yellow leaves longer in the fall. It has a narrower shape and a more delicate silhouette and is suitable for smaller front lawns.

Birch *(Betula* spp.). Birches are large trees with white or bronze, peeling bark that is particularly attractive against a dark evergreen background. They can be single or multi-trunked, and have simple, small-toothed green leaves in the summer, which turn yellow in the fall. Birches need deep watering, especially in a dry summer and in the fall before freeze-up. Birch trees that fail to leaf out at the top in the spring usually have not had sufficient water the previous summer or fall. They are subject to birch leaf miner, an insect that creates brown blisters in the leaves. It is controllable with a soil drench of a systemic insecticide each spring. (See chapter nine for more detail.) Cutleaf weeping birch *(B. pendula* 'Gracilis') has thin, flexible weeping branches and deeply cut leaves. European white birch *(B. pendula)* has pointed oval leaves, with branches that do not weep, and a more rounded shape. Paper birch *(B. papyrifera)* is similar, with a somewhat rough leaf. Young's weeping birch *(B. pendula* 'Youngii') is smaller, in an umbrella shape, with the leaf of a white birch and the weeping habit of the cutleaf weeping birch. The slender, twiggy branches of all birches look wonderful against a snowy background. 🌿

Bur Oak *(Quercus macrocarpa)*. Bur oak is a slow-growing, stately tree with deeply lobed glossy green leaves that turn an orange-brown in the fall. The rough grey bark is deeply furrowed when mature. Round acorns have a mossy fringe on the bottom half. Bur oak has a long tap root, which means it survives drought well. It ultimately becomes a large tree. It is the only oak hardy in our area. 🌿

Cherry *(Prunus* spp.). This group of trees has clusters of white flowers in May and small fruit that attract birds and can be used for jelly. An appropriate size for city gardens, these trees have something for every season. Amur chokecherry *(P. maackii)* is a tall, narrow tree with shiny copper bark that adds excellent winter colour to a landscape. It has fluffy flowers and dark fruit. 'Schubert' chokecherry *(P. virginiana* 'Schubert') is a smaller, more rounded variety with green leaves that turn purple in early summer after flowering. Mayday trees *(P. padus)* become quite wide, up to 8 m (25 ft), so they need a large area when mature. They are also available in a clump form, with several trunks. Pincherry *(P. pennsylvanica)* has shiny leaves that turn bright orange in the fall and small red fruit. It is a small tree with dark maroon bark, which is very attractive in winter. Unfortunately, it has a tendency to sucker. ✿

Crabapples, ornamental *(Malus* x *adstringens* cultivars). These crabapples are medium-sized trees with rounded heads, green or purple leaves, and flowers in varying shades of pink. They are often referred to as rosybloom crabapples. In May, when the crabapples are blooming in Calgary, the city seems to be covered in pink blossoms. Ornamental crabapples are compact trees, a perfect size for city gardening and a real joy to herald spring. They produce small red crabapples

Weeping birch needs adequate moisture to achieve the size of this specimen. <small>RUTH STAAL</small>

Rosybloom crabapples are Calgary favourites.

<small>RUTH STAAL</small>

that attract birds in the winter. Many cultivars are available, such as 'Thunderchild', with purplish green leaves and deep rose flowers; 'Hopa', with green leaves and purplish pink flowers; and 'Radiant', with bronze-coloured leaves and pink flowers with a white centre. 'Almey' has purplish red leaves in the spring that turn greenish bronze by mid-summer, and red flowers with a white base. 'Strathmore' is tall and narrow with pale pink blossoms. Siberian columnar crabapple (*M. baccata* 'Columnaris') is a narrow tree with showy white flowers and tiny yellow or orange crabapples. It is useful in areas with restricted space. 'Royalty' is not recommended because of its susceptibility to fireblight. ❁

Elm (*Ulmus* spp.). The elm is a large tree with a Y-shaped trunk and rough, serrated leaves. Elms can be pruned to take up little space at "people height," so they are useful where an overhead canopy of shade is desired but space is at a premium. They also make attractive boulevard trees. They are not suitable for windy areas as branch crotches are often narrow and susceptible to splitting. It is essential to prune them to the desired shape when they are young. American elm (*U. americana*) is a large tree with bigger leaves than the smaller Siberian elm (*U. pumila*). Siberian elm creates a dappled shade; American elm is useful where dense summer shade is desired and there is room for a larger tree. Brandon elm (*U. americana* 'Brandon') is a compact, dense form of American elm.

Hawthorn (*Crataegus* x *mordenensis*). Hawthorn is a small tree with coarsely toothed leaves and sharp thorns. It is attractive and tidy for small areas but has a tendency to sucker. It has clusters of long-lasting double flowers and showy fruit. 'Snowbird' flowers remain white; 'Toba' flowers emerge white, then turn pink after they open. Both have clusters of dark berries in the fall. ❁

Japanese Tree Lilac (*Syringa reticulata*). This small tree, often multi-stemmed, has dark green leaves and rich brown bark that is attractive in the winter. The conical clusters of fragrant, creamy white flowers appear in late June, the last of the lilacs to bloom. An attractive, compact tree, it deserves to be more widely grown. ❀

Little-leaf Linden *(Tilia cordata).* This compact tree has a dense, symmetrical crown, glossy green leaves, and tiny, yellowish white, fragrant flowers that hang in clusters. It needs a sheltered spot to survive here.

Manitoba Maple *(Acer negundo).* This maple is a very hardy, large tree with compound leaves that turn yellow in the fall. Unfortunately, it is subject to aphids, which exude a sticky honeydew that drips down on anything below it. An unattractive sooty mould also grows on the honeydew. Female trees produce seedlings that can easily be mown off the lawn but are a real nuisance in flower beds and vegetable gardens. A good tree for rural areas because of its hardiness, it is not the best choice for a tidy city landscape.

Mountain Ash *(Sorbus* spp.). Mountain ash are medium-sized, slow-growing trees with compound leaves and clusters of white flowers, followed by orange or red berries. The copper fall leaf colour and reddish brown bark are attractive in the winter, and the fruit stays on the tree, which attracts birds. All mountain ash require good drainage—they cannot survive in constantly wet soil. Their bark is prone to sun scald and splitting, so it is helpful to wrap the trunk in the winter if it is exposed to sun. Mountain ash are best planted where the trunk is shaded by a hedge or shrub. Damage is also common from weed whips and lawn mowers. The American mountain ash *(S. americana)* is a large variety with an oval head; European mountain ash *(S. aucuparia)* is often sold in a multi-stemmed form and is the largest variety; Russian mountain ash *(S. aucuparia* 'Rossica') is a tall, narrower species. ❦

Ohio Buckeye *(Aesculus glabra).* This large tree has big compound leaves; large, upright, cone-shaped inflorescence; pale yellow flowers in June; and prickle-covered fruit. Here it does best in sheltered areas.

Poplar *(Populus* spp.). Without poplars, early Calgary had few trees. The balsam poplar *(P. balsamifera)* and the trembling aspen *(P. tremuloides)* are native here. They grow very quickly, survive well, and are widely used for windbreaks. Still valuable in rural areas, the balsam poplar becomes far too large for small city lots, and the trembling aspen is a short-lived tree prone to fungal problems. Commonly planted in the 1970s, the very large 'Northwest' poplar *(Populus* x 'Northwest') is now being removed from most properties because of extensive root and suckering problems. 'Griffin' poplar *(P.* x 'Griffin') is a narrower tree, but has the same potential root problems as 'Northwest'. Silver poplar *(P. alba)* has glossy, three-lobed green leaves that are silvery white on the underside, and it is often confused with silver maple *(Acer saccharinum).* It is subject to winter die back and has a tendency to sucker. Two narrow varieties of poplar, however, are welcome additions to a garden: both resemble the Lombardy poplar *(P. nigra* 'Italica'), which isn't hardy here. 'Tower' poplar *(P.* x *canescens* 'Tower') is a narrow, columnar tree with wavy margins on oval green leaves. Foliage is retained down to the base. It is attractive in groups of three. Swedish columnar aspen *(P.*

tremula 'Erecta') is similar, with small rounded leaves that tremble in the wind. Their soft rust colour in the spring is particularly attractive. It has spiralled upper branches that are striking in the winter. Suckering is not a major problem, but be careful not to disturb the roots or bury them too deeply—this may trigger suckering. ❦

Russian Olive *(Elaeagnus angustifolia)*. Russian olive has long, narrow silver leaves and when mature, black bark. The fragrant yellow flowers produce dry, silvery fruit. This medium-sized tree is an attractive accent tree in the summer, especially against a dark background, and the dark bark is especially striking in the winter. Plant it in a sheltered area, away from strong winds. It does not do well in damp areas or in rich soil.

Willow *(Salix* spp.). Laurel-leaf willow *(S. pentandra)* is a very large, handsome tree, not suitable for most city properties because it can become 10 m (35 ft) wide. Leaves are long and shiny green and remain on the tree until well into fall. The smaller golden willow *(S. alba* 'Vitellina') is often multi-trunked, with silvery green leaves. The bright yellow bark is attractive in the winter. It is not fully hardy. The large weeping willows common in British Columbia are not hardy here. Willows require regular deep watering and do not do well in dry areas. The small branch ends break off in the wind, which can be a problem if there is a rock garden or pool nearby.

Fruit Trees

Many types and varieties of fruit trees grow well in Calgary. True, they do not produce the varieties of fruit we buy in grocery stores, but nevertheless, the fruit they produce is of good quality and the trees are easy to grow. All fruit trees need pollinators of the same genus but a different variety in order to produce fruit. Thus, an apple tree needs a different cultivar of the same genus. This could be another variety of apple, a crabapple, or an apple-crab. The pollinating tree does not need to be in your backyard, but does need to be in close proximity—about 30 m (100 ft). The trees must bloom at the same time, which is not usually a problem with apples or pears but can be with plums. You can graft branches of one variety onto another to give each a pollinator. Choose trees specifically for our area from reputable nurseries that specialize in prairie-hardy stock. Plant them in a sunny spot with lots of room for growth and learn about pruning techniques for fruit trees to create a well-lit space for fruit on a compact tree. (More details on pruning can be found in chapter nine.)

One of the major diseases that worries fruit tree growers is fireblight; however, many fruit trees diagnosed with fireblight actually have cytospora canker. This fungal infection is characterized by small black "pimples" (fruiting spores of the fungus) and reddish brittle branches. There is no cure, but it is not quite as contagious as fireblight. Aphids infest fruit trees but seldom do a great deal of harm. Be sure not to spray when the tree is blossoming, as pollination will be affected. (For more information on diseases and insect problems of fruit trees, see chapter nine.)

Apple (*Malus* spp.). Apples are available in many varieties, with a large range of size, flavour, keeping quality, and ripening time. New varieties are being introduced regularly and most nurseries can tell you what is currently available. 'Westland' is a large crisp apple for cooking that ripens in September and keeps well. It replaces 'Heyer #12', an old variety that ripens at the end of August and is often used for pies and applesauce but is not a good keeper. Some apples are very good for eating fresh: 'Goodland' has large red and green apples that ripen in mid-September; 'Norland' has smaller green apples with red stripes that ripen in mid-September on a dwarf tree, suitable for smaller areas; and 'Parkland' has smaller red apples that ripen in late August. These newer varieties generally keep well. Some apple trees produce so many apples that if they all survived the tree would not be able to support them. Often a tree loses a large percentage of the developing fruit in early summer. This is called June drop and it helps the tree produce fewer, larger apples. If some apples do not fall when the fruit first develops, it is best to remove a few from each cluster by hand to create the same result.

An apple-crab is a hybrid of an apple and a crabapple. Well-known varieties include 'Rescue', a yellowish green apple-crab with red stripes that ripens in late August; 'Kerr', with oblong red fruit; and 'Rosybrook', with greenish yellow, red-mottled fruit. These small apples are a good size for children to eat and also good for pies and applesauce; a few apple-crabs are suitable for jelly.

Edible-apple trees and apple-crabs always produce white flowers, whereas ornamental crabapple trees usually have pink flowers.

Apricot (*Prunus armeniaca*). Apricot trees are hardy here, but because the blossoms are some of the first to appear and are often lost to a late frost, the trees fruit roughly one year in four or five. As they are attractive, you might decide it is worth the unpredictable fruit and try them. Apricots need two varieties for pollination. 'Brookcot' and 'Westcot' are newcomers that produce flavourful fruit. 'Manchurian' seedlings are often available. Because they are hybrids, they have variable characteristics, but they can be good pollinators for other varieties. Learn as much as you can from reputable nurseries before planting.

Pear (*Pyrus* spp.). The fruit from pear trees grown here is not of the quality that is available for sale, and few varieties are available for cross-pollination, but the trees produce beautiful white flowers that are reason enough to plant them. 'Ure' is one variety that has small, juicy fruit suitable for eating fresh. Pollinators might be 'Golden Spice', which has spicy, tart fruit, or 'David' or 'John', both of which have hard, coarse-textured fruit that is not particulary good for eating fresh but is good for sauce and pies. New varieties are being developed constantly, so keep asking questions.

Plum (*Prunus* spp.). Plums are small, attractive landscape trees. They can be cultivars of native, Japanese, or American plums. Because parentage varies widely, trees bloom at different times; not only are two different cultivars of plum necessary for pollination, they must both bloom at the same time. For example, 'Brookred' can be pollinated by 'Pembina', 'Opata', or western sand-cherry (*P. bessyi*), which is a small shrub of the same genus as plums.

'Brookgold' can be pollinated by 'Pfitzen' or 'Dandy', but 'Brookred' will not pollinate 'Brookgold'. If you have two trees that do not bloom at the same time, try mulching the soil around the roots of the early-blooming tree to keep the soil cool longer and delay its flowering. If you are purchasing plum trees, ask for help in choosing two that will bloom together. There are many varieties with either red or yellow fruit; some are suitable for jams and pies and some are suitable for eating fresh.

Deciduous Shrubs

Deciduous shrubs are woody plants, usually with several stems, that lose their leaves in the fall. They add flowers to a garden in the spring and summer, a variety of leaf colour, winter bark colour, fruit, and fragrance. Shrubs vary a great deal in size; often, a shrub will be available that is a more appropriate size for a small area than a tree would be. Shrubs also vary in their preference for sun or shade, and moist or dry soil, so choosing shrubs that do well in a chosen area will improve their chance of success.

Note: A small shrub is considered to be less than 1.2 m (4 ft); a medium-sized shrub 1.2–2.5 m (4–8 ft); and a large shrub over 2.5 m (8 ft).

Buffaloberry *(Shepherdia argentea).* This large thorny shrub has long, narrow silvery green leaves, inconspicuous yellow flowers, and bright red clusters of fruit in the fall. The fruit is sour, but useful for jams and jellies. A male and a female plant are necessary to produce fruit, so they are more successful planted in groups. Buffaloberry is hardy and a good contrast plant with dark green evergreens. ❦

Burning Bush *(Euonymus* spp.). Both varieties available in Calgary are grown for their red fall colour and interesting fruit. The Turkestan burning bush *(E. nanus* 'Turkestanicus') is a small, fine-textured, sprawling shrub with long, narrow dark green leaves that turn pink in the fall. It has showy clusters of deep pink seed capsules. A little larger is the winged burning bush *(E. alata).* It has broader leaves, and corky ridges make the stems square. Some winter tip kill can be expected, but branches grow quickly in the spring. Both tolerate partial shade. ❦

Caragana *(Caragana* spp.) A large family of tough shrubs, all caraganas have small yellow flowers but vary considerably in size, shape, and leaf type. Common caragana *(C. arborescens)* is too large for most gardens and can sucker. It is best used for large hedges on rural property. There are several cultivars appropriate for city landscaping. Fernleaf caragana *(C. arborescens* 'Lorbergii') is a large, upright shrub with cascading branches; it has a delicate appearance and fine, very narrow leaves. Walker's weeping caragana *(C. arborescens* 'Walker') is a narrow-leaved caragana grafted to a straight stem to produce a slender, columnar, weeping shrub. Pygmy caragana *(C. pygmaea)* is a compact, round shrub with small leaves and thorns. It makes a good hedge. Pygmy standard caragana *(C. pygmaea* 'STANDARD') is a pygmy caragana grafted onto a straight stem to produce a tiny, treelike shrub. Weeping standard caragana *(C. arborescens* 'Pendula') is grafted to a straight stem to produce a weeping shrub with typical caragana leaves. Watch for suckers on the stems or at the base of grafted caraganas. They should be removed, as they will grow more quickly than the grafted portion. 'Sutherland' caragana *(C. arborescens* 'Sutherland') is a tall, narrow, upright shrub that is good where a narrow, hardy tree is desired.

Cotoneaster *(Cotoneaster lucidus* or *C. acutifolia).* Cotoneaster is a hardy, medium-sized to large shrub with small, leathery dark green leaves that turn orange-red in the fall. It has small pale pink flowers, followed by tiny dark fruit liked by birds. Easily pruned, it is our most common hedge, but it also makes a good specimen shrub. It tolerates shade but will grow almost anywhere. T● ❦

Cranberry *(Viburnum* spp.). There are several species of cranberry in Calgary; all have maple-shaped leaves, tolerate shade well, and need moisture. American highbush cranberry *(V. trilobum)* is a large shrub with white flowers, followed by red fruit, and leaves that turn red in the fall. Compact American cranberry *(V. trilobum* 'Compactum') is a smaller variety that has no flowers or fruit. Dwarf European cranberry *(V. opulus* 'Nanum') is a low-growing variety with no flowers or fruit; it turns reddish purple in the fall. Compact European cranberry *(V. opulus* 'Compactum') is a medium-sized variety with white flowers and red fruit that attracts birds. T● ❦

Currant *(Ribes* spp.). Currants tolerate shade and take to pruning well. They make good hedges as well as single specimen shrubs. Alpine currant *(R. alpinum)* is a medium-sized shrub with lobed green leaves and tiny green flowers but rarely any fruit. Golden-flowering currant *(R. aureum)* is medium-sized with light green leaves, fragrant yellow flowers, and large black berries that are good for jelly and jam. Currants planted in the sun are less susceptible to powdery mildew. T●

Daphne *(Daphne cneorum).* This very low shrub is actually a broad-leaved evergreen. Because it grows to only 20 cm (8 in.), it is often covered with snow in the winter, giving it the protection it needs. Winter protection is recommended, as snow is unreliable in Calgary. It prefers a

A shaded, moist location suits 'Annabelle' hydrangea, which blooms all summer until the hard frosts of fall. JUDITH DOYLE

sheltered, moist spot and produces fragrant bright pink flowers very early in the spring. ❀

Dogwood *(Cornus* spp.). There are several species and varieties of these hardy shrubs, varying in size and bark and leaf colour. All do well in shade and moist soil. Bark colour is showy in winter. Red osier dogwood *(C. sericea* or *C. stolonifera)* is a large shrub with green leaves and dark red bark. It has white flowers and bluish white fruit, and the leaves turn maroon in the fall. Siberian coral dogwood *(C. alba* 'Sibirica') is similar but slightly smaller, with bright red stems, white flowers, and bluish fruit.

Variegated or silver dogwood *(C. alba* 'Argenteo-marginata') is a smaller variety with variegated green leaves and white, yellowish green flowers, dark red bark, and bluish fruit. It isn't quite as hardy as Siberian coral, so requires a sheltered spot out of the winter wind. Yellow-twigged dogwood *(C. sericea* 'Flaviramea') is medium sized with green leaves, white flowers, and bluish white fruit. It has bright yellow bark that is attractive in winter. For all dogwoods, pruning out old wood encourages new growth, which has the most attractive fall colour. T● ⚜ ❦

Double-flowering Plum *(Prunus triloba* 'Multiplex'). This medium-sized shrub has double pink flowers along the stems in spring before the dark green leaves form. It is often the first shrub to bloom in the garden, greeting spring with masses of bright pink blossoms. It does not produce fruit. It prefers a sunny location and requires pruning to maintain an attractive shape. ✿

Elder *(Sambucus* spp.). This family includes several medium to large shrubs with compound green or yellow leaves. Red-berried elder *(S. racemosa)* is a large shrub with compound green leaves, clusters of cream-coloured flowers, and red berries. The fruit can be used for jelly or wine. It can be multi-stemmed or pruned to a single trunk like a small tree.

When golden elder *(S. nigra* 'Aurea'), a large shrub, is planted in a sunny spot, the leaves are yellow. White flowers are followed by black berries. It often dies back in the winter and new growth comes from the bottom. As the new growth is more attractive, it is often cut to the ground in the fall. Golden plume elder *(S. racemosa plumosa* 'Aurea') has deeply serrated gold-coloured leaves, cream flowers, and red fruit. ⚜

Forsythia *(Forsythia* spp.). Forsythia is a small- to medium-sized shrub with bright yellow flowers early in the spring, on bare branches, then simple green foliage the rest of the summer. *F.* x 'Northern Gold' is the only one likely to be successful here. It is not a reliable bloomer in the Calgary area, as late spring frosts can damage flower buds and tip kill is not uncommon. It is startling when it does bloom, with brilliant blossoms the length of the branches. Forsythia tolerates sun or partial shade. ✿

Golden Ninebark *(Physocarpus opulifolius).* Golden ninebark is a medium-sized shrub with three-lobed leaves that are yellow if planted in the sun. They turn bronze in the fall. Creamy white flowers are followed by showy red capsules. The bark is cinnamon coloured—an attractive winter contrast. 'Dart's Gold' is a smaller shrub with intensely golden leaves. There is also a green-leaved variety *(P. monogynus)* that turns orange-red in the fall. Some winter tip kill is to be expected, but it comes back easily from rootstock. ⚜

Honeysuckle *(Lonicera* spp.). There are several species of these medium to large shrubs that grow well in sun or shade. The largest is pink Tatarian honeysuckle *(L. tatarica),* with masses of pale pink flowers in June, followed by tiny red fruit. It is often used as a tall hedge but is subject to aphids, which fold the leaves up and curl the ends of the branches in a "shepherd's crook." 'Arnold Red' honeysuckle *(L. tatarica* 'Arnold Red') has fragrant red flowers and red berries that attract birds. It is supposedly more resistant to the honeysuckle aphid. Sweetberry honeysuckle *(L. caerulea edulis)* has creamy white flowers and dark blue berries. 'Clavey's Dwarf' honeysuckle *(L. xylosteoides* 'Clavey's Dwarf') is smaller, with velvety leaves and small white flowers, at about 1.5 m (5 ft). It can be used as a hedge. 'Miniglobe' honeysuckle *(L. xylosteoides* 'Miniglobe') is a miniature variety of 'Clavey's Dwarf', only 1 m (3 ft) tall.

Hydrangea *(Hydrangea* spp.) This shrub is related to the gift plants with big balls of pink or blue flowers, which are not hardy here. Two varieties do well in Calgary, in sheltered spots, moist soil, and partial shade. 'Annabelle' *(H. arborescens* 'Annabelle') is a larger shrub with large leaves and rounded, long-lasting clusters of white flowers. 'Pee Gee' *(H. paniculata* 'Grandiflora') is a small shrub with small leaves and showy pyramidal clusters of white flowers that turn pink in August as they age. ❀

Lilac *(Syringa* spp.). Lilac is a large genus of shrubs with plain green leaves and clusters of flowers, usually fragrant, blooming from May to July. Lilacs need a sunny place and often take several years after planting to bloom. Common lilac *(S. vulgaris)* is the old-fashioned lilac with fragrant purple or white flowers. As it produces many suckers, it is not recommended except on acreages or very large informal lots. The French hybrids of *S. vulgaris* are large shrubs, in many named varieties, with different coloured flowers, often double and not as fragrant. For example, 'Ellen Wilmott' is double white, 'Charles Joly' is double reddish purple, 'Blue Skies' is single lavender, 'Kathy Havemeyer' is double pink, and 'Sensation' is single purple with a white edge. Preston lilacs *(S. prestoniae)* are large shrubs, with leaves that are veined and slightly fuzzy, and single flowers in pink or purple that bloom later than French hybrid lilacs. There are several named varieties, such as 'Red Wine', with deep red blossoms; 'Minuet', with light purple; and 'James McFarlane', with rose. Villosa lilac *(S. villosa)* is a large shrub with dull green quilted leaves and plum-coloured flower buds that open to single pink flowers later than most other lilacs. It can be used as a tall hedge. Dwarf Korean lilac *(S. meyeri)* has a dwarf, rounded form, with tiny leaves and mauve flowers. It can be planted singly or as a hedge. It is ideal in a small spot where any other lilac would grow too big. 'Miss Kim' lilac *(S. patula* 'Miss Kim') is medium sized, with pale lilac flowers. It blooms a little later than other lilacs and the leaves turn purple in the fall. ❀ ❦

Mock Orange *(Philadelphus* spp.). Mock orange is a large shrub with simple leaves, twiggy branches, and large, very fragrant flowers resembling orange blossoms in June. The most hardy variety is the 'Waterton' mock orange *(P. lewisii* 'Waterton'), which has a single flower. Double varieties such as *P. virginalis* x 'Minnesota Snowflake' and virginal mock orange *(P. virginalis)* have double flowers, but are not as hardy in this area. They all tolerate partial shade. Regular pruning to remove older branches at the base encourages prolific flowering and maintains a more compact size. T● ❀

Nanking Cherry *(Prunus tomentosa)*. Nanking cherry is a large shrub with small quilted leaves and pale pink single flowers along the stems in May. The small bright red cherries can be eaten fresh or used for jelly and syrup. They also are loved by robins. It tolerates sun or partial shade and is very hardy. T● ❀

Potentilla (*Potentilla fruticosa* cultivars). These hardy, small, fine-leaved shrubs do well in sunny locations with good drainage. There are many named cultivars with different flower colours, mostly shades of yellow, but also white, orange, and pink; they bloom from late June to September. Read labels carefully for colour and height. Tall cultivars, to 1.2 m (4 ft), include 'Coronation Triumph', 'Goldfinger', and 'Jackmanii'—all with yellow flowers. Examples of medium cultivars, to 1 m (3 ft), are 'Abbotswood', with white flowers; 'Katherine Dykes', with light yellow flowers and grey green leaves; and 'Sunset Red', with brick-coloured flowers. Short cultivars are 'Moonlight', with pale yellow flowers and 'Red Ace', with orange red flowers that are yellow underneath—both to 75 cm (30 in.)—and 'Yellow Gem' and 'Sutter's Gold', both to 45 cm (18 in.) with yellow flowers. ✺

Purple-leaved Plum or Sandcherry (*Prunus x cistena*). A medium-sized shrub with dark purple leaves and small pale pink flowers in spring, it is a good contrast plant with greens, blues, or yellows. Some winter die back is to be expected, but pruning back to healthy growth restores it. It does best where there is persistent snow cover. The bark is dark purple, providing attractive winter contrast. ♠

Sea Buckthorn (*Hippophae rhamnoides*). This large, multi-trunked, thorny shrub has narrow grey green leaves and small yellow flowers. If there are both male and female plants in an area, female plants produce brilliant orange fruit that stays on the tree all winter. They do best in a sunny, well-drained location. Sea buckthorn is an aggressive grower and tends to produce suckers.

Spirea (*Spiraea* spp.). There are many species of these small-to-medium shrubs with varying leaf and flower colour. They do well in sunny spots. Bridal wreath spirea (*S. x vanhouttei*) is a medium variety, with small, oval green leaves and white arching flower clusters in June. Garland spirea (*S. x arguta*) is a compact shrub with narrow green leaves and a similar habit, and 'White Swan' spirea (*S. trilobata*) is a small, neat variety with fine green leaves. 'Anthony Waterer' spirea (*S. x bumalda* 'Anthony Waterer') is small sized, with green leaves and reddish new growth, and light red, fuzzy flowers in July and August. 'Froebelii' (*S. x bumalda* 'Froebelii') is similar, with pink flowers, and is a little hardier. 'Goldflame' (*S. x bumalda* 'Goldflame') is a compact shrub with yellow leaves tinged with red, and flat clusters of fuzzy pink flowers in July and August. 'Goldmound' (*S. japonica* x 'Goldmound') is a compact shrub with lime green leaves and light pink flowers. ✺ ♠

Wayfaring Tree (*Viburnum lantana*). This is a large-sized shrub with woolly grey green leaves that turn purple in the fall, showy clusters of white flowers, and scarlet berries that turn black as they mature. The fruit is attractive to birds. These shrubs do well in damp, shady places. T●

Weigela (*Weigela* spp.). A medium-sized shrub, it has large purplish green leaves. Large, funnel-shaped pink or red flowers appear in June on last year's wood. Keep new growth trimmed during the summer and remove old woody growth. Weigela often blooms again in the fall. It needs some sun and can tip kill over the winter. 'Centennial' has pink flowers and 'Minuet' has red flowers. ✺

Willow *(Salix* spp.). This can be a shrub as well as a large tree. 'Blue Fox' *(S. brachycarpa* 'Blue Fox') is a small, upright shrub with long, narrow blue grey leaves. It does well in moist, shady places and provides a pretty contrast with greens. Arctic willow *(S. purpurea* 'Gracilis') is a small shrub with very slender leaves. It often dies back in the winter, but grows well again the following spring. It is useful in damp, shady corners where little else thrives. 'Flame' willow *(S. x* 'Flame') is a large shrub with attractive orange red bark that stands out in the winter. Leaves are green in the summer and yellow in the fall. French pussy willow *(S. caprea)* is a large shrub with glossy green, oval leaves. The flowers are the soft, silvery tufts used in dried-flower arrangements or bouquets. T●

Perennial Vines

Vines, or climbers, add texture and colour to walls or fences, create privacy, act as a wind screen, or lend height to a landscape design without taking up much ground space. Some, such as Virginia creeper, leaf out each spring on old wood. Others, such as some clematis, die back to the ground and grow to quite a height in one summer. All except Engelmann ivy need a trellis or wire for support.

American Bittersweet *(Celastrus scandens).* This tall-growing climber has yellow orange capsules that split open to display red-coated seeds inside. They dry well and are used for bouquets. It needs a sturdy trellis as it produces a tangled mass of branches that have to be thinned and pruned occasionally. A male and a female plant are necessary to produce fruit, so several plants are usually grown.

Climbing Honeysuckle *(Lonicera* x *brownii* 'Dropmore Scarlet Trumpet'). Climbing honeysuckle has soft green leaves and trumpetlike orange flowers

Clematis weave a web of colour on a south-facing wall—'Jackmanii', 'Ville de Lyon', and 'Etoile Violette'. FRANK SCOTT

from early summer to a hard fall frost. It tolerates partial shade or sun and is very hardy. Old growth becomes woody, so prune it out occasionally to maintain fresh new growth that flowers well. Control aphids with flower insect sprays. ✿

Climbing Nightshade *(Solanum dulcamara).* Native to the area, this climber grows very quickly from the ground each spring to 3 m (9 ft). It has deep violet flowers, with the petals bent backward, and tiny red fruit. It continues to flower all summer, so will have flowers and fruit at the same time. This vine tolerates shade well. Although it is not readily available from nurseries, it is passed between gardeners regularly; cuttings root easily. T●

Engelmann Ivy *(Parthenocissus quinquefolia* 'Engelmannii'). This cultivar of Virginia creeper has smaller leaves and sucker pads that cling to rough wood or stucco. It does not need support once started up a wall, but be aware that it can invade the surface it is on and it cannot easily be removed. ❦

Hops *(Humulus lupulus).* These fast-growing perennials are used to screen an objectionable view or cover an unattractive building or wall. They are not often planted for landscape value. Hops are susceptible to powdery mildew and several insects, but as they are very hardy and drought resistant are useful on acreages where wind might be a problem. The fruit is used to flavour beer.

Virginia Creeper *(Parthenocissus quinquefolia).* This climber has compound green leaves, small, inconspicuous green flowers, and blue fruit. It turns red in the fall, tolerates shade well, and is quite hardy and drought resistant. It is slow growing, growing leaves on old wood, but can eventually reach the top of a two-storey building. It climbs using tendrils that cling for support. ❦

Clematis *(Clematis* spp.). Clematis are tall climbers with impressive flowers. They take very little space, so can be grown in the tiniest of gardens. Imagine them climbing a pillar, covering that blank wall, or arching over the garden shed. New clematis should be planted after all danger of frost has passed. Plant 5 cm (2 in.) deeper than they are in the container, into rich and deeply dug soil. Water generously and shade the roots with a thick mulch of leaves or gravel. If perennial groundcovers are planted close by, they can also help keep the soil cool and moist. Provide a strong trellis and assist the young shoots to scramble up it. Do not apply lime to your clematis, as they do not require it in our alkaline soil. Once established, clematis benefit greatly from an application of compost dug lightly into the soil surface every spring, along with a handful of bone meal. All large-flowered clematis should be grown against the house for best success. Species and smaller-flowered clematis can be grown out in the garden amongst shrubs or small trees, against fences, arbours, and pergolas. ✿

Clematis can be divided into two distinct groups. These are based on their pruning requirements and not the plants' ability to grow here. There are selections from each group that do equally well in Calgary.

The first group consists mainly of small-flowered species and hybrids that bloom early in the season. They are best left unpruned except for tidying them up to prevent them from being severely overgrown or taking over the garden. The plants are perfectly hardy here and seldom die back. The main flush of flowering takes place in May, after which the wayward growths may be pruned back lightly. New growth quickly takes over where the old growth was and may even sporadically bloom at its tips in late July into August.

C. alpina. Satiny blue, nodding flowers are usually surrounded by four well-developed sepals with a pale tuft in the centre. Cultivars to watch for are 'Frances Rivis' (blue), 'Ruby' (red), 'Willy' (pale pink), and 'Frankie' (mid-blue).

C. macropetala. Similar to *C. alpina* except that the flowers are usually fuller because the centre tuft is well developed. The species *C. macropetala* has double mauve and cream flowers. Cultivars to look for include 'Blue Bird' (blue), 'Maidwell Hall' (deep blue), 'Rosy O'Grady' (soft pink), and 'White Swan' (white).

C. tangutica. This hardy species can either be pruned or not, as it blooms on current growth only. It can be grown out in the open in exposed areas. The yellow, pendant flowers appear in late July and continue intermittently until frost. The attractive seed heads self-sow freely. *C. orientalis* is closely related.

The second group of clematis includes the large- and small-flowered hybrids that require heavy pruning. This is the better group for our climate, as all of the flowers are produced on the current season's growth. The plants may be pruned back severely in the fall or early spring. Several varieties sold by nurseries produce large flowers on their old growth, therefore being less successful for us, as the growth from last year usually winter kills. Flowering usually starts in mid-July and can continue to frost in certain cultivars. Recommended large-flowering hybrids are: 'Comtesse de Bouchaud', satiny, rose pink flowers; 'Etoile Violette', deep purple, floriferous; 'Hagley Hybrid' ('Pink Chiffon'), pale pink, fades in sun; 'Jackmanii', purple, very popular; 'Rouge Cardinal', glowing crimson red; 'Ville de Lyon', carmine red, choice, tall (can also bloom on old wood if protected); 'Huldine', small white flowers.

Of the smaller-flowering hybrids, selections from *C. viticella* do very well in Calgary. These can be planted in the garden and do not require the protection of a building except in the most inhospitable of locations. Choose from: *C. viticella* 'Kermesina'(rubra), deep crimson, floriferous; *C. vit.* 'Purpurea Plena Elegans', double violet purple; *C. vit.* 'Royal Velours', deep velvet purple; *C. vit.* 'Venosa Violacea', purple fading to white in the centre.

Love in the Garden: Roses

When considering roses for Calgary landscapes, the gardener may have heard that they are too much of a challenge, with a high failure rate. Not true! Hardy roses are no more difficult than any other shrub, and even the more tender types can be successfully grown here. Besides several time-tested old favourites, there are a great many new prairie-hardy roses to choose from. Most of these new hardy roses bloom throughout the summer in a sunny location, require little winter protection, and are relatively trouble free.

Note: In the listings, S means under 1 m (3 ft); M means 1–1.5 m (3–5 ft); and L means over 1.5 m (5 ft). DR means disease resistant.

Hardy Roses

These old favourites, long grown in Calgary gardens, bloom only once in a season, but heavily, with a fine show in June and early July.

'Persian Yellow' *(Rosa foetida* 'Persiana') has prickly canes and fine-textured, sweet-smelling foliage, covered with showy, bright yellow, double flowers. It is prone to blackspot. L

'Austrian Copper' *(R. foetida* 'Bicolor') has a brief blaze of colourful single roses, orange scarlet above and yellow below. The fine-textured foliage is prone to blackspot. L

Redleaf rose *(R. rubrifolia* or *R. glauca)* has arching purplish canes, ferny grey purple leaves, and delicate, single pink flowers in profusion, followed by hips. It is an elegant foliage plant. L/DR

Altai rose *(R. spinosissima altaica)* is vigorous and prickly, with fine-textured foliage, covered with highly scented, creamy white single flowers with showy yellow stamens. L/DR

'Harison's Yellow' *(R. harisonii)* has masses of semi-double, bright yellow blooms (the "Yellow Rose of Texas"). L/DR

Several rugosa rose hybrids flower all summer. Of all the hardy roses, rugosas have the greatest need for plenty of peat, compost, and acidifying fertilizer, or they may suffer from yellowing foliage (chlorosis).

'Hansa' has purplish pink, clove-scented flowers, deep green wrinkled leaves, and tough, grey prickly branches. M–L/DR

'Blanc Double de Coubert' has glistening white, richly fragrant flowers, and dark green, shining and crinkled leaves, with large orange hips in winter. M/DR

'Grootendorst' has clusters of small scentless flowers with serrated edges that look like carnations. M/DR

'Pink Grootendorst' has tight clusters of small double "carnations" all summer. S–M/DR

'F. J. Grootendorst' is similar, with red flowers. M/DR

'Therese Bugnet' (boonyay) is vase shaped, with dark red canes, elegant fine foliage, and densely double, fragrant pink flowers in June, and repeat bloom if well fed and watered. L/DR

Over the past several years, many new varieties of roses have been developed in Canada. Many of the 'Explorer' roses, named for early explorers in Canadian history, are hardy here, although they may exhibit considerable tip kill; however, they bloom on new growth that is vigorous and resistant to blackspot and powdery mildew. Most bloom all summer, or heavily in June with a repeat in August.

'William Baffin' is covered with raspberry pink, cream-centred, semi-double, lightly scented flowers that repeat bloom. The long lax canes can be tied to a support for a climber effect. L

'Henry Hudson' has pale pink buds, opening to white and fragrant blooms all season. It is excellent for small gardens. S, spreading

'John Davis' may be used as a pillar rose, with its dark red canes tied to a support. It is smothered with semi-double light pink flowers that have a delicate spicy scent. M–L

'Jens Munk' has bright green wrinkled foliage and is covered continuously with clear lavender pink semi-double blossoms with a strong spicy fragrance. It needs acidifying fertilizer. M

'David Thompson' is densely foliaged, with large, deep crimson, double flowers all summer. It is seldom without bloom. M

'John Cabot' is best tied to supports as a climber. It sports clusters of cherry pink semi-double flowers all summer, which contrast with the handsome bright green foliage. L

'John Cabot', a hardy shrub rose developed in Ottawa, has a long season of summer bloom, and can be tied to a trellis as a climber. KEN GIRARD

'Nearly Wild' is a compact mound of free-flowering, clustered, large, single pink roses, with nonstop bloom all summer. It is choice! S

The 'Parkland' series, developed at Morden, Manitoba, includes several well-known older roses; most are quite resistant to disease. They often tip kill in the spring, but grow back quickly to bloom on new wood.

'Adelaide Hoodless' has clusters of semi-double, rich red flowers in late June, repeating in early August. M

'Cuthbert Grant' has drooping clusters of compact, deep red, velvety flowers and glossy foliage. S–M

'Prairie Dawn' has clear bright pink, lightly scented flowers that repeat in August if deadheaded faithfully. L

In the ongoing 'Morden' series:

'Morden Centennial' has clusters of double pink roses, borne in profusion all summer, and fine foliage on dark red canes. M

'Morden Cardinette' has cardinal red double flowers all summer. Very hardy, it is suitable for massing in beds. S

'Morden Amorette' is covered with slightly fragrant, carmine (vivid crimson) double flowers all summer, if spent blooms are deadheaded. S

'Morden Blush' blooms all summer long, with clusters of exquisite, baby pink double flowers with a soft fragrance. S–M

'Morden Ruby' has clusters of luscious pink double flowers, speckled with red, all summer. Remove spent blooms to tidy it. M

Climbers are rarely successful here as they bloom on older canes that winterkill unless they are removed from their trellises and covered for the winter. In their place, some of the taller hardy roses such as 'William Baffin' and 'John Cabot' can be tied to supports. Many hardy roses not available locally are worth trying. Most mail-order businesses supply catalogues containing good descriptions and hardiness information.

CARE AND PLANTING OF HARDY ROSES

Although you may find some hardy shrub roses for sale bareroot (no pot, no soil, with the roots in damp sawdust in a sealed container) in the spring with the tender roses, most are available for sale in pots, along with other shrubs. They are best planted during May or June, before the hot summer weather. They need at least half a day of direct sun, and a healthy, well-drained soil, modified if necessary with added compost. Plant them in the same way as other shrubs, with the bud union slightly below soil level, in holes large enough for the roots to spread.

Most hardy roses do not require any specific winter protection. Mulching the soil around the roots with dry leaves or straw keeps the soil temperature more consistent during winter weather. Pruning is usually done just after they start to leaf out in the spring. Old, woody canes and those crossing or needing shortening are pruned out—cut back to an outward-facing bud. There will probably be some winter tip kill, which is also removed at this time. Since most hardy roses bloom on new wood, some winter die back and spring pruning cause no harm. Those that bloom only once a season should be pruned just after flowering.

Tender Roses

Although tender roses do require some attention in the fall to ensure winter survival, it is not difficult to overwinter them here. Many Calgary gardeners are successful, and some rose gardens are spectacular. Most tender roses will bloom from June into September, sometimes even October, with light frosts doing no damage.

Tender roses may be divided into three categories, based on their floral character.

Hybrid tea roses have large flowers on long stems, with double blossoms borne singly or with several side shoots, and are excellent for cutting.

Floribunda roses have smaller blooms, usually borne in clusters, with each cluster having several blooms open at one time.

Grandiflora roses are a combination of hybrid tea and floribundas. They have clusters of large flowers on long stems and are also good for cutting.

Hundreds of varieties of tender roses are available. At first, you will be more successful trying proven varieties that are known to do well here. Once you have been successful with these, you may enjoy experimenting with other, lesser-known varieties.

The tiny, miniature roses, less than 30 cm (12 in.) high, are surprisingly hardy and make a wonderful front border for larger tender roses. They are grown on their own roots, rather than being grafted, so they can experience considerable winter die back and still survive. There is a large range of colour variation to choose from. Miniature roses are commonly sold in 10-cm (4-in.) pots in May. Weather permitting, they bloom from July through September. They need to be covered in the winter in the same way as other tender roses do, but on a smaller scale. An ice-cream pail with the bottom removed, filled with about 15 cm (6 in.) of dry leaves, will do nicely.

PLANTING TENDER ROSES

Roses do best in full sunlight for at least 80 percent of the day. Inadequate light creates weak, spindly roses that are prone to mildew and have few blossoms. Tender roses benefit from some protection from north and west winds, and from soil free of roots from other trees and shrubs. Plants should be about 75 cm (30 in.) apart, at least 1 m (3 ft) from the foundation of the house. Roses planted too close to a sunny foundation may sprout during Chinooks and die during the next cold spell. Winter protection keeps the roots cold longer when they are planted in the open. The aim of winter protection is to keep the soil temperature consistent, rather than to keep the roots from getting too cold.

The best time to purchase plants is in May, when there is a good selection and the weather is usually moderate. Tender roses are available in three forms. In order of suitability, they are: potted and in leaf, bareroot, and individually packaged. Potted roses are the best choice for beginners, even though there is not as good a selection, as they can be seen to be growing and their health is relatively easy to determine. For the more advanced grower, there are rose nurseries that ship bareroot plants to customers. They often have a large inventory of hard-to-find varieties. The best time to order bareroot roses is fall or early winter, so that the plants can arrive in late April or early May. Packaged roses are often difficult to establish, as the roots have been cut off to fit into the package, and they could have been sitting on a shelf under less-than-ideal conditions.

'Portrait' is a hybrid tea rose that needs special care to prepare it for Calgary winters. FRANK SCOTT

Roses need lots of water but cannot tolerate constantly wet roots. If the subsoil is very hard and drainage is poor, remove the soil to a depth of 30 cm (12 in.) and replace it with good quality topsoil and compost. Dig some of this mixture into the soil at the bottom of the hole as well, to loosen it and improve the drainage.

The planting instructions that come with a tender rose will likely not be applicable to our climate. Tender roses must be planted so that the graft union (the swollen place where the tender rose is grafted on to a hardier rootstock) is 10 cm (4 in.) below the ground. Plant them at an upward angle, not straight up and down. This is called the slant method. This protects the graft union from sudden temperature changes during Chinooks. Firm the soil to eliminate air pockets and water well. It is a good idea to protect the exposed stems for a couple of weeks with a mulch or with earth piled up around them, to prevent them from drying out. This is the time to label the newly planted roses, either with permanent tags or by making a plan on paper and numbering the plants for a master list. Water newly planted roses well, as needed. The plants must neither become too dry nor become water-logged. As new shoots appear, remove the covering over the stems and prune back dead wood.

CARE OF TENDER ROSES

Roses should be watered deeply when the soil becomes dry, usually about every five to seven days in warm, dry weather. Frequent, light sprinkling should be avoided. Soaker hoses, drip irrigation, and very low sprinklers use water more efficiently than oscillating sprinklers with high streams of water. However, periodically giving the leaves a hard spray of water, especially on the underside, will do a great deal to prevent problems with spider mites and aphids. Water early in the day, on sunny days if possible, so that leaves and flowers dry quickly. Damp leaves in our cool evenings are much more prone to powdery mildew and blackspot.

Roses need fertilizer, but it does not have to be a fertilizer specifically for roses. Try water-soluble 20–20–20 or 15–30–15, or 16–20–0, which is sold in pelleted form. Manures and other natural fertilizers added to the soil help the plants make the best use of commercial fertilizers. Fertilize roses regularly, following label instructions, throughout the growing season until about August 15. After mid-August, fertilizer encourages too much new growth, which is harmed by early fall frosts. Do not overfertilize to make roses bloom; they bloom when there is adequate sunlight.

Winter protection is necessary for tender roses to survive in our climate. Most important is to keep the soil temperature consistent, as winter Chinooks can encourage new growth that will later be damaged by colder weather. A few degrees of frost in the fall establishes dormancy, but it is wise to cover tender roses before a sudden, hard frost—usually sometime in mid-October. It is easier to cover a rose that is not too tall, and as they die back a great deal anyway, you can cut them back to 45 cm (18 in.) at the end of the growing season. There is no need to remove all the leaves, unless they are diseased (in which case, be sure they are not left on the ground underneath the bush). Water roses before the first hard frost so that the soil is damp when they are covered. Each rose should have an inverted pot or 22-L (5-gal.) bucket with the bottom cut out, a rose collar, a Styrofoam rose cone (with holes cut into the sides or the top cut out for air circulation), or a heavy cardboard box placed over it. Then fill this covering with vermiculite, peat moss, straw, sawdust, or well-packed, dry leaves. If there are several plants in the same area, put straw between the pots to add more insulation. Cover the pots with anything made of cloth, not plastic—old carpet, several layers of burlap, landscape fabric, or old bedspreads. Frost blankets, layers of quilt batting sandwiched between burlap covers and stitched together, insulate well. Fabric insulating materials must be held down with rocks or pieces of wood to keep them in place over the winter. Some gardeners build plywood boxes with lids around a rose bed to enclose the insulating material.

Resist uncovering your roses too soon in the spring. Many people find that their roses die because they uncovered them to see if they were alive. If it becomes so warm that they could start to bud, remove the covering slowly, but keep it close at hand in case frost threatens. The rule of thumb is to uncover roses when the poplar trees leaf out in early May. Put any insulating material (peat moss, leaves, straw) into the compost for further use.

Prune roses when the winter protection is removed. It is then easy to see what shoots are alive, and to remove old, dead canes down to that point. Don't be too quick to discard a rose that has no shoots in the spring. Wait until mid-June before deciding it has not survived. Once roses are growing well, crossing canes or those growing outward can be shortened or removed, but little pruning is necessary.

Even if the tender rose dies back to below ground, as long as it survives above the graft, it will grow and bloom again. If it dies back to below the graft, the rose that grows will be the rootstock, which will not have attractive blooms as rootstock is chosen only for its hardiness. Suckers from the rootstock grow very rapidly. They have seven leaflets on a stem, whereas hybrid forms have five. If suckers are the only growth, remove the rose. Suckers can also grow along with the hybrid growth. Count the leaflets and remove any suckers directly from the root.

Roses are subject to insect problems, as are any flowering plants outdoors. Aphids, rose weevils, and leafhoppers can damage new leaves and flower buds. If a regular hard spray of water doesn't help, rose dust or rose and flower spray is a safe way to keep them under control. You may have to apply it several times for better control, particularly if rain or a sprinkler washes it off. Spider mites are not insects; they are closely related to spiders. They cause tiny light-coloured specks in the leaves, and a dusty, filmy web on the underside of the leaf. Insecticides won't have any affect; it must be a mite killer. Some roses are subject to blackspot, a fungal infection that causes black spots on the leaves. A systemic fungicide, used as soon as the first spots appear, will likely help, but applications may have to be repeated every two weeks for several treatments. Powdery mildew makes the leaves look like they have been dusted with icing sugar. A rose dust containing a fungicide that indicates it will control powdery mildew is effective if used soon enough and repeated periodically. When using chemicals to combat pests and disease, be sure to read all labels and follow instructions carefully.

TOP TEN TENDER ROSES FOR CALGARY			
Red	'Royal William'	**Pink**	'Electron'
	'Fragrant Cloud'		'Pink Peace'
	'Showbiz'	**Orange**	'Die Welt'
Yellow	'Peace'		'Ave Maria'
White	'Pascali'		
	'Sheer Bliss'		

SIX

Faithful Friends: Perennials and Hardy Bulbs

Using Perennials in Calgary Gardens

William Reader, Calgary Parks superintendent from 1913 to 1942, who built and planted a once world-famous rock garden on the north slope of Union Cemetery, was an ardent promoter of hardy perennials. He noted that no other class of plants delivers such good returns for such a small outlay of money and time. In a well-planned border, they give week-by-week interest from early spring to late fall. Even in Calgary, crocus, scilla, and hepatica are already in bloom by early April, and many plants, such as achillea, rudbeckia, and globe thistle are usually still in bloom as late as Thanksgiving.

By April 1, there is plenty to see in a perennial garden, where hardy shoots have been pushing up through the crumbling mulch since mid-March to form ever-larger mounds of green. There can even be a display of colourful flowers if hardy bulbs have been planted among the peonies, bleeding hearts, and other plants. A local bloom-time chart, averaged over eight years, lists forty-two plants in flower before May 24—all enduring frost and late snow storms without much trouble. With our brief frost-free growing season, local gardeners are warming to these faithful friends, which cheerily reappear in the most barren of seasons to provide bloom long before any tender flowers can be planted out.

Perennials are plants that live for an indefinite number of years on the same roots. Most herbaceous perennials die down in the fall for a period of winter dormancy, the hardy roots putting forth new growth the following spring. A few, such as pinks, rock cresses, and many alpine plants, remain green through the winter. There are hundreds of species and varieties of hardy perennials to suit almost every situation in the garden—from deep shade, whether dry or damp, to hot, dry, wind-swept spots. Perennials come in many heights, colours, and textures. Some are grown for their lovely flowers; others for their interesting or scented foliage. They have been developed from wild species from all over the world—peonies from China, tulips from Turkey, gaillardia from the Canadian prairie. Although initially more expensive to buy than annuals, perennials return every year (all being well). Also, gardeners love to share and trade plants, and horticultural societies set up plant exchanges for their members. As clumps increase and are divided, new plants provide interest on the initial investment.

Study the perennial beds in your garden—are they sunny and dry, shady all day, or low and wet?—and select plants to suit the conditions. Then amend the soil according to the plants' needs: from lean and fast draining, to moist and rich with organic matter. When designing flower borders, consider blooming time, height and spread, colour, and leaf texture. The new gardener will make plenty of mistakes, but all gardeners do, even after years of experience. Luckily, perennials are portable (some big ones only just) and moving the plants into better arrangements is part of the fun.

In the last few years, renewed interest in perennials has many gardeners thinking that they are much less work than the annual buying and planting of tender flowers. Those seeking a lower-maintenance garden must be cautioned. There are chores from March to October—spring clean-up, staking, mulching, watering, weeding, feeding, deadheading, fall clean-up, and preparation for winter—and the inevitable dividing and moving as perennials outgrow their spots or need to be relocated. For most gardeners, however, the effort is enjoyable in itself as exercise and as a chance to get close to the earth.

In this chapter, perennials are listed in alphabetical order by botanical (scientific) names as many species have no common names, or the common names are obscure and seldom used. Many plants have several different common names; also, some common names refer to more than one species (loosestrife can mean *Lythrum* or *Lysimachia*; poppy and lily are used with many plants that are not really poppies or lilies).

Perennials Recommended for Calgary Gardens

FLOWERS

Achillea spp. (yarrow). Most species form clumps of ferny, sometimes spicily pungent leaves, dark green to silvery grey. Woody stems support flat-topped heads of many tiny florets tightly clustered together. Most are medium to tall plants for the middle or back of the border. They bloom in summer. ○ D ✿ ✿ ❦

A. filipendulina, 75 cm (30 in.), has incised, fragrant leaves and yellow flowers from mid-summer onward. 'Coronation Gold' has large rich yellow flowers. Similar but more compact, *A. taygetea* 'Moonshine' has finely cut silver foliage and large pale primrose yellow flowers. A rapid spreader, *A. millefolium,* 60 cm (24 in.), comes in many pink-flowered varieties, often with conspicuous white eyes and deep green ferny leaves. New strains include 'Summer Pastels' and the 'Galaxy' series.

Quite different, *A. ptarmica* 'The Pearl' (sneezewort), 75 cm (30 in.), forms dense, spreading thickets of tall stems with narrow dark green leaves and sprays of tiny, white, double pompom flowers. For alpine beds or edging, early blooming

GUIDE TO ICONS

Full sun
○

Part shade
◉

Shade
●

Rock garden
RG

Cut flower
✿

Dried flower
❦

Woodland
W

Water garden
WG

Groundcover
GC

Poisonous
✖

Dry
D

Moist
M

Fragrant
✺

Border
✿✿✿

Meadow
❦

A. tomentosa, or woolly yarrow, 30 cm (12 in.), bears large bright yellow flowers above dense mats of silvery green filigree leaves. ○ D RG

Achilleas thrive in quick-draining, moderately fertile soil. Sand and grit lighten soil and improve drainage. Staking is essential for tall species.

Aconitum napellus (monkshood) 150 cm (60 in.). Rounded mounds of deeply divided leaves grow rapidly into impressive tall towers of glossy dark green, supporting racemes of knobby greenish flower buds. The

'Summer Pastels" yarrow is easily grown from seed to bloom that same season. JUDITH DOYLE

flowers, resembling a monk's cowl, open sequentially for many weeks from mid-July until late August, in shades of indigo or purplish blue, or blue and white *(bicolor)*. 'Newry Blue', a deep marine blue, flowers from June to September. More compact, at 90 cm (36 in.), are 'Blue Sceptre' (blue/cream) and 'Bressingham Spire' (violet blue). *A. henryi* 'Spark's Variety' has vivid purple blue flowers in June and July. Provide deep, well-drained soil enriched with organic matter, plenty of moisture, and a sunny or partially shaded site; stake; watch for and remove caterpillars from the flower buds in spring. All parts are poisonous. ○ ● M ✖

Actaea pachypoda and *A. rubra* (baneberry) 50 cm (20 in.). These native plants for the woodland garden require moist soil with some organic matter

---

CALGARY'S OFFICIAL FLOWER

Pulsatilla vulgaris rubra, formerly *Anemone pulsatilla rubra,* (red pasque-flower, windflower) 30 cm (12 in.). The affection of Calgarians for the brave little prairie crocus *(Anemone patens)* must have been the reason why so many voted its garden cousin Calgary's official flower. Early in spring, silvery shoots rise from thick woody crowns, the large silky flower buds in their feathery muffs racing ahead of the tufts of ferny leaves. The nodding, downy buds open to form deep, starry cups of ruby red sepals surrounding a showy boss of yellow stamens. White, mauve, purple, and rose forms are also available. Fading flowers are followed by fluffy plumes of long, silky-tailed seeds. The plants are covered with fine glistening hairs that protect them from drying wind and cold. Well-drained soil and an open sunny location suit these plants best. ○ RG

Calgary's official flower is *Pulsatilla vulgaris rubra,* a red form of pasqueflower that blooms early in spring. JUDITH REMPEL

While many plants have both common and botanical (scientific) names, some have only a botanical name. Many botanical names are already in common use (*Delphinium, Phlox*), or sound almost the same (*Paeonia*—peony, *Rosa*—rose), and so are already familiar. Some plants are actually more commonly known by their botanical name (hosta rather than plantain lily, bergenia rather than rockfoil). Common names vary from region to region and country to country, but all over the world, gardeners recognize the international system of botanical nomenclature.

The botanical name of Calgary's official flower is *Pulsatilla vulgaris rubra*, each word a description of the genus, species, and variety of this particular plant. A genus (plural genera) is a grouping of closely related specific plants; this first name is always written in italics (or underlined) and capitalized, unless it is also used as a common name—pulsatilla. A species (both a singular and plural word) is a specific plant within a genus. A variety is a further subclassification, indicating small but significant differences, such as colour (in this case *rubra*—red); naturally occurring varieties reproduce true from seed. Second and third names are always italicized or underlined but usually not capitalized.

Cultivated varieties, or cultivars, are developed from cuttings or divisions of superior varieties. They are given a capitalized name in single quotation marks but never italicized—*Pulsatilla* 'Camla' is a mauve-flowered cultivar. Hybrids are crosses (x) between species (interspecific) of the same genus (*Chrysanthemum* x *superbum* or Shasta daisy) or, more rarely, crosses between genera (x *Heucherella* 'Bridget Bloom', an intergeneric cross between *Heuchera*, coral bells, and *Tiarella*, foam flower).

Pulsatilla	the genus name
Pulsatilla vulgaris	the species name, meaning common
Pulsatilla vulgaris rubra	a red-flowered variety
Pulsatilla vulgaris 'Camla'	a mauve-flowered cultivar
Anemone pulsatilla rubra	former name of *P. vulgaris rubra*
Windflower, pasqueflower	common names

Whereas the common name may vary or identify more than one plant, the botanic name is unique and is given to no other plant.

added. Leaves are coarse and divided, with white flowers in spring followed by fruit: white in the species and red in the variety *rubra*. ● ◉ M W

Aegopodium podagraria 'Variegatum' (variegated goutweed, bishop's weed) 30 cm (12 in.). Use with care! Because of their rampant growth habit, these plants should be isolated by paving or deep barriers, or planted in deep pots sunk into the ground, so they cannot invade other territory. The frosty green and white variegated leaves are very attractive. Flat umbels of white lacy flowers appear in summer. It looks its best in moist shade. ● ◉ M GC

Ajuga reptans (bugleweed) 20 cm (8 in.). Spreading by above-ground stems (stolons), the rosettes of small, rounded, and wrinkled leaves are green, with a purple tint if given enough sun, or variegated with silver, pink, orange, white, or yellow, depending on the cultivar. Short spikes of flowers appear in June, usually blue or purple, with pink and white selections available. *A. genevensis* does not spread so fast; *A. pyramidalis* has flowers on longer stalks. All prefer moist, cool partial shade. ● ◉ M GC

Alcea rosea (hollyhocks) 180 cm (72 in.) or more. Tall wands bear large, out-facing single or double flowers in shades of white, pink, crimson, red, or yellow, opening in succession from the bottom to the top of the spires. The round, lobed leaves are rough in texture. They need a large space in full sun, sheltered from the wind, and rich, moist, well-drained soil; stake. Usually biennial in habit, they will reproduce from self-sown seed. ○ M

Alchemilla mollis (lady's mantle) 30 cm (12 in.). Shallowly lobed, toothed, fan-shaped leaves of softest grey green are crowned with a froth of tiny chartreuse flowers in late spring. It does best in partial shade in moist soil. Fading flowers should be removed or dozens of seedlings will be produced. ◉ M W

Anaphalis margaritacea (pearly everlasting) 45 cm (18 in.). In summer, long stems clothed with silvery grey downy leaves are topped by clusters of white papery bracts centred with tiny yellow flowers. One plant soon spreads into a good-sized clump, in dry or moist soil in a sunny or partly shaded position. ○ D ❧ ◗

Androsace spp. (rock jasmine) 15 cm (6 in.). These excellent rock garden plants grow in mounds. *A. carnea* has very tight growths of deep green glossy leaves and long-lasting white or pink flowers in May. *A. sarmentosa* has pretty rosettes of leaves that spread by stolons, with gorgeous pink flowers in May. *A. sempervivoides* has smaller rosettes with glossy leaves and pink flowers. ○ GC RG

Anemone sylvestris (snowdrop anemone) 30 cm (12 in.). Lovely large, white, cupped flowers appear over low mounds of deeply cut, ferny leaves in spring. It lights up a shady site and needs moist soil. Deadheading prevents unwanted seedlings. It also spreads by rhizomes. ● ◉ M W

Antennaria spp. (pussytoes) 20 cm (8 in.). In summer, the short woody stalks carry small clusters of fuzzy flowers in white or pink *(A. rosea)* above flat, creeping mats of tiny silver leaves. Foliage is persistent. It needs full sun and dry, gritty soil. ○ D GC RG

Anthemis tinctoria (golden Marguerite) 75 cm (30 in.). This sun-loving, drought-resistant, free-flowering daisy is happy in soil of low fertility. Short-lived, it self-sows if a few seed heads are left to develop, although deadheading is impor-tant to keep flowers coming. Anthemis has ferny foliage and sprays of short-rayed golden yellow daisies; 'Moonlight' is pale yellow, 'Kelwayi' more golden, and *A. sancti-johannis,* deep orange. ○ D ❧ ◗

Aquilegia spp. and hybrids (columbine) to 60 cm (24 in.). All have delicate, starry, spurred flowers and bluish green, fernlike foliage. Long graceful stems bear distinctive, often two-toned, flowers in late spring and early summer. Hybrids have larger flowers with longer spurs in shades of red/yellow, mauve/cream, blue/white, and solid colours. *A. caerulea* has showy blue and white flowers. *A. canadense,* a native species, has small red and yellow flowers. They all like lightly shaded, moist, rich soil. A few seed pods allowed to ripen will ensure a varied supply of these sometimes short-lived flowers. ◉ M ✿ W

Arabis caucasica or A. albida (rock cress) to 30 cm (12 in.). Spreading mounds of small grey green or variegated fuzzy leaves are covered with sprays of showy white or pink fragrant flowers in early spring. Foliage is evergreen and can be damaged without good snow cover. Arabis needs light, porous soil and full sun. ○ D GC RG

Arctostaphylos uva-ursi (bearberry, kinnikinnick) 15 cm (6 in.). A native plant with shining, rounded, evergreen leaves, brightened by tiny pinky white flowers in spring and red berries in fall. It thrives in dappled shade or full sun. Plant in areas with good snow cover to protect the foliage from burning and drying. ○ ◉ GC

A dry, exposed, sunny site suits snow-in-summer *(Cerastium tomentosum),* a creeping plant that needs to be confined. MAUREEN IRETON

Armeria juniperifolia (thrift) to 20 cm (8 in.). Rounded tufts of dense, fine leaves set off pink or white pom-pom flowers in spring. *A. maritima* is a larger species with bright pink flowers on long stems; deadheading prolongs the season of bloom. They need fast-draining sandy soil in full sun. Protect evergreen leaves with spruce or pine boughs in winter. ○ D RG

Artemisia spp. (sage). Sages are noted for their aromatic silvery foliage and hardiness in exposed, dry locations. They must have gritty soil and well-drained sites in full sun to be at their best. Southernwood or old man, *A. abrotanum,* 60 cm (24 in.), is very ferny with a strong medicinal aroma. *A. ludoviciana,* 60 cm (24 in.), has handsome, narrow silver leaves in large, upright, spreading thickets of stems; it should be contained. *A. schmidtiana* 'Silver Mound', 30 cm (12 in.), forms perfect domes of soft, feathery, fragrant silver leaves if the soil is not too rich. *A. stellerana* 'Silver Brocade', 30 cm (12 in.), spreads into a gleaming silver carpet of beautiful, deeply lobed leaves. ○ D ✸ RG ✿

Aruncus dioicus, formerly *A. sylvester,* (goatsbeard) 150 cm (60 in.). Stately aruncus grows into a massive rounded bush and occupies a wide space. In early summer, large flower plumes wave above the compound leaves, looking like lovely starbursts. The minute creamy white flowers are borne in loose panicles of long, frothy strands. *A. dioicus* 'Kneiffii', 75 cm (30 in.), with deeply incised leaflets, is similar but smaller. Tiny *A. aethusifolius,* 30 cm (12 in.), forms low clumps of fine, ferny foliage and creamy flowers. Aruncus have deep tap roots, which make moving them difficult. Rich, deep, moist soil high in organic matter, in semi-shade, is best. ◉ M W

Aster spp. (aster, starwort, Michaelmas daisy). Suitable for the border are the tall Michaelmas daisy types and compact mounding plants derived from crosses with smaller species. Asters bear dozens of small clustered daisies with white, pink, blue mauve, or purple ray petals and yellow centres, over a long season in summer. They prefer moist yet well-drained soil with a high organic content, and a sunny position. Alpine aster, *A. alpinus,* 30 cm (12 in.), a spring-flowering species with large mauve blue daisies, is suitable for rock gardens. ○ 🌸 🌿

Chrysanthemum leucanthemum, or ox-eye daisy, blooms in June. JOHN DOYLE

Astilbe hybrids (astilbe) 45–60 cm (18–24 in.). Hybrids of *A. japonica, simplicifolia,* and x *arendsii* provide flowers from mid-summer to fall. They grow well in cool and shady or sunny and boggy sites, sheltered from drying winds, in rich, moist soil amended with generous amounts of organic matter and mulch. Their fernlike leaves are dark green, with a hint of red in the red-flowered forms. In summer, fluffy, tapering plumes of white, pink, red, or magenta flowers have a long season. A tiny late-blooming species, *A. chinensis pumila,* is suitable for the rock garden. ◉ M W

Astrantia major (masterwort) 60 cm (24 in.). Mounds of three-lobed, toothed leaves are topped in June and July by long-lasting greenish pink flowers that are very delicate in appearance; the variety *rubra* is red. It needs only ordinary garden soil in a moist, partially shaded site. ◉ M W

Aubrieta deltoidea (purple rock cress) 15 cm (6 in.). Low, spreading mats of small grey green leaves are densely covered in early spring with hot pink, mauve,

A deep-pink form of the well-loved painted daisy (pyrethrum) lends its brilliant colour to the summer border. JUDITH DOYLE

rple flowers; a summer shearing triggers more bloom. It needs light, well-
d soil in full sun. *A. gracea* has smaller, less-fuzzy leaves but more prolific
wier flowers of hot pink and vibrant purple. ○ GC RG

nia saxatilis (basket-of-gold alyssum) 30 cm (12 in.). Early sprays of
bright yellow fragrant flowers foam above tough grey foliage. It must have a
sharply drained, sunny site; a rock wall for it to tumble down is ideal. Plants are
longer-lived if cut back by one-third after flowering. ○ D RG

Bergenia cordifolia and *B. crassifolia* (bergenia, rockfoil) 40 cm (16 in.).
These extremely hardy plants spread by rhizomelike stems to form large clumps.
The broad, rounded, leathery leaves, the size of dinner plates, are deep green in
summer, turning scarlet, then purple, as winter sets in. In spring, the limp foliage
comes back to life to set off clusters of small, scented pink, purple, or white flowers in May. Both species do best in moderately fertile, well-drained loam in a
semi-shaded position. An annual top-dressing of compost keeps the clumps
blooming for many years. ◉ RG

Brunnera macrophylla (brunnera) 45 cm (18 in.). Enduring dry shade under
shrubs, where it will self-sow, brunnera sends up loose sprays of tiny, bright blue,
forget-me-not flowers above rough, heart-shaped leaves in spring. ◉ W

Calceolaria spp. (slipperwort) 20 cm (8 in.). Intriguing little yellow flowers
with pouched lower lips are borne plentifully on short wiry stems above tightly
clustered leaves in summer. It likes moist, well-drained soil, enriched with organic
matter. ◉ M W

Caltha palustris (marsh marigold, king cup) 45 cm (18 in.). Early in spring,
shiny, deep green, round, and toothed leaves are soon followed by glossy, golden,
buttercuplike flowers. 'Flore Pleno' is the double form. It needs full sun and boggy
soil in spring and early summer. Sunken pails punched with a few holes make
good "mini" bogs and are easy to keep wet. Allow to dry in late summer. This is a
native plant in moist areas of central Alberta. ○ M WG

Campanula spp. (bellflower). Carpathian bellflower, *C. carpatica*, 30 cm (12
in.), is long-lived, hardy, and reliable. With daily deadheading, it flowers profusely
from July to frost. This little gem forms a neat mound of delicate rounded leaves
with fine, wiry branching stems that bear large china blue or white flowers.
Clustered bellflower, *C. glomerata*, 60 cm (24 in.), also known as Dane's blood
and twelve apostles, spreads rapidly to form large dense mats of coarse foliage. In
July, rough-textured leaves and tall stiff stalks are topped with large tightly packed
clusters of showy purple or white flowers. Both species demand full sun and well-
drained soil. ○ ❧

Peach-leaved bellflower, *C. persicifolia*, 75 cm (30 in.), has elegant spires of
large blue or white out-facing bells held well above low clumps of narrow leaves;
the variety *humosa* has double bells. Deadheading encourages more bloom.
Persistent foliage must be protected from drying out in winter with a covering of
evergreen boughs. This bellflower likes rich, moist soil in a sunny position that
receives some afternoon shade. ○ ◉ M ❧

An old favourite, Canterbury bells, *C. medium*, 75 cm (30 in.), has large single
or double flowers in shades of pink, violet, blue, and white. The variety *calycan-*

thema is the cup-and-saucer flower type. Canterbury bells are biennial so allow them to self-sow. Seeds produce basal rosettes the first year, then bloom prolifically the second year, set seed, and die.

The wee *C. cochlearifolia* (fairy bells), also called *C. pusilla*, 12 cm (5 in.), is a pretty little menace that can insinuate itself everywhere. Its mats of tiny bright green leaves are covered all summer with miniature blue or white bells. Similar in size but not invasive are *C. portenschlagiana (C. muralis)*, with bluish purple flowers; and *C. poscharskyana*, a low, sprawling plant with a profusion of large lilac flowers. In sunny, well-drained locations, both are vigorous and easy. ○ RG ❦

Catananche caerula (Cupid's dart) 45 cm (18 in.). Summer-blooming, sun-loving, and drought-resistant, with papery, tufted pale blue flowers and greyish grassy leaves, it is best in rock gardens. This short-lived plant may survive longer if it is planted in humus-enriched, well-drained, sandy soil. ○ ✑ D ❦

Centaurea spp. (cornflower, knapweed). *C. montana*, 75 cm (30 in.), bears a myriad of brilliant blue spidery flowers on leafy, floppy stems, in late spring. Cut it back hard after flowering as the foliage becomes unsightly. Fresh growth soon reappears and may rebloom. Pink centaureas, *C. dealbata* (similar to *C. hypoleuca* or 'John Coutts'), grow a little taller, with deeply cut leaves and feathery mauve pink flowers in June and July. The massive *C. macrocephala*, or golden knapweed, 120 cm (48 in.), is a robust plant for the back of the border. Its sturdy stems are clothed with husky, coarse leaves. Each bloom opens into a fluffy golden thistle in July and August. Centaureas require only ordinary soil, in full sun. They self-sow if not deadheaded. All but the yellow species need staking. ○ ◉ ❦

Cerastium tomentosum (snow-in-summer) 20 cm (8 in.). Spreading mounds of narrow silvery grey leaves are eclipsed in mid-summer by tiny, intensely white flowers. Although it is somewhat invasive, a dry, sunny spot and well-drained soil help keep it under control. It is perfect for a hot, barren, windy location. ○ D GC

Chrysanthemum morifolium cultivars (mums) 45–75 cm (18–30 in.). Prairie-hardy 'Morden Mums' are cushion mums that bloom from July until frost: 'Canary' (yellow); 'Cameo' (white); 'Gaiety' (bronze); 'Mertice Bottomley' (lavender); and others. They do best in full sun or partial shade, in rich, well-drained soil. Shallow rooted, they need frequent, plentiful watering. To keep them going, divide them every two years, replanting only young outer divisions. A taller hybrid that needs little care and blooms reliably every September is *C.* x *rubellum* 'Clara Curtis', 75 cm (30 in.). It has sprays of single pink daisies with yellow centres.

C. coccineum, also known as *Pyrethrum roseum* (painted daisy, pyrethrum), 90 cm (36 in.), has long floppy stems that bear dozens of daisies in early summer. Pink, red, or white ray petals surround yellow disks; the deep green foliage is dainty and carrotlike. Early staking is advised.

C. x *superbum* or *C. maximum* (Shasta daisy), 90 cm (36 in.), grows tall, robust thickets of strong stems clothed with dark green, narrow, toothed leaves that carry a huge quantity of large white daisies with yellow centres, in July and August. 'Alaska' is one of the hardiest cultivars. Very similar, but blooming earlier, the ox-eye daisy, *C. leucanthemum*, must be deadheaded to prevent copious self-sowing.

These last two plants need well-drained fertile soil and regular watering; staking is not necessary. ○ ◉ M ⚘

Cimicifuga racemosa (bugbane) 120 cm (48 in.). These plants have handsome compound leaves and multiple spires of tiny, fluffy white flowers in September. Moist, fertile soil in half shade is best, as they must receive some sun to bloom before frost. The *simplex* species fails to bloom in Calgary. ◉ M ⊛ W

Clematis spp. (clematis). Low-growing clematis species, while floppy, can be staked to take their place in borders: *C. recta*, 90 cm (36 in.), can support itself on other plants or trail from a low wall. It bears small white or cream flowers in early summer. *C. integrifolia*, 60 cm (24 in.), bears enchanting, deep blue, nodding, flared bells on wiry stems. *C. heracleifolia davidiana*, 90 cm (36 in.), is shrubby with scented blue flowers. All like a sunny position in cool, moist (mulched) soil that is well drained. ○ M ⚘

Maiden pinks *(Dianthus deltoides)* flower in July and self-sow generously. JUDITH DOYLE

Convallaria majalis (lily-of-the-valley) 20 cm (8 in.). An old favourite with its upright, pointed leaves and racemes of tiny, white, pendant flowers, it quickly spreads to form a luxuriant carpet of green. The flowers appear from late May into June and are exceedingly fragrant. Perfect for shaded areas, it is best confined with deep wood or concrete edging. ● ◉ GC ⊛

Coreopsis grandiflora or *C. lanceolata* (tickseed) 60 cm (24 in.). These short-lived, sun-loving, floppy plants are covered with yellow wide-rayed daisies in summer. Some of the smaller cultivars, such as 'Gold-fink' and 'Baby Sun', are longer-lived. Thread-leaved coreopsis, *C. verticillata*, 45–60 cm (18–24 in.), has lemony or golden yellow flowers on wiry stems with fine leaves, all summer. Coreopsis needs only moderately fertile soil and good drainage. ○ ⚘ ❦

Dianthus 'Spotty' is a modern cultivar of old-fashioned garden pinks. MAUREEN IRETON

Corydalis lutea (golden corydalis) 30 cm (12 in.). Low mounds of delicate, ferny, blue green foliage are sprinkled with drooping clusters of small, tubular yellow flowers over a long period in early summer. It thrives in shady, moist, well-drained locations. ◉ M W

Delphinium spp. and hybrids. Delphiniums appear early in spring, soon forming large mounds of pale green, lobed and toothed leaves that darken with maturity. Long racemes crowded with individual single or double florets top the tall, brittle stalks in summer. Many hybrids do well here. Of the Giant Pacific hybrids, 180 cm (72 in.), the 'Round Table' series, mostly doubles in shades of white, pink, lavender, pale and dark blue, violet and purple, is popular: 'King Arthur' (purple); 'Black Knight' (deep violet); 'Galahad' (white); and 'Guinevere' (mauve pink). Most of these have florets with a small central cluster of short petals, called a "bee," in a contrasting colour. 'Summer Skies' is soft blue with a white bee. For small spaces, the Dwarf Pacifics, 60 cm (24 in.), are useful: 'Blue Fountains' (in mixed blues) and 'Blue Heaven' (sky blue). The Belladonna hybrids are a little taller and bushier, in shades of light blue ('Belladonna'), dark blue ('Bellamosa'), or white ('Casa Blanca'). For earlier bloom in the middle of the border, the 'Connecticut Yankees', 75 cm (30 in.), offer single white, blue, lavender, and purple flowers. The shorter kinds are a little less demanding and just as colourful as the tall ones.

D. nudicaule is a delightful small species with bright orange red flowers, produced in great abundance when located in full sun and good drainage.

These plants flower so magnificently that they are well worth the attention they demand. The planting location should be in full sun most of the day, yet sheltered from strong winds. They grow best in deep, rich, moist soil with regular annual applications of fertilizer and mulch and need plenty of water during hot, dry weather. Staking is a must, with several long, strong sticks. The back of the border is the best place for them. Their worst enemy is the caterpillar of the delphinium moth, which attacks the plants just as the clumps are developing, eating the flower buds and deforming the leaves. Simply cut the plants to the ground when they are 30 cm (12 in.) high. This starves the larvae. The plants soon restore themselves and bloom as if nothing has happened. ○ M ⚘

Dianthus barbatus (sweet William) 45 cm (18 in.). Small fringed flowers are massed in large up-facing heads on tall leafy stems that rise from low mounds of foliage. Very sweetly scented, the flowers come in solid colours (white through pink and crimson) or with a deep pink stripe. Biennial, they

Leopard's bane, the earliest of the yellow daisies, lights up a shady corner in early spring. KEN GIRARD
DORONicum

decline after blooming. Usually, self-sown seedlings replace the older plants. ○ ⚘ ✿

Dianthus spp. (pinks). Maiden pinks, *D. deltoides,* 20 cm (8 in.), sport masses of tiny brilliant dark pink, cerise, or white flowers above mats of dark green ferny foliage in early summer. They self-sow generously. Cheddar pinks, *D. gratianopolitanus (D. caesius),* 15 cm (6 in.), are covered with clove-scented, fringed pink or white flowers that almost hide the blue green mounds of narrow leaves in summer. The double 'Tiny Rubies' is exquisite. Taller cottage pinks or grass pinks, *D. plumerius,* form low clumps of sharply pointed, narrow blue leaves topped with highly scented pink, white, crimson, or striped fringed flowers. They like full sun and gritty, well-drained soil. Evergreen foliage should be protected from winter sun with spruce branches. ○ D ✺ RG

Dicentra spectabilis (bleeding heart) 90 cm (36 in.). Emerging very early in spring, fleshy pink stems and ferny fronds of deeply divided leaves grow rapidly into large spreading clumps. The arching stems bear long drooping racemes of heart-shaped pink and white pendant flowers. The white-flowered variety is a little less hardy. In deep, well-drained, moist soil in light shade, the foliage stays fresh and green for most of the summer. *D. eximia* and *D. formosa,* both 30 cm (12 in.), are similar but daintier, with ferny leaves and tiny clustered flowers held above the foliage on delicate, nodding stems. These clump-forming woodsy plants have pink or white flowers in late spring; cherry red 'Luxuriant' flowers all summer. ◉ M W

Dictamnus albus or ***D. fraxinella*** (dittany, burning bush) 90 cm (36 in.). In June, spires of massed pink or white recurved flowers rise high above neat bushes of glossy, ashlike compound leaves. Bronze green ornamental seed pods follow. The dark green pungent foliage of this spectacular garden plant remains handsome until frost. A sunny, well-drained site with deep, fertile soil should be chosen as the long tap root makes moving it difficult. All parts are poisonous. ○ ⚘ ✺ ✖

Digitalis grandiflora syn. ***D. ambigua*** (foxglove) 90 cm (36 in.). This long-lived hardy foxglove has pale yellow, funnel-shaped flowers, sprinkled inside with brown spots, over dense tufts of long, pointed leaves. They bloom in July for several weeks, with the flowers opening gradually from bottom to top and drooping from one side of each of the many stems. Of the more tender fox-gloves, the beautiful cultivar 'Foxy', 90 cm (36 in.), blooms in July from seedlings started in mid-February (15–20) and set out late in May. White, cream, pink, carmine (crimson), or maroon flowers, uniformly spotted, appear five months after sowing. Foxgloves do best in moist, well-drained soil in dappled shade. A few seed pods left to mature will ensure a crop of new rosettes near the parent. Mulch lightly over winter. These plants are poisonous. ◉ M W ✖

Doronicum caucasicum (leopard's bane) 50 cm (20 in.). Low-spreading clumps of heart-shaped, toothed leaves appear very early in spring, then sport dozens of narrow-rayed yellow daisies for several weeks. They like cool, moist, rich soil and are striking in a partially shaded area. Remove faded flowers and stems after blooming. ◉ M ⚘ W

Draba **spp.** (draba) 8–12 cm (3–5 in.). Drabas bloom very early in the season, when sprays of tiny flowers all but cover the plants. Flowers are usually bright yellow, but there are some white-flowering species. The tiny leaves are massed in small tight mounds or spreading mats. They are best in rock gardens. ○ M

Echinacea purpurea, formerly ***Rudbeckia purpurea,*** (purple coneflower) 90 cm (36 in.). Established plants form clumps of large, pointed, hairy leaves and bloom from mid-July to October. The large daisy flowers are composed of ray petals of deep pink that flare downward from cone-shaped, bristly disks of stiff coppery florets. Each flower is very long lasting. Cultivars have larger flowers in shades of pink to purple. White-petalled forms have coppery, orange, or green cones. Coneflowers need well-drained, sandy loam in full sun. Mulch young plants to ensure survival through winter. ○ ◉ ✿ ❦

Echinops ritro (globe thistle) 120 cm (48 in.). Big rounded clumps of deeply toothed and bristly leaves are topped all summer with round, prickly flower heads that are a lustrous metallic blue from the bud stage right through to frost. Tiny starlike flowers emerge from the dozens of tightly packed spines that make up each flower head. Hardy and drought and heat tolerant thanks to its deep roots, it requires only a sunny position in ordinary, well-drained soil. Plants grown in rich soil may spread and flop; wire cages or stakes will hold them. Deep-rooted clumps of long-lived globe thistles can be left undisturbed indefinitely, a good thing as they are hard to move. One plant is enough in a small garden. ○ D ❦ ✿

Epimedium **spp.** (barrenwort) 30 cm (12 in.). These valuable foliage plants have dangling, dainty, heart-shaped leaves on thin wiry stems. E. *grandiflorum* has large, pink, spurred flowers; E. x *rubrum* has small deep pink flowers and red-tinted leaves. Both bloom in early spring. They tolerate dry shade but prefer deep, rich soil. ◉ M W

Erigeron **hybrids** (daisy fleabane) 60 cm (24 in.). In summer, thickly petalled daisies in shades of white, blue, lavender, and pink are borne in profusion on clumps of floppy, leafy stems that should be staked. These daisies have more and narrower ray petals than asters. The central disk is prominent and always yellow. They do best in full sun, in light, well-drained, not too fertile soil. ○ ✿ ❦

Eryngium **spp.** (sea holly) 90 cm (36 in.). This striking border plant is sturdy, drought tolerant, and a magnet to bees. It provides interest from early summer to the last days of fall. Mounds of dark green leathery leaves are surmounted by thickets of stiff, silvery branching stems clothed in jagged silvery green leaves and topped by many small prickly silvery blue flowers, each with a starry ruff. The flower heads are perfect for drying. They are hard to move because of their deep, fleshy roots, and any pieces of root left behind send up a forest of new plantlets. Eryngiums need plenty of space, in full sun and well-drained, not too fertile soil. ○ D ✿ ❦

Euphorbia epithymoides, formerly *E. polychroma,* (spurge) 40 cm (16 in.). Brilliant, eye-catching colour very early in spring is the hallmark of this unusual bushy plant. Rounded domes of leaves are crowned with showy chartreuse yellow, petal-like bracts over a long period. It is best grown in well-drained soil of only average fertility, in an open spot that receives afternoon shade. It wilts in hot sun. The taller *E. griffithii* 'Fireglow' has orange bracts. Tiny *E. cyparissias* grows in tufts. It has very fine leaves and yellow bracts and is very invasive. ○ ◉ RG

Filipendula rubra (meadowsweet, queen of the prairie) 180 cm (72 in.). This truly spectacular plant is stately and long-lived. Spreading thickets of strong, ribbed stems carry large dark green jagged leaves. In mid-July, tiny dark pink buds slowly develop into large arching sprays of fluffy shell pink flowers. Filipendula prefers deep, humus-enriched soil and plenty of moisture. It flowers best in full sun and needs staking. ○ M ❦

F. ulmaria (queen of the meadow), 120 cm (48 in.), is a smaller filipendula that prefers boggy soil in full sun or a moist, lightly shaded location. The coarsely serrated leaves are dark green on top and paler beneath. Dense, feathery panicles of creamy white fragrant flowers appear in August. 'Flore Pleno' has double flowers; 'Aurea', yellow leaf variegations. ○ ◉ M WG

Hardy and drought-resistant purple coneflower blooms from mid-summer to frost. KEN GIRARD

The lovely cultivar *Erigeron* 'Pink Jewel', or flea-bane, bears a huge quantity of fluffy pink daisies in July. KEN GIRARD

F. vulgaris or *F. hexapetala* (drop-wort), 60 cm (24 in.), is suitable for the front of the border. Its large flat rosettes of ferny carrotlike foliage remain attractive all summer. Small creamy white flowers, clustered in fluffy panicles, are carried high above the foliage on slender, clean stems. The commonly available double 'Flore Pleno' may need light staking. It requires only ordinary, fertile soil and tolerates dry conditions. ○ ⚘ ✿

Gaillardia hybrids (blanket flower) 15–90 cm (6–36 in.). These large, brilliant, summer-blooming daisies have bronze prickly centres and deep red ray petals tipped with yellow. 'Burgundy' and 'Yellow Queen' have solid colours; 'Baby Cole' and 'Goblin' are low and compact. Most are short-lived; however, a yearly division that discards woody centres will keep them going. They are longer-lived in light, well-drained soil in an open, sunny position. ○ D ⚘ ✿

Galium odoratum, formerly *Asperula odorata,* (sweet woodruff) 20 cm (8 in.). Narrow glossy leaves in whorls on creeping stems are topped by small fragrant white flowers in late spring. They need a partly shaded position and light, moist soil. Deep snow cover or straw mulch protects the crowns in winter. Plants exposed to drying winds may die. They can be planted above spring bulbs. ◉ GC ✺

Gentiana spp. (gentian). A most desirable blue gentian, G. *acaulis*, hates our alkaline soil, but its very similar cousins G. *angustifolia* and G. *clusii* like it. These gentians form large mats of dark green leaves with large, up-facing, bell-shaped flowers in May and early June. Other early bloomers, G. *verna* and its varieties, form wonderful little mats of leaves covered with very pale to mid-blue flowers. Fairly delicate and short-lived, they can be divided and potted up in a gritty mix for a supply of new plants. One of the easiest summer-flowering species is G. *cru-*

ciata, which has small bright blue flowers borne in pleasing quantity on sprawling rosettes of glossy leaves. ○ RG

A taller summer-blooming gentian for the border is *G. lutea,* 120 cm (48 in.), with yellow flowers and large glossy leaves. This plant is hard to move because of its long tap root (the source of bitters). The willow gentian, *G. asclepiadea,* and the bottle gentian, *G. andrewsii,* 60 cm (24 in.), are suitable for moist, woodsy areas. Both bloom in late summer, with the long flowers of the graceful willow gentian growing in the axils of the leaves and the purple blue flowers of the bottle gentian remaining partially closed. A late-summer bloomer, the floppy *G. septemfida* is easy to grow, and cultivars and varieties of this species do well here. They lie flat in pinwheels, with the flowers facing upward. ◉ M W

Most gentians require gritty soil that drains well (with additions of granite chips for most species). The border types prefer well-drained, fertile loam. They all like bright light but dislike intense heat.

***Geranium* spp.** (cranesbill). The dainty, saucer-shaped flowers of hardy geraniums are borne in clusters above dense foliage. They range in colour from white and blue to every shade of pink, mauve, and purple, most with characteristic veining in a deeper shade. The handsome, sometimes aromatic leaves, deeply lobed and toothed, form perfect mounds of deep green. These easy plants thrive in full sun or partial shade in well-drained soil.

A typical border geranium, *G.* x *magnificum,* 75 cm (30 in.), a hybrid of *G. ibericum* and *G. platypetalum,* has heavy clusters of fuzzy flower buds that open into large deep violet saucers veined with deeper purple. The flowers come on all at once in late June in great abundance and last for two to three weeks. Some geraniums bloom all through the summer. Trailing mounds of *G. endressii,* 30 cm (12 in.), sport small pale pink flowers lightly veined with red that bloom all

Gaillardia 'Goblin', a compact form of blanket flower, blazes away all summer; it prefers a dry, well-drained site. JUDITH DOYLE

summer; cultivars offer a range of pink shades. *G. macrorrhizum* 'Ingwerson's Variety', 30 cm (12 in.), has pink lilac flowers and strongly scented foliage in large mounds that turn scarlet in fall; it spreads to form a good groundcover. *G. pratense*, 90 cm (36 in.), has light blue flowers on very long stems; this meadow cranesbill needs lots of space. *G.* x 'Johnson's Blue', 60 cm (24 in.), has bright blue long-lasting flowers with darker veining. *G. sanguineum* or bloody cranesbill, 30 cm (12 in.), has large pale pink to reddish purple flowers all summer and leaves that turn red in autumn. ○ ◉ ✿

Small geraniums for rock gardens or raised alpine beds include: *G. cinereum* 'Ballerina', 15 cm (6 in.), rosy purple flowers, veined and centred in deeper crimson; *G. dalmaticum*, 15 cm (6 in.), large rose pink or white flowers; *G. renardii*, 25 cm (10 in.), pale lavender flowers with fine purple veining and greyish textured leaves; *G. sanguineum lancastriense*, 15 cm (6 in.), rose pink veined with crimson, or white flowers; *G. sanguineum prostratum*, 10 cm (4 in.), pale pink flowers on dense, leafy mats. ○ RG

Geum spp. (avens). The native *G. triflorum*, 30 cm (12 in.)—three-flowered avens, prairie smoke, or old man's whiskers—has purplish pink nodding flowers, three to a stem, and blooms on open grasslands in May and June. Its finely dissected leaves, unusual rounded flowers, and silky seed whiskers are most attractive. *G.* x *borisii*, 40 cm (16 in.), is a hardy little gem with downy leaves, irregularly lobed and toothed, that form dense clumps. Dozens of small, flat, upfacing flowers are held well above the foliage on long stems, in a steady succession of brilliant orange bloom that lasts several weeks. Other geums, 'Mrs Bradshaw' (scarlet) and 'Lady Stratheden' (double yellow), are short-lived in Calgary gardens. Easy-care geums prefer rich, moist loam that drains well. Afternoon shade helps prolong blooms. ○ ◉ ✿ ✿

Gypsophila paniculata (baby's breath) to 90 cm (36 in.). Airy clouds of hundreds of tiny flowers stand above loose mounds of fine foliage in summer. Double white and double pink cultivars are available. Soil should be deep and very well drained but moisture retentive—that is, with plenty of organic matter. Alkaline soil is to their liking. These tap-rooted plants are hard to move; choose a permanent place in full sun. Staking is essential to avoid storm damage. ○ ✿ ✿ ✿ The darling little *G. repens* is low and trailing, covered in spring with sprays of tiny white or pink flowers. ○ RG

Helenium autumnale cultivars (helenium) 90 cm (36 in.). These unique daisies flower from late July to late September. The downward-flaring, notched ray petals of clear yellow or combinations of yellow, orange, bronze, reddish brown, and crimson surround a prominent globular hub or disk, which is often a contrasting or darker colour. *H. hoopsii* is smaller with yellow daisies in spring. All like a sunny position in moist, humus-rich soil. They need staking. Frequent division keeps the plants thriving. ○ M ✿ ✿

Helianthus hybrids (sunflower) to 150 cm (60 in.). These are tall bushy plants with large bright yellow daisies, single or double, depending on the cultivar. They bloom in summer in a sunny position with well-drained soil. They need staking. ○ ✿ ✿

GROUNDCOVERS

An asterisk indicates those particularly suited for shady areas.

- *Archangel (Lamiastrum galeobdolon)
- Arctic phlox (Phlox subulata)
- Bearberry or kinnikinnick (Arctostaphylos uva-ursi)
- *Brunnera (Brunnera macrophylla)
- *Bugleweed (Ajuga reptans)
- Cliffgreen (Paxistima canbyi)
- *Cranesbill (Geranium macrorrhizum)
- Creeping Jenny (Lysimachia nummularia)
- Creeping phlox (Phlox stolonifera)
- Daylilies (Hemerocallis spp.)
- *Dead nettle (Lamium maculatum)
- *Epimedium (Epimedium spp.)
- Fairy bells (Campanula cochlearifolia)
- *Forget-me-not (Myosotis spp.)
- *Goutweed (Aegopodium podagraria 'Variegatum')
- Hen and chicks or houseleek (Sempervivum spp.)
- Himalayan fleeceflower (Polygonum affine)
- Japanese spurge (Pachysandra terminalis)
- *Lily-of-the-valley (Convallaria majalis)
- *Ostrich fern (Matteucia struthiopteris)
- *Periwinkle (Vinca minor)
- *Primroses (Primula spp.)
- Purple rock cress (Aubrieta spp.)
- Ribbon grass (Phalaris arundinacea picta)
- Rock cress (Arabis caucasica)
- Sheep's fescue (Festuca ovina glauca)
- Snow-in-summer (Cerastium tomentosum)
- Stonecrop (Sedum spp.)
- *Sweet woodruff (Galium odoratum)
- Thyme (Thymus spp.)
- *Violet (Viola spp.)

Heliopsis scabra (perennial zinnia) 120 cm (48 in.). Another tall, sun-loving yellow daisy, with a long show of colour from summer to late September. This hardy species tolerates dry soil, but does better with regular watering. All daisies benefit from deadheading. Cultivars offer variations in flower colour and style.

Hemerocallis spp. (daylily—so-called as individual blooms last for one day in the species). Because hemerocallis is quite pest- and disease-resistant, hybridizers have been able to concentrate on enhancing the beauty of the plant. There is now a choice of height, extended and varying bloom periods, fragrance, and size and style of flower—including ruffled and "spider," with recurving petals. Varieties bloom at different times to provide constant and spectacular colour throughout the summer; some even rebloom later in the season. 'Stella d'Oro' is such a performer, a reliably hardy and proficient bloomer, compact in size, with fragrant yellow flowers.

The species have their uses, being very hardy and reliable, and are usually obtainable free from other gardeners, as they spread generously. *H. lilioasphodelus (flava)*, scented lemon lily, blooms in late spring with clusters of long yellow trumpets, each lasting only a day but replaced for weeks. *H. fulva,* the indestructible tawny daylily, blooms later with dusty orange flowers. With reasonably fertile, well-drained, moist soil and a warm, sunny location—at least half a day of sun—hemerocallis provide carefree patches of summer colour. When not in bloom, they have attractive, reedlike foliage.

The earliest of the nonbulbous flowers, blooming in the second week of April, is *Hepatica* x *media* 'Ballardii'. Judith Doyle

Many species have been used to develop thousands of modern cultivars in a stunning array of forms and colours, in every shade but pure white and blue. Most are 75–100 cm (30–40 in.) tall with arching grassy leaves in dense clumps, but some are dwarf. Some bloom early; others bloom in summer or even later. Mass-planted daylilies are effective groundcovers for large areas; select species and varieties that spread through rhizomes. ○ ◉ ⚘

***Hepatica* spp.** (liverwort) 20 cm (8 in.). One of the first spring flowers, the dainty little hepatica blooms as early as the second week of April. The starry flowers are small, with narrow petals (actually sepals) flaring from a tiny boss of prominent stamens. The usual colour is an intense lavender blue, although white and pink forms occur. Fresh green leaves of elegant design appear with the flowers, forming beautiful low mounds that gradually eclipse the dying blooms. *H. nobilis, H. triloba,* and *H. americana* are similar woodland species with long-stemmed, deeply lobed leaves. Cultivars, both single and double, include white, pink, deep rose, mauve, and purple flowers. The hybrid *H.* x *media* 'Ballardii' has very handsome toothed and lobed leaves and large china blue, starlike flowers. Hepatica thrive in cool, dappled shade, in moist, porous soil, generously amended with peat, sand, and fine, sharp gravel to allow good drainage and a deep root run. ◉ M GC W

Hesperis matronalis (sweet rocket) 75 cm (30 in.). This old-fashioned favourite has loose heads of fragrant white, mauve, or purple cross-shaped flowers in June. The leaves are dark green and lance shaped. It grows best in light, moist loam in a sunny position; it self-sows and spreads by rhizomes. ○ M ⚘

Heuchera sanguinea (coral bells, alum root) to 45 cm (18 in.). Heuchera takes the stage in mid-June with a profusion of dainty flowers that often continue all summer. From low mounds of small, rounded, scalloped leaves rise slender leafless stalks, bearing open panicles of tiny, bright, bell-shaped flowers that tremble and sway in the lightest breeze. Cultivars such as the Bressingham hybrids are tall and showy with colours from white through all shades of pink to blood red. Other hybrids of *H. americana* and *H. micrantha,* such as 'Palace Purple', offer attractive silvery or purple foliage with and without variegations. An intergeneric hybrid, x *Heucherella* 'Bridget Bloom' has dainty sprays of light pink flowers and soft pale green leaves. Coral bells need full sun or partial shade and light, well-drained soil.

Annual top-dressings of rich loam or compost keep them blooming well. Dead-heading prolongs bloom and prevents inferior seedlings growing up. Winter mulching helps prevent frost from heaving the plants out of the ground. ○ ●
RG 🌿

Hosta spp. (plantain lily, funkia) 15–90 cm (6–36 in.). Interesting foliage plants for shade gardens, hostas do well if given the proper conditions—dappled to light or even deep shade; moist, organic, fertile soil; and protection from wind and hail. Once well established, they usually produce beautiful leaves and flowers for many years.

Leaf styles vary from narrowly lance shaped to almost round, with an enormous range in size. They have shiny or matte, smooth, ribbed, or quilted surfaces, and some have wavy or twisted edges. Foliage colour ranges from plain shades of green, blue, and gold, to fanciful variegations with white, cream, or gold, either along the leaf edges or spreading out from the midrib. The lighter shades can stand more sun, but the blues retain their colour best in deep shade. Many hostas flower, usually in July and August, in shades of white, cream, or lavender, in graceful racemes above the foliage. Some are fragrant.

Many species and cultivars are grown here, including: *H. undulata*, low, twisted white and green leaves; *H. undulata* 'Albo-marginata' ('Thomas Hogg'), wavy-edged, white-margined, deep green leaves; *H. fortunei* 'Aureo-maculata', ribbed yellow and green leaves, and 'Francee', green leaves with white margins; *H. sieboldiana* 'Elegans', large, round, puckered blue leaves, and 'Frances Williams', very decorative, large gold and green leaves; *H. plantaginea* 'Royal Standard', large, pointed green leaves and tall fragrant flowers, and 'Honeybells', also fragrant. 'Tee Tiny', 'Tiny Tears', and 'Snowflake' are miniature varieties; 'Ginko Craig' and 'Dorset Blue' are mid-sized; and 'Sum' and 'Substance', 'Big Mama' and 'Big Daddy', and 'Krossa Regal' are large.

Iris setosa brings delicate beauty to the June garden. MAUREEN IRETON

Before planting (in a well-drained spot), the soil should be amended with large amounts of peat moss and well-rotted manure or compost, and bone meal for flowering varieties. Hosta roots are planted with the crowns just below soil level, then watered in well. Mulch with compost or rotted manure in early spring.

Hostas are considered to be gourmet food by slugs; early and continued control of these pests is advised. ● ◉ M W

Iberis sempervirens (candytuft) 30 cm (12 in.). Low mounds of dark evergreen leaves on woody stems are crowned in spring with clusters of white double flowers. It needs full sun and moist, well-drained soil; plants may winterkill if there is insufficient moisture during the growing season or if they stand in soggy soil during spring thaws. Good in rock gardens. ○ RG

Iris **spp.** (iris). The most familiar and reliable iris in the Calgary area is the bearded iris, *I.* x *germanica;* however, there are many others of varying hardiness and suitability. Irises grow from rhizomes—thick, fleshy, elongated stems that grow along or just under the soil—or from bulbs. Rhizomatous irises have leaves that are usually linear and flat, and arranged in fans; bulbous irises have long thin leaves like grass or onions. Rhizomatous irises are classified into two groups: bearded or beardless, referring to the fuzzy beard on the three down-facing petals.

Thousands of cultivars of bearded irises offer a wide choice of colour, size, and hardiness. Many have spectacular flowers with large ruffled and flaring petals,

---

LOW-GROWING PERENNIALS FOR ROCK GARDENS OR EDGING

- Alpine primroses (*Primula* spp.)
- Avens (*Geum* x *borisii*)
- Baby's breath (*Gypsophila repens*)
- Basket-of-gold alyssum (*Aurinia saxatilis*)
- Bellflowers, small (*Campanula* spp.)
- Bitterroot (*Lewisia* spp.)
- Blue-eyed grass (*Sisyrinchium montanum*)
- Campion (*Silene* spp.)
- Candytuft (*Iberis sempervirens*)
- Cinquefoil (*Potentilla* spp.)
- Cupid's dart (*Catananche caerula*)
- Draba (*Draba* spp.)
- Dwarf iris (*Iris pumila*)
- Edelweiss (*Leontopodium alpinum*)
- Gentians (*Gentiana* spp.)
- Geraniums, small (*Geranium* spp.)
- Hen and chicks or houseleek (*Sempervivum* spp.)
- Phlox (*Phlox stolonifera, P. subulata*)
- Pinks (*Dianthus* spp.)
- Purple rock cress (*Aubrieta deltoidea*)
- Pussytoes (*Antennaria* spp.)
- Rock cress (*Arabis caucasica*)
- Rock soapwort (*Saponaria ocymoides*)
- Rockfoil (*Saxifraga* spp.)
- Slipperwort (*Calceolaria* spp.)
- Snow-in-summer (*Cerastium tomentosum*)
- Speedwell, low (*Veronica* spp.)
- Stonecrop (*Sedum* spp.)
- Thrift (*Armeria juniperifolia*)
- Thyme (*Thymus* spp.)

three upright standards, and three down-curving falls, in a wide variety of colours and patterns. Miniature dwarf bearded iris, 20 cm (8 in.), are a good choice for rock gardens and dry areas. Available in many colours, they bloom from April to mid-May. Standard dwarf bearded iris, 20–30 cm (8–12 in.), are vigorous and prolific bloomers with a diverse colour range. They bloom from mid-May into June and are ideal for naturalizing. Intermediate bearded iris, 40–75 cm (16–30 in.), usually flower from mid-May to mid-June. These do very well in Calgary. Border bearded iris, 40–75 cm (16–30 in.), have larger flowers and bloom later than the intermediate, usually in mid-June. Many of these are old tried-and-true varieties. Miniature tall bearded iris, 40–75 cm (16–30 in.), have smaller and more delicate flowers than the tall beardeds and appear in mid-June. Some varieties of tall bearded iris, over 75 cm (30 in.), can reach 120 cm (48 in.) when in bloom. They bloom in almost every colour of the rainbow and the more vigorous varieties may have up to twelve flowers on one stem. The very tall bearded irises may need staking. Developed and selected for flower size and colour rather than winter hardiness, they require ideal conditions to survive our winters.

All bearded irises like plenty of sun and good drainage. Amend heavy clay soil with sand or other materials, such as perlite, to improve drainage; raised beds also help. Plant irises purchased bareroot in the late summer or fall as soon as possible to allow good root development before winter. You can also purchase irises by mail order from specialty nurseries, which can advise the best time to plant. Potted irises are available in spring and summer at garden centres.

Plant iris so that the top of the rhizome is slightly exposed. Dig a trench about 15 cm (6 in.) deep, leaving a ridge in the middle. Sprinkle a little bone meal on both sides of the ridge, cover it with 2.5 cm (1 in.) of soil, and then place the rhizome on top of the ridge, spreading out the roots below. The top of the rhizome should be flush with the surface of the soil. Firm the soil and water well. Mulch newly planted irises with leaves or straw the first winter so that frost will not heave them out of the ground. They can be fed in late spring with fertilizer such as compost, well-rotted manure, or a balanced, water-soluble fertilizer. After flowering, cultivate bone meal into the surrounding soil.

Remove untidy dead leaves when the blooms are spent, but leave the green leaves as the iris needs them to store food so it can bloom next year. Overgrown clumps that have died out in the middle can be divided and replanted. Bearded irises are best divided every three years, ideally four to six weeks after flowering. Dig up the entire clump, cutting the leaves 20 cm (8 in.) above the rhizome. Separate into single fans of leaves, each with a piece of rhizome; dust the cut ends with bulb dust in case of disease spores and allow them to dry for several hours before replanting. ○ ❧ ❀

Grassy-leaved Siberian iris, *I. sibirica*, 120 cm (48 in.), are beardless iris. They start to bloom just as the standard bearded types finish, in late June or early July. The flowers appear on tall spikes, usually two per spike in the species, up to five in the more vigorous hybrids. The most common colours are purple, blue, and white, but hybridizers are working on shades of pink, red, and yellow, and on mauve, plum, and cream. A few cultivars proven in Calgary include 'Blue Burn' (light blue/white); 'Butter and Sugar' (white/yellow falls); 'Dreaming Yellow' (white/yellow crest); 'Ego' (famous old blue hybrid); 'Super Ego' (pale blue); 'Floating Island' (white/falls tinged yellow); 'On and On' (violet); 'Ruffled

Iris x *germanica* 'Bounty' is an old-fashioned, reliably hardy, bearded iris with scented flowers. JUDITH DOYLE

Velvet' (velvety purple); 'White Magnificence' (extremely large flowers). If the conditions Siberian iris require are met, most will perform well and produce a lavish show of bloom. They need several hours of full sun, plenty of moisture in spring and summer, lots of organic matter to make the soil neutral, and soil that drains well even in winter. They rot if standing in too much water. After six years or so, when the iris clump centres start to die out, divide and replant outer portions with six or more growths in mid- to late August. Water in well to establish healthy new roots. ○ ◉ M WG

Beardless spuria irises also do well here, although you may need to order them from specialty nurseries. Recommended small rock garden varieties are *I. graminiae* and *I. ruthenica,* with dark glossy green leaves and small purple, plum-scented flowers that appear in mid-June. Larger species in this group that do well in dry areas are *I. halophila, I. spuria, I. musulmanica, I. crocea,* and *I. orientalis.* These irises must go into winter on the dry side to prevent rot. Move or divide them only when absolutely necessary.

You can also try: *I. laevigata,* 60–90 cm (24–36 in.), grows in ponds, with blue-purple or white flowers; yellow flag, *I. pseudacorus,* grows to 180 cm (72 in.) in water, less on land, with yellow flowers in June; *I. versicolor* grows in water or on land and has blue, white, or red flowers; *I. setosa,* 15–100 cm (6–40 in.), is a hardy species from temperate northern regions with pale blue to rich blue purple flowers; and *I. cristata* and *I. lucustre,* 15 cm (6 in.), are suitable for dappled shade, with purple, blue, or white flowers.

Bulbous spring iris are the earliest blooming iris. The bulbs, covered in netting that should not be removed, are planted in the fall and mulched well to keep them from growing too early. They need replacing about every three years. Two popular species are *I. reticulata* (purple) and *I. danfordiae* (yellow).

Lamiastrum galeobdolon (archangel) 25 cm (10 in.). Mounds of silver-streaked green leaves are brightened by short spires of yellow flowers in early summer. It spreads quickly by stolons to cover the ground in moist, semi-shaded areas. ◉ GC W

Lamium maculatum (dead nettle) 20 cm (8 in.). These wide-spreading mounds of beautiful leaves variegated with silver are topped with small clusters of white or pink flowers. Cultivars vary in the amount of leaf variegation and flower colour. Try 'White Nancy', 'Beacon Silver', or 'Roseum'. The stems root into the ground wherever they touch. It can also be propagated by cuttings. Partial to deep shade and moist, well-drained soil, lamium makes a good groundcover. ● ◉ M GC

Lathyrus latifolius (everlasting pea) 180 cm (72 in.). A vining plant with long flat stalks, leaves in pairs, and clusters of deep pink scentless flowers on wiry stalks from late June to September, there are white and red to purple forms. A sunny position is best, in fertile, well-drained soil with plenty of moisture in summer. Support plants with a trellis or allow them to ramble about among other flowers or down steep banks. Remove faded flowers to prolong bloom. ○ M ✿ ❦

Lavandula angustifolia (lavender) 30 cm (12 in.). Famous for its fabulous scent, lavender is also ornamental with its narrow spikes of tiny, clustered blue violet flowers and grey aromatic leaves. The dwarf blue variety, 'Munstead', is hardy in a sheltered, sunny, well-drained position. ○ D ✹ ✿

Leontopodium alpinum (edelweiss) 30 cm (12 in.). Small tufts of long, narrow grey leaves are topped in summer by large, flat, star-shaped silvery bracts, centred with tiny yellow flowers. It must have light, sharply drained soil in full sun. It is a good plant for rock gardens and edging. ○ D RG

Lewisia spp. (bitterroot) 10 cm (4 in.). These alpine plants grow small rosettes of leaves with large, showy pink flowers. *L. cotyledon* is the largest. They all like good soil, good drainage, and a sheltered but sunny location. ○ RG

Liatris spicata (gayfeather, blazing star) 90 cm (36 in.). Wonderful spiky plants for grouping in sunny borders, their long spires of unusual fuzzy pink, mauve, or white flowers open from the top down, from tightly packed buds, from summer into fall; 'Kobold' has dark purple flowers. The grassy leaves grow in low mounds. They prefer deep, sandy soil and tolerate drought. ○ ✿ ❦

Ligularia spp. (golden groundsel). These large, showy plants have handsome foliage and spikes of yellow to orange flowers in July and August. *L. przewalskii* (sha VAL ski), 150 cm (60 in.), is magnificent in the back of the border, in moist, semi-shaded locations. In July, strong black flower stalks rise above large mounds of deeply lobed

The spectacular golden torches of *Ligularia przewalskii* (golden groundsel) show to advantage against a dense background of cotoneaster. JUDITH DOYLE

leaves, bearing hundreds of tiny propeller-shaped blooms that open gradually to form blazing yellow torches. A similar plant, *L. stenocephala* 'The Rocket', has large, heart-shaped, toothed leaves.

Other hardy species are *L. dentata,* 150 cm (60 in.), and the smaller *L. hodgsonii*, with leathery, heart-shaped leaves and clustered yellow daisies on long, strong stems. 'Desdemona', 'Othello', and 'Gregynog Gold' are handsome cultivars. They need a sunny or partially shaded position and deep, moist soil that never dries out; the north side of a fence is a good site. These easy-care plants need no staking, despite their height. ○ ◉ M W

***Lilium* spp. and hybrids** (lilies). Lilies are summer-flowering perennials that grow from bulbs. Some bloom early in June; others in July and through to late August. A choice of varieties will ensure a long season of lilies.

Asiatic hybrids, 30–120 cm (12–48 in.), are the most reliable lilies for the Calgary area. They have up-facing, out-facing, or down-facing flowers in many colours—white, yellow, gold, orange, pink, red, and lavender, some with spots, stars, or stripes on the petals; blooming periods vary. They prefer fairly bright light and plenty of morning sun; some shade during the hottest part of the afternoon helps blooms to last longer.

Oriental lilies, to 120 cm (48 in.), are large and fragrant. They are the last of the lilies to bloom, producing (usually) white or pink flowers in July and August. Ideally located in dappled shade, they require plenty of winter protection and deteriorate over time. In the Calgary area, they are best planted in the spring.

Several species lilies are hardy in local gardens. *L. martagon,* 180 cm (72 in.), is large and dramatic with whorled leaves and upright stems. The flowers may be pink, red, maroon, orange, yellow, white, or ivory, some with spots, and they appear in June or July. They thrive in a shady spot amidst ferns and other foliage. A thick winter mulch prevents them from emerging too early in the spring and being damaged by late frosts. The easy-to-grow *L. regale,* 180 cm (72 in.), the regal lily, has white flowers. *L. cernuum,* 30–50 cm (12–20 in.), is a sun-loving lily with lilac flowers, often with spots. *L. lancifolium,* 120 cm (48 in.), the familiar orange tiger lily, now has black-spotted flowers in shades of white, cream, yellow, pink, and red. *L. duchartrei* has white, down-facing Turk's cap flowers. It spreads by stolons and is best planted in an area where it can be allowed to run. *L. henryi* has orange down-facing flowers and *L. tigrinum,* orange up-facing flowers.

Lily bulbs should be handled carefully as they are never dormant, are easily bruised, and die if allowed to dry out. Some lilies prefer sun, and some, partial shade; all require good drainage and cool roots, and fare badly close to south-facing walls. Plant lily bulbs in the fall or early spring in a slightly raised bed or on a slight slope, for good drainage. Add sand or vermiculite if the soil is heavy, as well as organic matter such as compost or peat moss. Bone meal may also be added. Use manure only as a top-dressing as it can introduce pathogens that may rot the bulbs. Dig a hole at least 15 cm (6 in.) deep and plant small bulbs 25 cm (10 in.) apart and large ones 45 cm (18 in.) apart to allow plenty of space to multiply. Pour water into the hole to check if water drains away quickly, adding a layer of coarse sand when the water has soaked away. Powder the bulbs with bulb dust, set them in the hole, and cover them with 2–3 cm (1 in.) of sand. Cover with soil and water thoroughly. If lily beds are topped with aged manure or compost each fall, they do not require much extra fertilizing.

To keep lily roots cool in summer, overplant with low-growing groundcovers such as creeping baby's breath, rock cress, mother of thyme, or annual alyssum. Cut off spent flowers but not the leaves, as they must feed the bulb for next year. Lift and divide lilies when the centre of the clump becomes hollow. This is best done immediately after flowering.

Lilies may be affected by botrytis, indicated by browning leaves or brown dots on the flowers. General garden cleanliness, proper growing conditions, minimal handling of the bulbs, and plenty of air circulation help. If all else fails, use fungicides. Lilies may also be infected by viruses that cause stunted growth and deformed or streaked flowers. The only cure for viruses is removal of the infected plant. ○ ◉ M 🌸

Limonium latifolium (sea lavender, statice) 75 cm (30 in.). In summer, tall stems bear a cloud of tiny lavender blue flowers above a large mound of long, pointed leaves. In spite of their height, their flower sprays are so insubstantial that they can be planted in the front ranks of borders, where they can be seen to advantage. The flowers dry well. Plant in deep, sandy loam, to accommodate the long tap root, in a sunny, well-drained spot. ○ D 🌿 🌿

Linum perenne (flax) 45 cm (18 in.). In late spring and summer, vase-shaped bunches of wiry stems, clothed with fine, thready leaves, are topped with drooping clusters of small, sky blue, saucer-shaped flowers. Fresh flowers open each day if there is sunshine; buds remain closed on dull days. Although short-lived, flax sows plenty of seed and seedlings can be left to replace the worn-out parent. As flax is drought tolerant and revels in light, sandy soil of low fertility, well-drained, sunny, and open sites are best. A yellow-flowered species, *L. flavum*, 30 cm (12 in.), is a bright, bushy little plant with dark green leaves. ○ D 🌿

Lupinus varieties (lupins) to 120 cm (48 in.). Lupins are distinctive, from the digitate, pleated leaves to the huge spikes of pealike flowers in shades of pink, cream, mauve, red, and purple, and combinations of these. Although they soon sulk in Calgary gardens, they can be grown. The main problems are alkaline soil and dry conditions. Dig soil amendments such as peat moss, leaf mould, and compost deeply into the soil in generous quantity and supply plentiful water. Because they need lots of sun but hate dry heat, a site with afternoon shade is best. As lupins become increasingly yellow (chlorotic) and infested with aphids, they should be regularly replaced by year-old plants, which are easily grown from seed in pots in a cold frame or vegetable row. Stake tall varieties with slender bamboo sticks to prevent disaster just as the flowers are at their best. At 60 cm (24 in.), the dwarf 'Minarette' types may be easier to grow. ○ ◉ M 🌸

Lychnis spp. (campion, Maltese cross). Several species of lychnis (lik' niss) are hardy in Calgary gardens. An old favourite, *L. chalcedonica*, 120 cm (48 in.), is tall, with small neat tufts of narrow leaves that appear early in spring. The stiff, rapidly growing stems need early staking to prevent sprawling. In July and

August, the stems are topped by large rounded heads of tiny scarlet flowers, each shaped like a Maltese cross, the common name for this brilliant plant. There are also pink and white forms. They like ordinary, well-drained soil in full sun or partial shade, plenty of water, and deep mulch. ○ ● M ✿✿ Smaller relatives are *L. x arkwrightii,* 45 cm (18 in.), with purplish green leaves and large, brilliant scarlet orange flowers from June to August, and *L. haageana,* which has a single large scarlet flower on the tip of each stem. In complete contrast, *L. coronaria,* rose campion, 75 cm (30 in.), sports silver-felted leaves, an open branching shape, and single, magenta or white, saucer-shaped flowers. It is short-lived, usually biennial, but self-sows. It requires light, dry soil in full sun, where it will bloom all summer. ○ D ✿ In the front of the border, the spring-flowering *L. viscaria,* catchfly, 30 cm (12 in.), provides hazy drifts of pink blooms on sticky stems above low grassy mounds of leaves. It needs full sun and good drainage.

Lysimachia punctata (yellow loosestrife) 90 cm (36 in.). Charming yellow flowers are clustered in leaf axils along tall stems, their cheerful starry cups peering out on all sides, opening slowly from the bottom-up for a long season of bloom. Another species that may be less hardy, *L. clethroides,* 90 cm (36 in.), has graceful goose-necked spires of small white flowers. The leaves in both species grow in whorls along the stems. They prefer a sunny or half-shaded location with moist to wet soil, heavily amended with peat moss and compost. ○ ● M ✿✿✿

A prostrate species, *L. nummularia,* creeping Jenny or moneywort, has the same sunny flowers and little round leaves on stems that hug the ground. It spreads quickly into many joined rosettes. A perfect groundcover under shrubs, it should be kept out of the flower border. A glowing yellow-leaved variety, *L. nummularia aurea,* is especially handsome. ○ ● GC

Macleaya cordata (plume poppy) 180 cm (72 in.). This gigantic plant forms

***Lilium* 'Duet' is an elegant representative of the hardy, summer-flowering lilies grown in Calgary gardens.** KEN GIRARD

thickets of long tough stems bearing large lobed leaves of greyish green with silvery undersides. The small white flowers, incidental to the superb foliage, are borne in dainty plumes in summer. Macleaya is best planted where its foliage can show to advantage. It grows in sun or partial shade in ordinary soil. ○ ◉ ❁❁❁

Malva moschata (musk mallow) 90 cm (36 in.). Although short-lived, it sows enough seed to renew itself in the garden. Single hollyhocklike flowers are produced prolifically in summer, in white and shades of soft pink, on bushy plants with deeply cut dark green leaves. Their rapid, lush growth needs deep, moist, and well-drained soil, enriched with humus, and a sunny position. ○ M 🌿

Meconopsis cambrica (Welsh poppy) 45 cm (18 in.). Dainty pale yellow or pale orange poppies are borne in profusion above mounds of ferny foliage all summer long if dead flowers are removed. Light shade and good, moist soil ensure success. They self-sow generously. For the well-tempered gardener, there are the Himalayan blue poppies, *M. betonicifolia*, or the less hardy *M. grandis*, which must have acidic soil (heavily amended here) in a moist, semi-shaded location to be at their bluest. ◉ M W

Mertensia virginica (Virginia bluebell) 60 cm (24 in.). Drooping clusters of pale blue bells appear in April, last-

A brilliant cultivar of bee balm lends fiery colour and spicy fragrance to summer borders. MAUREEN IRETON

One of the early-blooming peonies, *Paeonia tenuifolia laciniata,* has single flowers and deeply cut leaves. JUDITH DOYLE

ing into early May. If interplanted with late-emerging hostas, there will be foliage and flowers even after the bluebells have gone dormant and vanished underground for the summer. For fall division, mark clumps with labels before they disappear. ◉ M W

Monarda didyma (bee balm, bergamot) 90 cm (36 in.). Flamboyant monarda blooms from early July through August. Tall square stems bear lance-shaped leaves that give off a pleasant spicy aroma when touched. The shaggy flower clusters have tubular florets that sprout in whorls from a pincushionlike head. The brilliant 'Cambridge Scarlet' needs full sun, rich moist soil, and frequent division to flower well in local gardens. Several pink, white, and purple selections are hardy and more drought tolerant. Hot pink 'Marshall's Delight' is hardy, vigorous, and resistant to the common scourges of powdery mildew and rust. The new 'Panorama' strain can be grown from seed; other named varieties can be

propagated from small divisions. ◯ ◉ M ✿ ✱✱✱ The native, lilac-flowered
M. fistulosa (horsemint), adapted to the drier soil and hot summers of the
prairie, is easier to grow. Monardas need moist soil, high in humus, and a sunny
location that has good air circulation to avoid problems with fungus. Mulch
heavily with organic matter. Frequent division—replanting young outer
shoots—keeps these plants vigorous. ◯ 🌿

Myosotis spp. (forget-me-not) 25 cm (10 in.). This self-sowing biennial has
masses of early-blooming blue flowers on small bushy mounds of foliage. The
pink form is just as pretty. It loves moist conditions in either sun or partial
shade. Seedlings replace worn-out parents. ◯ ◉ M W

Nepeta x faassenii or *N. mussinii* (catmint) 45 cm (18 in.). The first plant
may be preferable as it is sterile; the second self-sows, somewhat too vigorously.
Both plants are bushy, with stiff, square stems and small, grey wrinkled leaves
that give off a pungent aroma that cats love. Tiny lavender flowers appear in
spring and early summer. For a second flush of bloom, cut the plants back by
half after the first flowers fade. Catmints need only a sunny spot in light, well-
drained soil. ◯ D ✿ 🌿

Oenothera missouriensis (sundrops). Long stemmed but sprawling, these
trailing plants tolerate hot sun, drought, and poor soil. They are good for low
walls or broad paths, where their large up-facing flowers can best be seen. On
summer days, saucer-shaped yellow flowers appear at the tips of the leafy stems;
other species bloom in the evening. ◯ D RG

Omphalodes verna (blue-eyed Mary) 15 cm (6 in.). This woodland plant has
soft green pointed leaves and sprays of tiny pure blue flowers in spring. It roots
from nodes on the creeping stems and spreads happily in a shady, moist location. ◉ M GC W

Pachysandra terminalis (Japanese spurge) 20 cm (8 in.). A handsome
groundcover for dappled shade, it needs the protection of deep snow or thick
mulch as the leaves persist through the winter. In spring, cut back damaged
foliage. The palmately divided leaves are apple green, maturing to a darker
green; the small flowers are insignificant. ◉ GC W

Paeonia spp. (peony) 90 cm (36 in.). Some of the best-loved of all perennials are the familiar double white, pink, and red peonies. There are also single
early, Japanese (Imperial), fern-leaf, cut-leaf, and tree peonies, mostly available
in hybrid form. Of the many species, *P. anomala,* one of the earliest to bloom,
has finely divided leaves and single pink flowers in late May. The similar *P.
veitchii* grows a little taller and has paler pink flowers. Another species, *P. mollis,*
is smaller but has impressive flowers, blooming later in a darker shade. The fern-
leaf peony, *P. tenuifolia,* also blooms early in the season. Its bright red flowers,
either single or double ('Plena'), are carried above finely dissected, threadlike
leaves. Similar plants have leaves that are more broadly segmented. These are
referred to as cut-leaf peonies *(P. tenuifolia laciniata).*

One of the species used in hybridizing, *P. officinalis,* is quite variable with
white, pink, and red blooms in mid-season. Several forms have fully double
flowers. The pleasantly fragrant *P. lactiflora* is the main species used in hybridiz-

ing the large double, mid- to late-season peonies, the ones most commonly offered at garden centres—the lush double white, pink, and crimson varieties. Some named varieties have to be ordered from specialty nurseries. There are hundreds of gorgeous varieties offered, many new ones and old favourites such as 'Festiva Maxima', double white with crimson flecks and heavenly scent; 'Sarah Bernhardt', shell pink, double, and fragrant; and 'M. Jules Elie', crabapple pink, double, and ruffled with smooth, silvery pink guard petals.

Japanese peony hybrids have large guard petals surrounding the outside of the flower and several smaller petals in the centre. Some are single peony types, others are almost as full as the common hybrid doubles.

Peonies are very long-lived and should be planted with care. The crown should be just below soil level and no deeper than 5 cm (2 in.). Planted too deeply, they fail to bloom; too shallow, the crown and roots are exposed to winter cold and dehydration. Peonies need rich loam and lots of sun to do well, although some of the early-blooming species thrive in the dappled shade of a woodland garden. When preparing the soil, add organic matter and bone meal. Every few years, in early spring, cultivate some bone meal in around the plants—but not too close to the crowns, which are easily damaged—and top dress the plants with compost.

Most peonies are best staked as the blooms can be very heavy, particularly the double ones. Peony rings or large twiggy branches both work well. Spent blooms or seed pods should be removed. In early October, remove spent foliage but do not compost it—peonies are highly susceptible to botrytis and other fungal pathogens, so it is best to dispose of foliage in the garbage. Botrytis shows itself in two ways: the buds get to about pea size, then turn brownish red and develop no further, and spots develop on petals of open flowers. Affected plants can be treated in early spring with a fungicide recommended for botrytis.

Peonies do not need to be divided to maintain their vigour. If they must be moved or divided, do so very early in the spring or, preferably, in the fall after frost has damaged the leaves. Cut back the stems and dig up the plant, taking care not to break the brittle roots. If it was blooming well, replant at exactly the same depth as before. Before dividing, let the roots wilt in the sun for a few hours as wilted roots will not break so easily. Split into large divisions, with five or more "eyes" or growth tips. ○ 🌿 ✽ ✿✿✿

Papaver spp. (poppy). The long, deeply toothed leaves of the oriental poppy, *P. orientale*, 90 cm (36 in.), form large spreading clumps that die down after the flowering period. Tough hairy stems rise above the mounds in June, each bearing a large, fuzzy, drooping bud that slowly splits to reveal the bloom, tucked and pleated like a parachute. The crumpled satiny tissue of the petals opens to form a large bowl of shimmering colour, commonly bright orange and blotched at the base, surrounding a purplish black mass of stamens. Cultivars offer shades of carmine pink, blood red, scarlet, orange, soft pink, white, and salmon. The large seed pods are decorative. Ordinary, well-drained soil in a sunny location is suitable. It is best to divide old plants that seem crowded or fail to bloom well in August when they are dormant. Stake flower stems as they develop.

The Iceland poppy, *P. nudicaule,* 45 cm (18 in.), is indispensable in the spring garden. These poppies bloom on and on throughout summer, making a brilliant show when planted in generous groups. Over tufts of soft, deeply lobed leaves, dozens of slender stems carry a myriad of cup-shaped flowers in yellow, orange, and white. Cultivated varieties offer larger flowers in more colours, including pink, apricot, and scarlet. Deadheading encourages continuous bloom, but a few pods should be left to self-sow to replace the short-lived parents. Perfect drainage and full sun will ensure success.

Tiny alpine poppies, *P. alpinum,* 20 cm (8 in.), are also short-lived but may self-sow. Their leaves are finely dissected and milky green below dainty pastel flowers. They require well-drained, gritty soil and a sunny, sheltered location. ○ ❀❀❀ ⚘

Paxistima canbyi (cliffgreen) 25 cm (10 in.). A small, evergreen, woody plant, it has small hollylike leaves that persist for many years. Its flowers and small green fruit are inconspicuous. Slow growing, it can be used as a natural ground-cover in exposed dry areas or light shade; many plants are needed to produce a massed effect quickly. It propagates easily from cuttings taken in mid-summer. ○ ◉ GC

Penstemon barbatus (beardtongue) 45 cm (18 in.). This is one of the hardiest of the penstemons, which, as a group, do not tolerate extreme heat or cold. Short-lived, they do best in full sun, in well-drained soil of low to average fertility. The many slender stems, with their narrow shining leaves, end in racemes of bright pinky scarlet flowers, which are tubular in shape with flared lips. Borne in profusion, the flowers delight bees and hummingbirds. Other species and cultivars offer a range of pinks and reds. ⚘

Petasites japonica (coltsfoot) 150 cm (60 in.). This monster plant has huge hairy leaves over 90 cm (36 in.) in diameter, that appear after flowering. In May,

A beautiful double-flowered peony, *Paeonia officinalis rosea-plena,* blooms in June. KEN GIRARD

the many purple flowers are produced on stalks that emerge from the ground looking like some strange creature! It loves boggy areas. If it gets too dry, it will wilt, but it recovers rapidly with a thorough soaking. With its tendency to spread, it is not recommended for small gardens. ◉ M W

Phlox spp. (phlox). Tall border phlox, *P. paniculata,* 90 cm (36 in.), provides masses of beautiful, sweetly scented flowers in summer. Large panicles of flat, out-facing florets are clustered on tall leafy stems, in shades of white, pink, mauve, magenta, red, and orange. There are many cultivars to choose from. To perform their best, they must have deep, moist, fertile soil in sun or half-day shade, with thorough watering through the summer.

Wild sweet William *(Phlox divaricata)* blooms in May. KEN GIRARD

Powdery mildew may attack drought-stressed plants, especially in hot weather. In spring, remove a number of stems in each clump to provide better air circulation and encourage larger flowers. Stake plants to support the heavy flowers in windy, wet weather. ○ ◉ M ❀ ✿✿✿

A smaller spring-flowering species, *P. divaricata,* 30 cm (12 in.), with clusters of pale lilac blue flowers, grows well in sunny or partly shaded sites that have good moisture. Even smaller, the prostrate *P. stolonifera* forms creeping mats with small round leaves and star-shaped flowers in pink, blue, mauve, or white. Moss or arctic phlox, *P. subulata,* is also prostrate in habit, with evergreen-needly leaves completely covered, in early spring, with bright pink, mauve, or white flowers. These three rock garden types like full sun and light, well-drained soil. ○ RG

Physostegia virginiana (obedient plant) 90 cm (36 in.). This valuable late-summer bloomer adds colour to tired borders. Its bright pink or white tubular flowers are packed tightly together in wide spires atop long, leafy, stiff, square stems. 'Variegata' has white-edged leaves. They do best in moist soil and plenty of sunshine. The common name refers to the unusual flowers, which stay in position if pushed to one side or other of the stem. ○ M ⚘ ✿✿✿

Platycodon grandiflorus (balloon flower) 45 cm (18 in.). The flower buds, which resemble inflated balloons, get ever larger until they finally open into star-shaped, deep blue flowers in summer. There are pink and white cultivars. As they are late to appear in spring, mark them with permanent labels so they are not damaged by early cultivation. Full sun or partial shade, in light soil amended with plenty of peat moss, suits them. Move these deep-rooted plants with care to avoid damage. ○ ◉ ✿✿✿ ✹

Polemonium caeruleum (Jacob's ladder) 60 cm (24 in.). Woodland plants with simple elegance, their compound leaves are arranged in opposite pairs of leaflets, like a ladder. Blooming in early summer, the small, nodding, clustered flowers are china blue. There is a white form. Greek valerian, *P. reptans,* 15 cm (6 in.), is spreading and ferny, with pale violet blue sprays of flowers in spring. Polemoniums need moist, humus-rich soil in light shade. ● M W

Polygonatum (Solomon's seal) 15–60 cm (6–24 in.). The stems, leaves, and flowers of these graceful woodland plants are all loosely arching. In spring, pairs of delicate creamy white bells dangle downward from each leaf axil. The large, pointed leaves are attractive all summer. In deep, moist soil and dappled shade, the plants slowly increase to good-sized patches. They are easily divided. ● W

Polygonum bistorta 'Superbum' (fleeceflower, snakeweed) 75 cm (30 in.). Only two polygonums are recommended for Alberta gardens as the others are far too invasive for flower borders. This beautiful June-blooming species spreads gradually and wayward shoots are easily discouraged with a sharp hoe. The basal leaves form good-sized clumps of long, arching, pointed leaves that ruffle slightly from a strong central rib. Tall stems rise above the foliage to display the unique, tightly packed flower spikelets, composed of many tiny pink flowers all crammed together at the end of the stems like bottle brushes. This variety needs moist to wet soil in a semi-shaded position. ● M W A handsome, low groundcover for full sun and a well-drained site, *P. affine* 'Donald Lowndes' or 'Darjeeling Red', 30 cm (12 in.), offers shining green leaves that turn bronze in the fall, surmounted by low-growing spikes of rose pink flower clusters. ○ D GC

Potentilla spp. (cinquefoil) 45 cm (18 in.). Related to the shrubby potentillas and resembling geums, named varieties have small, brilliant flowers, single or double, in shades of pink, crimson, red, orange, and yellow, in late spring and summer. Five-toothed leaflets (cinquefoil) radiate from the tips of the slender stems, which are arranged in sprawling rosettes. They look best in groups along rock walls. Although they need sun to bloom, they are best shaded in the afternoon. *P. recta* 'Warrenii', 60 cm (24 in.), has bright yellow flowers in summer on upright, bushy plants that like a sunny location. ○ RG M

Primula spp. (primrose). Many species of primula do well here if their needs are met. Most require deep, loamy soil in cool, moist locations. The alpine types like a more gritty, well-drained compost. The bog lovers must have deep, constantly moist loam. Light or dappled shade suits all but the sun-loving alpines.

Primulas form basal rosettes of leaves, some fleshy and evergreen, some with a mealy coating (farina), others deeply crinkled or scalloped, in various shades of green. Leafless stalks support single flowers or loose clusters, round heads, or tiered umbels of flowers in every colour but true red or blue. The flowers often have toothed, ruffled, or fringed edges. Candelabra primroses bear tiers of nodding flowers on long wiry stems and bloom later than other species.

Primula species and varieties can provide flowers from late April or early May through mid-July. Unfortunately, the 'Pacific Giant' polyanthus primulas are not consistently hardy here, but can be bought for a touch of spring. The cowslip, *P. veris*, 40 cm (16 in.), is a show-stopper with large clusters of cool yellow, delicately scented flowers from early May to early June. There are also brick red and orange colours. *P. vulgaris*, the common primrose, usually pale yellow, also comes in soft pinkish mauve, with a single flower to each stem. *P. elatior*, or oxlip, has umbels of palest yellow flowers rising above dark, somewhat downy foliage. All benefit from a top-dressing of compost each year and a winter mulch of leaves.

P. auricula, a tough, easy plant, is quite different, with thick fleshy leaves covered in mealy powder and large clusters of two-toned cupped flowers. Blooming for about one month from mid-May on, the scented flowers range in colour from dark maroon and purple, to yellow, pink, and even green, most with a creamy eye. The leaves stay green all winter if mulched with leaves. Varieties of P. marginata resemble tiny, compact auriculas, with fine silver edges along the somewhat toothed, fleshy leaves. They need lean gritty soil and the protecting shade of small rocks. Another tough, reliable primrose that tolerates even dry conditions is P. x juliae 'Wanda', a wonderful magenta colour. The drumstick primula, P. denticulata, with its dramatic round umbels of mauve or white flowers, is also forgiving and easy.

Of the later-blooming primulas, the fairy primrose, P. cortusoides, and the very similar P. saxatilis are delicate pink primulas that like damp, peaty shade. Their pale scalloped leaves form rosettes topped with loose clusters of dainty flowers in June. Both self-sow quite readily if seed pods are left.

Many primulas prefer boggy conditions, and this need can be met by digging down about 45 cm (18 in.), lining the hole with several layers of plastic perforated in a few places, and backfilling with damp peat and compost, over a layer of coarse gravel. The unusual P. vialii with its erect purple flower clusters likes such a bed, along with P. florindae, a tall plant with graceful yellow-flowered umbels, blooming the first three weeks of July, and P. sieboldii, with clusters of rosy purple flowers.

Primulas are left undisturbed until flowering becomes sparse or the clumps die out in the middle. Divide immediately after blooming and replant rooted divisions in soil enriched with compost or well-rotted manure. The only pests are slugs, which can be picked off and destroyed. ○ ◉ M W

Prunella grandiflora (self-heal) 30 cm (12 in.). These quiet little plants have short spears of pouched and hooded violet blue flowers over low clumps of leaves. They do well in lightly shaded areas in moist, rich soil. 'Loveliness' hybrids offer shades of white, pink, and pale mauve. ◉ M W

Pulmonaria officinalis (lungwort) 30 cm (12 in.). Shade-loving plants of early bloom and easy culture, P. officinalis and the similar but more refined P. saccharata are remarkable for their low mounds of long, pointed, arched leaves, which are green dappled with silver. These appear very early in spring along with pink funnel-shaped flowers, which are borne in drooping clusters on leafy stalks. The flowers turn blue as they mature so that the plants appear to bear blooms of two colours. Cultivars offer a range of flower colours and leaf variegations. P. rubra has plain unmarked leaves and deep pink flowers fading to blue. P. angustifolia, with dark green bristly leaves, has vivid blue flowers; 'Munstead Blue' is reputed to be as blue as gentians. Also blue flowered, P. longifolia has long narrow leaves. Lungworts appreciate spring sunshine in the blooming period. The soil should be enriched with organic matter and kept evenly moist. ◉ M GC W

Ranunculus acris 'Flore Pleno' (buttercup) 90 cm (36 in.). Blooming for weeks in late spring and early summer, dozens of tiny double buttons of shining gold ride high on long stems above dense, spreading clumps of beautiful three-lobed, toothed leaves. The unique flowers are composed of many tightly overlapping waxy petals. They need only reasonably moist soil in full sun. ○ ❦ ❧

Hardy primulas *(Primula auricula)* bear flowers in clusters early in May; the fleshy foliage is evergreen. JUDITH DOYLE

Rudbeckia fulgida (coneflower, black-eyed Susan) 75 cm (30 in.). Flowering over a long season, from summer right up to the hard frosts of October, long-lasting daisies have bright golden yellow ray petals surrounding a hard, cone-shaped black disk, on strong branched stems. The broad, pointed leaves are rough to the touch. 'Goldsturm' is a superior variety. An old garden favourite, *R. laciniata* 'Golden Glow', 180 cm (72 in.) or more, is a true giant with shaggy, double, yellow daisies and deeply lobed leaves. Best in the very back of the border, it needs annual thinning to no more than a dozen stems and long stout stakes to support it. A similar species, *R. nitida*, has lemon yellow double flowers in late summer. Rudbeckias need well-drained but moist soil and full sun. ○ ❦ ❧

Salvia* x *superba (salvia, sage) 30–45 cm (12–18 in.). Hardy in a sunny, sheltered position with reliable snow cover, they tolerate drought and prefer light, well-drained soil. Because of their small size and deep colour, they look best grouped in front of white, pink, or pale yellow flowers. The tiny purple or

Dainty *Primula cortusoides* enjoys a moist, shady location. KEN GIRARD

dark violet blue flowers, so vivid they seem to glow, are borne in many tightly packed spires on compact little bushes. ○ ✿✿✿ ✺

Saponaria ocymoides (rock soapwort) 20 cm (8 in.). Spreading mounds of tiny leaves show off clouds of tiny pink flowers in early summer. It trails beautifully over rock walls and prefers sunny, well-drained soil. Although it self-sows copiously, unwanted seedlings are easily hoed out. ○ RG

Saxifraga spp. (rockfoil) to 20 cm (8 in.). Mossy saxifrages such as S. x *arendsii*, S. *canaliculata*, and S. 'Bob Hawkins' have tight mounds of finely divided, "mossy" leaves, covered in late spring with a profusion of dainty white, pink, or dark red flowers. They can suffer severe foliage burn without deep snow cover. They need a sheltered location in partial shade and light, well-drained soil. ◉ RG Encrusted saxifrages such as S. *paniculata*, S. *longifolia*, and S. *hostii* have toothed, "encrusted" leaves in clustered rosettes and sprays of tiny creamy white flowers in late spring. These are sun-loving plants for rock gardens and edging. ○ RG

Scabiosa caucasica (pincushion flower) 60 cm (24 in.). Blooming from summer until hard frost, this conversation piece is notable for its large flowers. Frills of irregular, overlapping petals surround pincushionlike mounds of smaller, tightly packed petals and stamens, usually powder blue or mauve. Cultivars offer shades of white to deeper blue. Flowers are borne on long floppy stems over grassy mounds of leaves. Light soil, with lots of sharp sand and grit worked in, and a sunny location suit these plants best. The fantastic giant scabious is of another genus, *Cephalaria gigantea*, 180 cm (72 in.) or more, with similar flowers in pale yellow and large, deeply divided leaves. ○ ✿✿ ✺

Primula vialii **is an excitingly different primrose; it prefers a semi-shaded, boggy situation.** KEN GIRARD

Sedum spp. (stonecrop). Taller varieties are useful in borders. They have succulent leaves and small star-shaped flowers massed in large heads. S. *aizoon*, 40 cm (16 in.), is spring blooming, with large flat clusters of bright yellow flowers, for a sunny, dry spot. The late-blooming hybrid S. x 'Autumn Joy', 60 cm (24 in.), has large, clustered pale pink flowers that turn copper in the fall. S. *spectabile* 'Brilliant' and 'Meteor' are similar, with deep pink flowers. Floppy S. *rosea atropurpureum* has dark red

For pure golden splendour in the garden, *Solidago* **hybrids are unsurpassed; unlike wild goldenrod, garden forms are not invasive.** MAUREEN IRETON

foliage and pink flowers, and needs support. Tall sedums like full sun, good drainage, and more moisture than most succulents. ○ ◉ ✿✿✿

There are many mat-forming and low-mounding sedums with succulent leaves for rock gardens and edging borders. Growth habits range from neat and tidy to overly rambunctious *(S. acre)*. Leaves can be needlelike, flat, or round like bean seeds. Heads of tiny, clustered, starry flowers appear in early spring to late fall, in white, pink, red, and yellow. They need well-drained, light soil in a sunny position. ○ GC RG

Sempervivum spp. (houseleek, hen and chicks). Low, clustering rosettes of fleshy green or red-tinted leaves are spread by stolons, growing baby rosettes around and within the mother rosette. In summer, many varieties sport clusters of star-shaped flowers on fleshy stalks. There are many varieties of leaf forms, textures, colours, and sizes, including the elegant, silvery, cobwebbed *S. arach-noideum.* They do well in sunny, exposed positions but tolerate some shade. Too much shade and the rosettes become smaller and dull in colour. ○ GC RG

Sidalcea malviflora (prairie mallow) 90 cm (36 in.). Tall, spiky, bright pink, sun loving, and summer blooming, sidalcea has small flowers that resemble miniature hollyhocks. Rounded leaves, delicately scalloped and ridged, form loose, basal clumps. Tall branching stems sparsely arrayed with small, lobed leaves support loose racemes of dainty flowers that open almost flat. They fade from deep magenta to soft pink as they mature. If faded flowers are removed, the season of bloom lasts from July to September. Ordinary, well-drained, moist soil in a sunny position, sheltered from wind, suits them. Taller varieties need light staking. ○ ◉ ✿✿ 🌿

Silene spp. (campion) to 20 cm (8 in.). Low-growing foliage and star-shaped flowers with inflated or tubular calyces mark these variable plants. Moss campion, *S. acaulis,* 5 cm (2 in.), grows in prostrate cushions of tiny, tightly packed leaves spotted with bright pink flowers in late spring. Sea campion, *S. maritima,* 15 cm (6 in.), has low, sprawling mounds of pale green leaves, covered with tiny, inflated white flowers in summer. *S. hookeri,* 20 cm (8 in.), has clusters of bright magenta flowers above low rosettes of grey hairy leaves in late spring. These tough little plants grow in any ordinary, well-drained soil in a sunny position. Campions are especially useful in rock gardens and as edging plants. ○ RG

Sisyrinchium montanum (blue-eyed grass) 20 cm (8 in.). Tidy tufts of grey blue grassy leaves and stalks are topped with tiny blue flowers that last only one day. Full sun and good drainage are all this good edging or rock garden plant needs. ○ 🌿

Smilacina racemosa (false Solomon's seal) 90 cm (36 in.). A woodland plant for a shaded, moist area, its requirement for slightly acidic soil can be satisfied with large additions of peat moss and leaf mould. Its bright green, veined, and pointed leaves appear to zigzag up stems topped by short spires of tiny, fluffy white flowers. ◉ W

Solidago hybrids (goldenrod) 30–75 cm (12–30 in.). Easy plants that require minimal care, they need only moderately fertile soil in a sunny position. The self-supporting, stiff stems, well clothed with dark green, lance-shaped leaves, bear unique star-burst sprays of tiny, fuzzy golden flowers in July and August. Many native species can be invasive. ○ ✿ 🌿

x *Solidaster luteus* 90 cm (36 in.). This intergeneric hybrid of *Aster* and *Solidago* has lemony flower buds that open over a long season to form sprays of tiny white or cream asters in September. Its weak stems need support. Wire tomato cages work well. ○ ✿ 🌿

Stachys spp. (betony). Lambs' ears, *S. byzantina*, formerly *S. lanata*, 45 cm (18 in.), is grown mainly for its wonderful velvety leaves, which form spreading clumps that slowly expand into dense carpets of silver. The leaves are long and tongue shaped, densely covered with white silky hairs and downy to the touch. Quiet and unobtrusive in their silvery muffs, the small purplish flowers are borne in whorls atop long woolly spikes. 'Silver Carpet' is a nonflowering variety. Very hardy if planted in fast-draining soil that is not too fertile, lambs' ears endures dry spells and heat. It needs full sun most of the day. ○ D RG Quite different in appearance, *S. macrantha (S. grandiflora)*, or big betony, 50 cm (20 in.), is compact and bushy, with deep green, wrinkled, and scalloped triangular leaves, and showy whorls of purplish pink tubular flowers. This betony appreciates a lightly shaded spot with evenly moist soil. ◉ M ✿ Wood betony, *S. officinalis*, is very attractive in herb gardens, borders, or wild meadows. It has reddish purple tubular flowers borne on stiff, square stems above clumps of long, toothed leaves. A moderate water user, like most herbs it needs full sun. ○ ✿ 🌿

Tanacetum vulgare 'Crispum' (tansy) 90 cm (36 in.). Tansy has rounded, ferny, aromatic leaves on strong stems, topped in summer with clusters of little yellow buttons that dry well. In full sun and dry, well-drained, not too fertile soil, it is not too invasive; still, it is best not planted among other flowers. ○ ✿ 🐝 🌿

Thalictrum aquilegifolium (meadow rue) 150 cm (60 in.). This tall, elegant background plant grows well in semi-shaded borders. In late April, fat, blanched buds emerge from the cold earth, quickly developing into tall strong stalks arrayed with ferny, columbinelike foliage. The fluffy panicles of bloom open in June, in shades of white, mauve, pink, or purple. A smaller species that blooms later, *T. dipterocarpum* or Yunnan meadow rue, is a choice plant with tender stems that require support. The ferny leaves and tiny mauve pink flower sprays are very dainty. 'Album' has white flowers and 'Hewitt's Double', little mauve powderpuffs in airy sprays that last well into September. Both species prefer rich, moist, well-drained soil that is mulched annually with peat and compost. ◉ 🌿 W

Thermopsis caroliniana (Carolina lupin) 90 cm (36 in.). This member of the pea family has long spires of yellow lupinlike flowers in late spring. It does best in light, well-drained, poor to moderately fertile soil in full sun. Amend clay loam with sand and grit. ○ D M

Thymus spp. (thyme) 6 cm (2–3 in.). Creeping, mat-forming thyme has tiny, aromatic evergreen leaves, variously shiny green, variegated, or woolly, covered in spring with tiny pink, magenta, red, yellow, or white flowers. It likes full sun and well-drained soil. This versatile groundcover is perfect between stepping stones or covering dry slopes as it tolerates light foot traffic and most types release a rich fragrance when brushed against or walked on. ○ D RG ❀ GC

Fragrant thyme is at home in rock gardens or between paving stones in a path. <small>KEN GIRARD</small>

Tiarella **spp.** (foamflower) 30 cm (12 in.). Closely related to heucheras, hybrids have been produced between the two genera. Small white flowers are produced in profusion in mid-summer, giving it its common name. It likes a shady, moist location. ● M GC W

Tradescantia **hybrids** (spiderwort) 60 cm (24 in.). Grassy, spidery leaves and wavy stems set off small three-petalled flowers that open from clusters of buds over many weeks in early summer. The sky blue, deep blue, mauve, purple, cerise, violet, or white flowers last only one day but are constantly replaced. They like moist, even boggy, soil in light shade. ◉ M ❀❀❀

Trollius **spp.** (globeflower) 60 cm (24 in.). Clumps of deeply divided ferny leaves develop early in spring, soon pushing up long stems bearing large globular flower heads of incurving satiny petals. Various species and cultivars provide glowing shades of pale to deep yellow and orange, in May and early June. 'Ledebour' globeflower blooms later, with more open flowers and prominent petals. To look their best, they must have rich, moist soil in partial shade. ◉ M W

Valeriana officinalis (garden heliotrope) to 240 cm (96 in.) in black loam. Strong, ribbed, tubular stems support large, sky-scraping, flat clusters of tiny

Among the first flowers of spring, 'Johnny jump-up' violas will continue to bloom all summer long if sheared back after the first flush of bloom is over.
<small>JOHN DOYLE</small>

Purple loosestrife *(Lythrum salicaria)* has been declared a noxious weed under the *Noxious Weeds Act* of Alberta. Under this act, noxious weeds must be controlled to prevent their rapid spread. An introduced species, lythrum is able to replace native marsh plants because of its aggressive nature and prolific seed production. As native plants are replaced, wildlife and water-fowl decline due to habitat destruction.

The ability of wild species to breed with tame cultivars and produce viable seed is of concern to gardeners. Garden hybrids and cultivars, so-called self-sterile hybrids, frequently set copious seed when cross-pollinated. There is a great possibility that some of the seed produced on garden plants through insect cross-pollination will eventually find its way into wetlands. While fully appreciating the value of this plant as a garden ornamental, The University of Alberta Devonian Botanic Garden has advised that the propagation, sale, and growing of all forms of purple loosestrife, including 'Morden Pink' and other cultivars, should cease immediately. The Garden dug up and destroyed its collection of lythrum species and cultivars in 1992. Most garden centres no longer sell the plant.

The brilliant pink spires of this lythrum cultivar might soon be only a memory in Calgary gardens; all forms of lythrum (purple looses-trife) are now classed as noxious weeds in Alberta. FRANK SCOTT

Unfortunately for gardeners, purple loosestrife is a hardy and very attractive herbaceous perennial that has been popular in prairie gardens for many years. To be on the safe side, all types should be removed and disposed of (in sealed, opaque plastic garbage bags for delivery to a landfill site). Burning is a good method where regulations permit. It will be difficult to replace the brilliant, long-lasting pink or purple spires of lythrum in summer borders. Other pink summer flowers you can try include aster, chrysanthemum, and phlox. Spiky plants with pink and purple flowers are liatris and sidalcea, fireweed *(Epilobium),* and hollyhocks.

pinkish white flowers that scent the whole garden in early summer. The large leaves are deeply cut. It needs full sun or light shade in any well-drained soil. It is less tall in lighter soils. Deadhead this self-sower before seed is formed. ○ ●
❀ 🌿

Verbascum nigrum (mullein) 150 cm (60 in.). This species is reliably peren-nial in light, well-drained soil of low fertility and full sun. A dramatic plant, its basal leaves are large, broad, and pointed, grey green and rough in texture. Stout stems soar high above them, bearing dozens of nubbly buds that open randomly into little yellow saucers. Also perennial, *V. chaixii*, has yellow or white, purple-centred flowers. *V. phoeniceum,* 75 cm (30 in.), blooms in shades of pink to pur-ple in June and July. It needs a hot, dry spot and well-drained soil. ○ D 🌿

Veronica spp. (speedwell). Veronicas bring a touch of soft, hazy blue to the garden. In the upright species, the leaves are narrowly lance shaped and serrated, glossy or dull mid-green in colour. The tiny flowers are arranged in terminal racemes that taper to narrow spires as they unfold from the bottom to the top.

V. incana or woolly speedwell, 40 cm (16 in.), has narrow silvery leaves form-ing neat tufts that support many spikes of contrasting deep blue flowers in June. ○ D RG ⚘ There are also pink forms. It needs lean soil, good drainage, and full sun. Similar in size, Hungarian speedwell, *V. teucrium,* has brilliant clear blue flowers in lavish quantity, in late spring. These floppy plants need to be propped with twiggy branches or sited on the edge of a low wall where they can tumble freely. 'Crater Lake Blue' is a vivid blue. Another small species, *V. gentianoides,* is named for its broad, gentianlike leaves. Blooming in late May, it has delicate pale blue flowers.

Taller is spike speedwell, *V. spicata,* 60 cm (24 in.), with dense racemes of blue in summer. The many hybrids of this species with *V. longifolia* have resulted in a variety of colours—pale pink, deep pink, lavender, and white. Clump speedwell, *V. longifolia (V. maritima),* can grow as tall as 120 cm (48 in.), with racemes of dark lavender blue. Cultivars offer many pastel shades. Another tall species, *V. grandis holophylla,* has long-lasting deep blue flowers in summer. ○ ◉ M ⚘

Of the many rock garden species, the easiest are *V. pectinata,* with prostrate mats of woolly grey leaves and deep blue flowers with a white eye, and *V. pros-trata (V. rupestris),* a creeping form with short spikes of deep blue, showy flowers. ○ RG

Sun-loving border veronicas are long-lived and restrained in growth. Ordinary soil can be enriched with rotted manure or compost for border types, which need both good drainage and moisture retention to cope with summer heat. Rock gar-den types grow profusely, preferring less fertile, well-drained soil in full sun.

Vinca minor (periwinkle) 15 cm (6 in.). Lax, creeping stems and dark green glossy leaves that persist throughout the growing season make for a good ground-cover. The small star-shaped flowers appear in mid-spring and sporadically throughout the growing season right to frost. Usually blue, there are also purple and white cultivars. It needs moist, well-drained soil in partial shade. Good win-ter snow cover or mulch protects the evergreen leaves from drying winter winds. ◉ M GC W

Viola spp. (violet, viola) to 30 cm (12 in.). Western Canada violet, *V. rugulosa,* is very attractive in spring, with dense mounds of large heart-shaped leaves and tiny white and mauve flowers. ○ ◉ ⚘ A determined spreader, it should be confined to small patches in a shaded area. 'Johnny jump-ups', *V. tricolor,* are like miniature pansies with tiny yellow and purple or plain purple flowers borne in profusion from very early spring on. Once in the garden, they self-sow with aban-don. They like more sun than other violets. ◉ W GC

Yucca filamentosa (Adam's needle) foliage to 60 cm (24 in.). A desert plant with stiff, spiky foliage, the leaves are rigid and sharply pointed, the margins edged with thready, curling filaments. Flowers are borne high on woody stems, in pyramidal spires of creamy pendant bells. Only mature plants (eight to ten years old) bloom. The much hardier southern Alberta species, *Y. glauca,* is smaller, with narrow, white-edged, greyish leaves in pincushionlike mounds. It bears spires of clustered greenish white flowers in July. Yuccas must have full sun and sandy, well-drained soil low in humus. Drought tolerant, yuccas are good for barren, exposed slopes. They are best planted as specimens so that their whole form is visible. ○ D 🌿

ORNAMENTAL GRASSES

Ornamental grasses provide year-round interest in the garden and need little maintenance. In the fall, they can be left uncut to bend and rustle in the breeze, lending texture and subtle colour to the winter landscape. Grasses can be used in borders with other plants; try small ones in groups for edging or setting off other plants. Large specimens can mark a driveway entrance or fill a sunny corner. Most require ordinary, well-drained soil in an open, sunny position and are suitable for meadow gardens.

The following grasses grow very well in Calgary, even though books list them for more temperate zones. It is worthwhile to test the limits of hardiness of the plants we read about. Young grasses should be watered well until established; then, only occasionally. Disease and pest free, virtually their only problem is the invasiveness of certain species *(Bromus* and *Phalaris).* This tendency can be curbed by planting in a very dry area or within artificial constraints. The other grasses listed here have perfect manners.

Arrhenatherum elatius bulbosum 'Variegatum' (variegated bulbous oat grass) 75 cm (30 in.). This grass has a pale, cool, refined look. The striped leaves have white margins and grow in loose tufts. It needs moist soil and afternoon shade to stay vigorous.

Briza media (quaking grass) 40 cm (16 in.). A small grass with erect slender stems, flat, tapering light green leaves, and heart-shaped florets, it lives up to its name in the lightest breeze. In summer, ornamental panicles of purple brown spikelets dangle on threadlike stalks.

Bromus inermis 'Skinner's Gold' (golden brome) 75 cm (30 in.). Invasive as quack grass, it is best planted in a large sunken pot with the bottom removed. It is very striking in summer with its glowing yellow-green striped leaves, tall stems, and feathery flower panicles.

Deschampsia caespitosa (tufted hair grass) 75 cm (30 in.). This grass forms mounds of long, narrow, green leaves with very fine open heads of delicate flowers on long stalks. It grows in sun or light shade, in moist or dry soil.

Festuca ovina glauca (sheep's fescue) 25 cm (10 in.). Low tussocks of fine silvery blue leaves keep their colour all winter. Feathery flowers rise above the mounds in summer. Suitable for sunny banks and edging, this plant is trouble free as long as the soil is light. Divide them every three to five years or when the clumps die out in the middle. In spring, shear them back by about half their height. *F. tenuifolia,* or green fescue, is an even smaller tufted grass with threadlike leaves of bright emerald green. This little gem belongs in a rock garden or raised bed.

Helictotrichon sempervirens (blue oat grass) 90 cm (36 in.). Neat arching clumps of tough, narrow blue grey leaves are topped by loose clusters of buffy oatlike spikelets in summer. With its fine texture and quiet colour, this grass is best used by itself and not crowded by other plants.

Molinia caerula variegata (purple moor grass) 40 cm (16 in.). Densely tufted, its long fine leaves are striped with creamy yellow. Purplish pink flowers are borne on long stalks in summer. It prefers moist soil, amended with plenty of peat moss. Planting it close to evergreens sets off the lovely colour.

The cool green and white stripes of ribbon grass are most decorative. MAUREEN IRETON

Phalaris arundinacea picta (ribbon grass) 90 cm (36 in.). This handsome tall-growing grass spreads rapidly through creeping rhizomes. It should be confined by barriers such as a large plastic container sunk to the rim in the ground. Its cool green and white stripes make the extra planting effort worthwhile. In July, numerous flower panicles stand well above the foliage on tall stalks. These remain attractive all season and into winter, when the whole plant turns a beautiful buffy colour. It is useful to control erosion on slopes and areas where it is hard to maintain other plants. In dry conditions, it spreads less easily.

FERNS

A few ferns can be grown in our gardens, even though Calgary would not seem to have an ideal climate for their cultivation. They thrive in moist, semi-shaded locations with well-drained soil rich in organic matter. They are best planted in areas that are covered in snow all winter, as winds can dry out the crowns or roots. Lacking snow cover, they should be mulched heavily with leaves in late fall.

Other than the ferns in the following list, you may also like to try: male fern, *Dryopteris filix-mas,* 50 cm (20 in.), a mid-sized, robust, spreading fern; royal fern, *Osmunda regalis,* a large fern, close to 90 cm (36 in.) tall when its requirements are met; hay-scented fern, *Dennstaedtia punctilobula,* 40 cm (16 in.), with lacy fronds, which makes a good groundcover; sensitive fern, *Onoclea sensibilis,* 30 cm (12 in.), with broad lime green fronds; and fragile fern, *Cystopteris fragilis,* 20 cm (8 in.), with finely divided, almost frothy leaves.

Adiantum pedatum (maidenhair fern) 30–50 cm (12–20 in.). This mid-sized fern has a mounding habit. Black stalks emerge in spring, eventually opening into beautifully fresh apple green fronds, which have several pinnae radiating from one side, like fingers from a spread-out hand. The clumps are best left undisturbed for years as they improve with age. They thrive in light to heavy shade and must be kept evenly moist.

Athyrium filix-femina (lady fern) 50–75 cm (20–30 in.). When mature, this is a rather large vase-shaped fern. Twice-divided fronds (bipinnate) give it a lacy appearance. It grows from a creeping rhizome, which should be planted just below the soil surface. Kept moist, it will tolerate quite a bit of sun, but it also does well in the shade.

Athyrium niponicum pictum syn *A. goeringianum* (Japanese painted fern) 30 cm (12 in.). The beautifully coloured fronds of this mid-size fern are wine red when emerging, eventually opening to a silvery green with red stems. The colour is best in light shade or a location with morning sun. In too much shade, the red colour does not develop; too much sun causes the colours to fade.

Dryopteris dilitata (broad buckler fern) 60 cm (24 in.). This mid-size fern with deep green, finely cut fronds likes bright shade. Narrow buckler fern, *D. carthusiana* syn *D. spinulosa*, 40 cm (16 in.), is a more delicate fern with finely divided mid-green fronds. It prefers humus-rich, acidic soil.

Cinnamon fern requires cool, moist, organically rich, and somewhat acidic soil. KEN GIRARD

Matteucia struthiopteris (ostrich fern, fiddlehead fern) 90–150 cm (36–60 in.). Easy to grow, these tall vase-shaped ferns spread by underground stolons, one plant eventually becoming a large colony. The large pale green fronds emerge in the form of fiddleheads, which are followed in late July by dark brown or black fertile fronds. They need light, bright shade with enough moisture to keep the fronds from yellowing. To prevent rot, plant so that the top of the crown is slightly above soil level.

Osmunda cinnamomea (cinnamon fern) 50–80 cm (20–30 in.). This large fern likes wet springs, moist summers, and dry falls. In early spring, fertile fronds push up out of the ground. These are a light reddish brown, hence the common name. Once the spores have been released, the green, sterile, vegetative fronds emerge, growing quite tall in good conditions. They must be kept evenly moist in acidic soil. They are best planted in an area that stays frozen all winter, with snow cover or plenty of leaf mulch.

Tulipa tarda, a wild tulip species from Turkey, forms spreading colonies by self-sown seed and bulb division. MARGARET BROWN

HARDY BULBS

The surest way to have a colourful spring garden is to plant bulbs in the fall. There is a tempting variety that will withstand Calgary winters and suit any size or type of garden. These bulbs are equally at home massed in formal beds or naturalized under trees in a woodland garden. Blooming periods vary, so it is easy to achieve continuous spring bloom by choosing an assortment. Bulbs may be ordered from tantalizing catalogues or bought in local garden centres, where boxes of bare bulbs are displayed with seductive photographs, encouraging gardeners with visions of their garden next spring.

Hardy bulbs for spring flowering are best planted in early to mid-September, as bulbs benefit from having six to eight weeks to establish roots before the ground freezes. Daffodils in particular prefer to be planted while the soil is still warm. Bulbs prefer a sunny location, but as many emerge before trees, shrubs, and perennials have leafed out, areas that will be shaded later in the season are suitable. Those in the warmest locations bloom earliest and it is wise to avoid overly warm locations, such as against a south-facing foundation of a house. Chinooks, mild winters, or warm early springs may cause bulbs in these locations to emerge too early and freeze.

Bulbs in flower beds look best as eye-catching blocks of colour. Avoid stringing them out in single file. Plant small groups in a random manner around trees and shrubs or in grassy areas. Bulbs are attractive naturalized this way and later leaf growth will camouflage the spent leaves.

Bulbs prefer a rich, well-drained soil. Remove heavy clay and replace it with soil enriched with compost or peat moss. You may add 9–6–6 fertilizer mixed 15 mL per tenth of a square metre (1 tbsp. per sq. ft) into the soil under the bulb. Plant bulbs pointed end up, flat side down, and sprinkle them with bulb dust to prevent damage from insects or disease. Planting depths vary, but the larger the bulb, the deeper it should be planted. A rule of thumb is to plant bulbs at a minimum depth of three times the bulb's height. In the Calgary area it does not hurt to plant large bulbs slightly deeper; if they are not deep enough, they may grow prematurely during Chinooks and be damaged by frosts. Cover bulbs with soil, press down firmly, and water well. To prevent bulbs from coming up too early in the spring, it is important to mulch bulb beds with at least 8 cm (3 in.) of leaves, straw, or evergreen branches after the ground has frozen.

In the spring, water bulbs well when the ground thaws out. When shoots emerge, fertilize with a fertilizer high in phosphorus and potassium (4–10–8) Bone meal may also be used, but it is slow-acting. When blooming has finished cut off stems with spent flowers and seed pods. Leave the foliage to die down naturally as the leaves will store food for the bulb for next year. Fertilizer (4–10–8) may be added to assist this process. Do not remove foliage until it turns yellow or brown and can be picked off easily. This may take a long time as daffodils, for example, often do not ripen until August. Annuals may be planted to disguise foliage not hidden by perennials.

Tulips (*Tulipa* spp.). Tulips are the most popular and familiar bulbs with Calgary area gardeners. Harbingers of spring, they can be among the first flowers to appear, and a proper selection of varieties can ensure bloom right into late June. Tulips can be short (10 cm/4 in.) or tall (60 cm/24 in.). Colours range from pure snow white to a purple so dark it is almost black. The shapes and sizes of the flowers are almost as variable as the colours. The rock garden or species tulips can have small flowers, such as *T. tarda*, or large ones, such as *T. weinlandiana*. Most species are single-flowered, but there are a few that have multiple blooms per stem. One of the best of these is *T. praestans* and its varieties.

Tulips do well in Calgary, especially those closely related to the species, as they tend to naturalize themselves and multiply. Planted in the early fall, the small bulbs should be approximately 10 cm (4 in.) deep. Large-flowered hybrids and species should be planted at least 15–20 cm (6–8 in.) deep. Like most bulbs, tulips enjoy areas where the soil drains freely and resent having wet feet. Species tulips keep growing year after year, with more flowers each spring. The showier hybrid tulips eventually need to be dug up, separated, refertilized, and reset into the ground. Some gardeners replace these bulbs completely after about three years in the garden.

New varieties of tulips are available at garden centres every year and many gardeners plant a few every fall alongside the tried-and-true varieties.

RECOMMENDED DAFFODILS FOR CALGARY GARDENS

- ❧ **Rock garden** (15–25 cm/6–10 in.): 'February Gold' (early); 'Hawera', 'Minnow', 'Pipit', 'Thalia', 'Tete-a-Tete' (mid-spring)
- ❧ **Trumpet** (45 cm/18 in.): 'King Alfred', 'Unsurpassable', 'Mount Hood' (mid-spring)
- ❧ **Large-cupped** (25–45 cm/10–18 in.): 'Carlton', 'Ice Follies', 'Scarlet Elegance' (mid-spring)
- ❧ **Small-cupped** (40 cm/16 in.): 'Barrett Browning', 'Flower Record' (mid-spring)
- ❧ **Bunching-flowered** (35–45 cm/14–18 in.): 'Cheerfulness', 'Yellow Cheerfulness' (mid-spring)
- ❧ **Double** (35–45 cm/14–18 in.): 'Dick Wilden' (early), 'Ice King' (mid-spring)

Daffodils (*Narcissus* spp.). These popular spring bulbs are available in many colours, shapes, and sizes. Most are hardy, tolerant, and adaptable plants that will grow in almost any situation except heavy shade or badly drained soil. They can be used in mixed borders or naturalized in meadows and open woodlands.

Narcissus poeticus **'Actaea' is a sweetly scented daffodil.** JUDITH DOYLE

Smaller varieties can be planted in rock gardens. Most daffodils remain in bloom for three to four weeks in early spring.

Daffodils grow from bulbs that vary from pea size to 13–15 cm (5–6 in.) in circumference. Wild daffodils increase by seed, but garden bulbs develop offset bulblets produced on the two opposite sides of the parent bulb. The grey green leaves are all basal, usually flat in common daffodils, and as long as the flowering stalks. Flowers are most frequently yellow and white but colours can range from cream through pink, orange, and scarlet. Many varieties appear in catalogues, from dainty little *N. minimus*, at 8 cm (3 in.) a tiny perfect replica of tall yellow trumpet daffodils, and *N. cyclamineus* with its startled swept-back petals, to towering large-flowered cultivars 45 cm (18 in.) in many different colour combinations.

Plant daffodils in rich, well-drained soil supplied with organic matter and bone meal in a sunny location or where light shade is cast by trees or taller plants. They do not thrive in hot, starved soils. They should be planted as soon as the bulbs become available in late August and early September. Choose large, firm bulbs free from rot or discolouration. A fertilizer with potassium and phosphate can be worked into the soil. Arrange the bulbs in informal groups of each

'Apeldoorn' is a deservedly popular, May-flowering tulip. KEN GIRARD

type. Large bulbs need to be planted at least 20 cm (8 in.) deep, smaller bulbs 10 cm (4 in.) deep, and the tiniest bulbs need only 8 cm (3 in.) of depth. Space according to size so there will be room for some increase—although daffodils may not multiply into clumps in the Calgary area—and be sure to mulch well. In spring, daffodils may be fertilized and they should be watered regularly until the leaves die back.

When plantings become crowded and the number and size of the flowers deteriorate, it is time to lift, separate, and replant the bulbs. Replanting in enriched soil every three or four years will ensure optimum results. This is best done just as the leaves die down, when it is easy to find the bulbs. The bulbs may also be stored in a warm, dry place—with withered leaves, skins, and roots removed—and then replanted in August. Do not separate offsets from the parent bulb until they have developed a basal plate—the flat bottom from which roots grow. Bulbs are toxic, so ensure they are kept away from children and pets.

SMALL HARDY BULBS

Besides the familiar tulips and daffodils, there are many miniature bulbs that can fill the gaps in the spring garden, although it would be a shame to think of these dainty little flowers only as gap-fillers. They are beautiful in their own right and many are inexpensive enough that a good number may be planted to make a drift of colour. Most are very cold hardy, and many multiply to provide veritable carpets of bloom in a few years.

Most of these smaller bulbs like warm, well-drained areas where the early spring sun can coax them into pushing their frail little heads out of the cold soil. It is a good idea to place them in groups next to walkways and areas where they can be easily seen and enjoyed from inside the house. They also work well in

The first flowers of spring are the cheery species crocus and hybrids, in shades of white, mauve, purple, and gold. MAUREEN IRETON

shrub borders and around trees, where they receive enough light through the bare branches in early spring. By the time the trees and shrubs have leafed out and cast heavy shade, the bulb leaves have withered and the bulbs remain dormant until next spring. Remember to use a light winter mulch. The following small bulbs are worth trying.

Crocus *(Crocus* spp.). Crocuses are actually not bulbs but corms—thickened underground stems capable of producing roots, leaves, and flowers. The two main types of crocus are the large-flowered Dutch hybrids, *C. vernus,* and the smaller flowered species crocus. The species types, once established in the garden, will produce for many years, whereas the larger hybrids may eventually fade away as they deplete themselves. Nevertheless, some gardeners have great success with the Dutch types, which come in a pleasing range of mauve, purple, stripes of the two, and white and gold. To get a good show, try planting twenty-five to fifty bulbs, as they are quite inexpensive. They are most successful planted near a warm house foundation and should be mulched well, preferably by shovelling snow over them whenever possible. Squirrels love to eat crocus corms and may dig them all up.

Glory-of-the-snow *(Chionodoxa luciliae).* Only 10 cm (4 in.) tall when in full bloom in April and May, these bulbs have tiny flowers in blue, purple mauve, or pink. They do well in either sun or partial shade and should be planted in generous drifts in easily visible locations in shrub borders or under trees, or in small groups in the rock garden.

Grape Hyacinth *(Muscari armeniacum).* These bloom from early to mid-May, later than other small bulbs, although the handsome tufts of grassy leaves appear in early April. As the flower spikes emerge, reaching a height of 15–25 cm (6–10 in.), the leaves fall flat to display to full advantage the tightly clustered tiny bells, which are commonly blue but may also be white *(M. botryoides* 'Album'). There is also a species that has dark blue, almost purple, flowers on the lower half of the inflorescence and light blue flowers on the upper half *(M. latifolium,* sometimes called Oxford and Cambridge). These bulbs increase year after year and require little care. They often send up leaves in the fall, but this does not seem to harm them. They are excellent for edging walkways, in rock gardens, and massed under spring-flowering shrubs such as plums and cherries.

Ixiolirion *(Ixiolirion).* These easy-to-grow, hardy plants have grasslike leaves. They produce trumpet-shaped lavender blue flowers on 30-cm (12-in.) stems in June. Plant them in a sunny location and mulch to protect leaves from spring frosts.

Siberian Squill *(Scilla sibirica).* Delightful and exceedingly hardy, these will do well for years, soon increasing into large colonies and lakes of bright blue nodding bells. They are about 15 cm (6 in.) in height, bloom very early in April, and last about three weeks. There is a white form and a larger blue one.

Snowdrop *(Galanthus nivalis).* Related to daffodils, snowdrops come up in early spring, blooming in April and May. These dainty plants grow about 15 cm (6 in.) tall and have bluish green leaves and nodding white bell flowers with a small green dot on the petals. They look best if planted in groups. To establish these bulbs in the garden, force them indoors for the first season so that they root out properly. After flowering, they should be kept cool and moist in bright light and then placed outside in May. Most garden centres sell the bulbs in the fall, but they are best planted outside after blooming, any time up to mid-summer. If they are planted in the fall, they may not have time to develop a strong root system and could rot away. If they do not come up, there is still hope; one Calgary gardener finally had blooming snowdrops three years after planting them and they have even increased into a modest patch.

Striped Squill *(Puschkinia libanotica* or *P. scilloides).* These little treasures are not used enough in Calgary area gardens. Grassy-leaved, the plants are about 15 cm (6 in.) tall when in bloom. The flowers are white with a bright blue stripe in the middle of the petals, the overall effect being a soft icy blue. They do well in many types of location but must have some sun. Not at all fussy, these bulbs grow in almost any soil from gravelly to rich loam. They are among the first flowers in early April.

The following bulbs are larger and generally succeed, so are worth trying in Chinook zone gardens:

Alliums *(Allium* spp.). These beautiful ornamental cousins of onions, garlic, and shallots do well in Calgary area gardens, blooming in late spring or summer. The bulbs should be planted in early September in rich, well-drained soil, preferably in full sun. Plant large bulbs 10 cm (4 in.) deep, small bulbs 5–8 cm (2–3 in.) deep. Water well during growth, then allow to dry after flowering.

Three common Alberta species are the pink *A. cernuum* or nodding onion; *A. schoenoprasum sibiricum,* chives; and *A. textile,* white prairie onion. These can be seen on sunny hillsides, indicating the whole family's preference for sunny, well-drained locations. The leaves arise at ground level and are grassy or strap shaped, releasing an onion odour when crushed. The flowers are in loose, semi-cylindrical or ball-shaped clusters and range in colour from white, pale pink, rose and red to mauve, violet, blue, and yellow. Some are fragrant; all are long-lasting as cut flowers and work well in dried flower arrangements. If left to form seed, some alliums make elegant everlasting decorations. Alliums range from dainty plants suitable for rock gardens to veritable giants.

For alpine beds or rock gardens, try *A. karataviense,* 23 cm (9 in.), with white-shaded lilac pink flowers and large bluish leaves; *A. narcissiflorum,* 30 cm (12 in.), with white or pink flowers; and *A. cyaneum,* a tiny blue plant. Alliums for naturalizing or grouping in front of borders, all about 30 cm (12 in.), are the blue *A. caeruluem,* yellow *A. flavum* and *A. moly* 'Luteum', and the rose pink *A. ostrowskianum.* Recommended large alliums are *A. aflatunense,* which is 60–90 cm (24–36 in.) with round purple flower heads; *A. sphaerocephalum,* 60 cm (24 in.), with red purple, drumstick-shaped flower heads; *A. tuberosum,* or garlic chives, 45 cm (18 in.), with white lace caps; and *A. christophii,* the star of Persia, 60 cm (24 in.), with silvery purple flowers.

A. giganteum, 120 cm (48 in.), has enormous spherical heads of rosy purple. In the Calgary area this big allium is not reliable as the bulbs are large and need ideal conditions to prepare themselves for the next year's bloom. Freshly planted bulbs will almost always bloom the next spring, but after that may only send up green leaves with no flowers. Heavy feeding, plenty of sun, and well-drained soil may help in keeping this giant performing; if not, try the similar but smaller *A.*

aflatunense (75 cm/30 in.) or its cultivar 'Purple Sensation', as it not only survives the winter after blooming but increases as well.

Fritillaries *(Fritillaria meleagris)* 30–45 cm (12–18 in.). Checkered lilies are unusual flowers with wiry stems and sparse, grasslike leaves. They are best planted in generous groups. The large nodding flowers, which appear in mid-May, are mottled with purple burgundy on a pale creamy background. Some forms are a pale yellowish white. Fritillaries are long-lived once the bulbs are established and prefer a semi-shaded woodland setting. *F. michailowskyi* is a small rock garden species that does well in dry, well-drained areas, blooming in early May with purple flowers tipped with yellow. *F. pudica* is a small yellow-flowered species native to southern Alberta that is also suited to rock gardens. The Siberian fritillary *(F. pallidiflora)* produces yellow flowers on 60-cm (24-in.) stems in early spring. Not only is it hardy, it soon multiplies.

Chionodoxa are dainty but hardy little bulbs for the rock garden. MAUREEN IRETON

Hardy little Siberian squills bloom very early in April and rapidly form large colonies. JUDITH DOYLE

Earliest to bloom of the ornamental alliums is the decorative 'Purple Sensation'. KEN GIRARD

BLOOMCHART FOR HERBACEOUS PERENNIALS

NAME		BLOOMTIME						COLOURS						
BOTANICAL	COMMON	APR	MAY	JUN	JUL	AUG	SEP	WHI	PNK	RED	PUR	BLU	YEL	ORG
Crocus hybrids	Crocus	xxxx	x					x			x	x	x	
Hepatica spp.	Liverwort	xxx	xxx					x	x		x	x		
Puschkinia libanotica	Striped squill	xxx	xxx					x						
Scilla sibirica	Siberian squill	xxx	xxx					x				x		
Papaver nudicaule	Iceland poppy	xx	xxxx	xxxx	xxxx	xxxx		x					x	x
Viola tricolor	Johnny jump-up	xx	xxxx	xxxx	xxx			x			x	x	x	
Pulsatilla vulgaris	Windflower	xx	xxxx	xx				x	x	x	x	x		
Tulipa kaufmanniana	Waterlily tulip	xx	xx					x	x				x	x
Galanthus nivalis	Snowdrop	xx	xx					x						
Arabis spp.	Rock cress	x	xxxx	xx				x	x					
Tulipa praestans	Fusilier tulip	x	xxx							x				
Aubrieta deltoidea	Purple rock cress		xxxx	xxxx	x				x		x	x		
Geum triflorum	Three-flowered avens		xxxx	xxxx				x						
Bergenia spp.	Rockfoil		xxxx	xx				x	x		x			
Tulipa spp.	Species tulip		xxxx	xx				x		x			x	x
Primula denticulata	Drumstick primrose		xxxx	xx				x	x	x	x			
Narcissus (varieties)	Daffodil		xxxx	x				x					x	x
Draba spp.	Draba		xxxx					x					x	
Tulipa fosteriana	Foster tulip		xxxx					x	x	x			x	x
Vinca minor	Periwinkle		xxx	xxx				x				x		
Veronica pectinata	Speedwell		xxx	xx								x		
Pulmonaria spp.	Lungwort		xxx	xx				x	x			x		
Euphorbia spp.	Spurge		xxx	xx									x	
Narcissus (small types)	Dwarf daffodil		xxx	x				x					x	
Iris pumila	Dwarf iris		xxx	x				x	x	x	x	x	x	
Dicentra eximia	Dwarf bleeding heart		xx	xxxx	xxxx			x	x					
Nepeta mussinii	Catmint		xx	xxxx	xx			x				x		
Dicentra spectabilis	Bleeding heart		xx	xxxx	x			x	x					
Doronicum caucasicum	Leopard's bane		xx	xxxx	x								x	
Viola rugulosa	Wood violet		xx	xxxx				x						
Phlox subulata	Moss phlox		xx	xxxx				x	x	x	x			
Geum x *borisii*	Avens		xx	xxxx										x
Convallaria majalis	Lily-of-the-valley		xx	xxxx				x						
Trollius spp.	Globeflower		xx	xxxx									x	x
Primula auricula	Primrose		xx	xxx				x	x	x	x		x	
Muscari spp.	Grape hyacinth		xx	xx				x				x		
Tulipa (darwin types)	Darwin tulip		xx	xx				x	x	x	x		x	x
Clematis alpina, macropetala	Clematis		xx	xx				x	x		x	x		
Anemone sylvestris	Snowdrop anemone		xx	xx				x						
Caltha palustris	Marsh marigold		xx	xx									x	
Primula acaulis	Primrose		xx	xx				x	x	x	x	x	x	
Armeria spp.	Thrift		x	xxxx	xxxx	xxxx		x	x					
Myosotis spp.	Forget-me-not		x	xxxx	x				x			x		
Primula veris	Cowslip		x	xxxx									x	x
Androsace sarmentosa	Rock jasmine		x	xxx					x					
Fritillaria meleagris	Fritillary		x	xx				x			x			
Ranunculus acris	Buttercup			xxxx	xxx								x	
Alchemilla mollis	Lady's mantle			xxxx	x								x	
Saxifraga x *arendsii*	Rockfoil			xxxx				x	x	x				

| NAME | | BLOOMTIME | | | | | | COLOURS | | | | | | |
BOTANICAL	COMMON	APR	MAY	JUN	JUL	AUG	SEP	WHI	PNK	RED	PUR	BLU	YEL	ORG
Ajuga spp.	Bugleweed			XXXX					X			X		
Verbascum phoeniceum	Mullein			XXXX				X	X		X			
Paeonia tenuifolia	Fern-leaf peony			XXX						X				
Iris x *germanica*	Intermediate			XXX				X	X		X	X	X	
Meconopsis cambrica	Welsh poppy			XXX	XXXX	XXXX	XX						X	
Heuchera sanguinea	Coral bells			XXX	XXXX	XXXX		X	X	X				
Thymus serpyllum	Thyme			XXX	XXXX			X	X	X	X			
Gypsophila repens	Baby's breath			XXX	XXXX			X	X					
Allium schoenoprasum	Chives			XXX	XXX						X			
Saponaria ocymoides	Soapwort			XXX	XXX				X					
Achillea tomentosa	Woolly yarrow			XXX	XXX								X	
Symphytum spp.	Comfrey			XXX	XXX			X				X		
Geranium spp.	Cranesbill			XXX	XXX			X	X		X	X		
Centaurea montana	Cornflower			XXX	XXX			X				X		
Hesperis matronalis	Sweet rocket			XXX	XXX				X					
Chrysanthemum coccineum	Pyrethrum			XXX	XXX				X					
Polygonum bistorta 'Superbum'	Fleeceflower			XXX	XX				X					
Antennaria spp.	Pussytoes			XXX	XX			X	X					
Dianthus gratianopolitanus	Cheddar pink			XXX	X				X					
Iris x *germanica*	Tall iris			XXX	X			X	X	X	X	X	X	
Dictamnus albus	Dittany			XXX	X			X	X		X			
Silene hookeri	Campion			XXX	X				X					
Hemerocallis flava	Daylily			XXX	X								X	
Aster alpinus	Alpine aster			XXX	X							X		
Papaver orientale	Oriental poppy			XXX	X			X	X	X				X
Allium aflatunense	Ornamental onion			XXX							X			
Primula cortusoides	Fairy primrose			XXX					X					
Sisyrinchium montanum	Blue-eyed grass			XX								X		
Campanula cochlearifolia	Fairy bells			XX	XXXX	XXXX	XXXX	X				X		
Polemonium spp.	Jacob's ladder			XX	XXXX	XXXX	X	X				X		
Silene maritima	Sea campion			XX	XXXX	XXXX		X						
Rosa 'Therese Bugnet'	Rose			XX	XXXX	XX			X					
Thalictrum aquilegifolium	Meadow rue			XX	XXXX	X		X	X		X		X	
Aquilegia hybrids	Columbine			XX	XXXX	X		X	X	X	X	X	X	
Leontopodium alpinum	Edelweiss			XX	XXXX	X		X						
Primula vialii	Orchid primrose			XX	XXXX						X	X		
Lonicera x *brownii*	Dropmore scarlet honeysuckle			XX	XXXX						X			
Sedum aizoon	Stonecrop			XX	XXXX								X	
Cerastium tomentosum	Snow-in-summer			XX	XXXX			X						
Monarda didyma	Bee balm			XX	XXXX			X	X	X	X			
Allium ostrowskianum	Ornamental onion			XX	XXXX				X	X				
Galium odoratum	Sweet woodruff			XX	XXXX			X						
Dianthus deltoides	Maiden pink			XX	XXXX			X	X	X	X			
Chrysanthemum leucanthemum	Ox-eye daisy			XX	XXXX			X						
Lychnis viscaria	Catchfly			XX	XXX			X	X	X	X			
Veronica teucrium	Hungarian speedwell			XX	XXX							X		
Paeonia lactiflora hybrids	Peony			XX	XXX			X	X	X				
Penstemon barbatus	Beardtongue			XX	XXX				X	X				

BOTANICAL	COMMON	APR	MAY	JUN	JUL	AUG	SEP	WHI	PNK	RED	PUR	BLU	YEL	ORG
Dianthus barbatus	Sweet William			xx	xxx			x	x	x				
Delphinium elatum	Delphinium			xx	xx			x	x		x	x		
Campanula medium	Canterbury bells			xx	xx			x	x		x	x		
Saxifraga hostii	Rockfoil			xx	xx			x						
Primula sieboldii	Japanese star primrose			xx	x			x	x		x			
Catananche caerula	Cupid's dart			x	xxxx	xxxx	xxxx	x				x		
Salvia x superba	Sage			x	xxxx	xxxx	xx				x	x		
Campanula persicifolia	Peach-leaved bellflower			x	xxxx	xxxx	xx	x				x		
Potentilla fruticosa hybrids	Shrubby cinquefoil			x	xxxx	xxxx		x		x			x	
Lychnis chalcedonica	Maltese cross			x	xxxx	xxxx		x		x				
Gaillardia aristata	Blanket flower			x	xxxx	xxxx				x			x	
Centaurea dealbata	Cornflower			x	xxxx	xxx			x					
Iris hybrids	Tall border iris			x	xx			x	x	x	x	x	x	x
Achillea spp.	Sweet yarrow				xxxx	xxxx	xxxx	x	x	x			x	
Campanula carpatica	Carpathian bellflower				xxxx	xxxx	xx	x				x		
Lysimachia spp. (low)	Creeping Jenny				xxxx	xxxx	x						x	
Linum perenne	Flax				xxxx	xxxx						x		
Achillea ptarmica	Sneezewort				xxxx	xxxx		x						
Linum flavum	Yellow flax				xxxx	xxxx							x	
Digitalis grandiflora	Foxglove				xxxx	xxxx							x	
Erigeron hybrids	Fleabane				xxxx	xxx			x		x			
Veronica incana	Woolly speedwell				xxxx	xxx			x			x		
Valeriana officinalis	Garden heliotrope				xxxx	xx		x	x					
Thalictrum dipterocarpum	Yunnan meadow rue				xxxx	xx		x			x			
Malva moschata	Mallow				xxxx	xx		x	x					
Delphinium hybrids	Delphinium				xxxx	x		x	x		x	x		
Campanula glomerata	Clustered bellflower				xxxx	x		x			x			
Clematis integrifolia	Clematis				xxxx	x					x	x		
Lilium hybrids (Asiatic)	Asiatic lily				xxxx	x		x	x	x			x	x
Sedum spp. (low-growing)	Stonecrop				xxxx			x	x	x			x	
Thermopsis caroliniana	Carolina lupin				xxxx								x	
Allium moly	Yellow lily leek				xxxx								x	
Aruncus spp.	Goatsbeard				xxx			x						
Iris sibirica	Siberian iris				xx			x	x	x	x	x	x	
Lychnis coronaria	Rose campion				xxx	xxxx	xxxx	x	x					
Chrysanthemum x Superbum	Shasta daisy				xxx	xxxx	xx	x						
Verbascum nigrum	Mullein				xxx	xxxx	x						x	
Monarda fistulosa	Horsemint				xxx	xxxx					x			
Heliopsis scabra	Perennial zinnia				xx	xxxx	xxxx						x	
Anthemis tinctoria	Golden Marguerite				xx	xxxx	xxxx						x	
Coreopsis verticillata	Thread-leaved coreopsis				xx	xxxx	xxxx			x			x	
Eryngium planum	Sea holly				xx	xxxx	xxxx					x		
Clematis hybrids	Large-flowered clematis				xx	xxxx	xxxx	x	x	x	x	x		
Sidalcea malviflora	Prairie mallow				xx	xxxx	xx	x	x					
Solidago hybrids	Goldenrod				xx	xxxx	xx						x	

NAME		BLOOMTIME						COLOURS						
BOTANICAL	COMMON	APR	MAY	JUN	JUL	AUG	SEP	WHI	PNK	RED	PUR	BLU	YEL	ORG
Scabiosa caucasica	Pincushion flower				XX	XXXX	XX	X			X	X		
Phlox paniculata	Phlox				XX	XXXX	X	X	X	X	X			
Ligularia spp.	Golden groundsel				XX	XXXX							X	
Aconitum spp.	Monkshood				XX	XXXX		X			X	X	X	
Veronica spp. (tall)	Speedwell				XX	XXXX		X	X			X		
Filipendula rubra	Meadowsweet				XX	XXXX			X					
Echinops ritro	Globe thistle				X	XXXX	XXXX					X		
Centaurea macrocephala	Golden knapweed				X	XXXX	XX						X	
Echinacea purpurea	Purple coneflower					XXXX	XXXX	X	X		X			
Rudbeckia laciniata	Golden glow					XXXX	XXXX						X	
Rudbeckia fulgida	Coneflower					XXXX	XXXX						X	
Aster spp. (tall)	Aster					XXXX	XXX	X	X		X	X		
Thalictrum delavayi	Hewlitt's double meadow rue					XXXX	XX				X			
Physostegia virginiana	Obedient plant					XXXX	XX	X	X					
Gypsophila paniculata	Baby's breath					XXXX		X	X					
Liatris spp.	Gayfeather					XXX	XX	X	X		X			
Sedum spectabile	Stonecrop					X	XXX	X						
Tanecetum spp.	Tansy						XXXX						X	
Chrysanthemum rubellum	Chrysanthemum						XXXX	X						
Helenium hybrids	Helenium						XXXX			X			X	X

❧ In the "colours" portion of the chart, white includes green/white, and purple includes mauve and violet.

❧ Each "x" refers to the week in which the plant shows significant blooming in a typical Calgary year.

❧ The data used to develop this chart were collected over eight years.

SEVEN

Infinite Variety:
Annuals and Tender Bulbs

Annuals sprout in spring and flower during the summer to produce seed for the next generation. They come in every imaginable colour, size, and shape, making it a simple task to translate a gardener's whims into reality—the perfect plant can be found for every corner of the garden. Even the most ardent of perennial aficionados plant lavish pots of annuals to ensure brilliant, continuous colour from early summer until the first frost and beyond, or to bridge the gaps in perennial bloom succession.

Once seeds have been sown or seedlings transplanted, annuals require only regular watering, fertilizing, and removal of spent blossoms (deadheading) to do what they are supposed to do—provide us with endless pleasure. Deadheading prevents seed from forming and so prolongs the period of blossom production. Many plants that are not truly annuals are treated as such in Calgary. Some, such as geraniums and tender herbs, are perennial in warmer climates. Others are tender bulbous-rooted plants, such as dahlias and gladioli, that must be taken indoors if they are to survive the long, cold winter. It is easy to mistake annuals that self-sow seed (for germination the following year) for perennials. To encourage repeat performances of your favourites, leave the spent blossoms in late summer to allow seed formation. Finally, remember that annuals die at the end of their one and only growing season so there is no need to arrange for winter protection.

Annuals can fill flower beds and borders to overflowing; cascade from window boxes and hanging baskets; hide the dying foliage of spring-flowering bulbs; cover the ground between small, newly purchased shrubs until they grow into their allotted spaces; or surreptitiously creep their way into the cracks and crannies of a stone wall or a brick pathway. If experimentation and change please you, there is always next year to try something entirely different. Familiar annuals are appearing in new guises as hybridizers have fun creating new colours, sizes, and shapes. One catalogue offers forty-four varieties of marigolds alone, ranging in height from 15 to 90 cm (6–36 in.), with 2.5-cm (1-in.) single to 15-cm (6-in.) double blooms, in numerous shades of yellow and orange, even white.

Hybridizing not only provides a greater range of colour and size, but also increases disease and frost resistance. The All America Selections is a nonprofit organization with professional plant judges across North America who help identify outstanding developments in annuals. The Calgary Zoo is a display garden for the All America Selections, so drop by each year to see new varieties being demonstrated. With the variety of cultivars available, it is almost impossible to remember which impatiens you grew or liked elsewhere last year. Jot down pertinent information as the season progresses, such as size, colour, and desirable characteristics. Be aware that the weather can have a strong effect on success, and don't judge a particular plant without taking that season's growing conditions into consideration. Also be aware of the microclimates in your own garden. A plant that is only marginally successful in one area might do better out of the wind, in a spot where the soil warms up sooner, where water doesn't puddle after a rain, or even where you will remember to water it!

Annuals are classified as hardy, half-hardy, or tender. These terms define the range of temperatures required for seeds to germinate and sprout, and the ability of seedlings to withstand frost. Hardy annuals are the most cold tolerant, with young seedlings able to withstand the effects of a light frost. You can seed many of these outdoors several weeks before the last spring frost, or well after the first fall frost for germination the following spring. Half-hardy annuals tolerate periods of cold but not frost. These seeds should be started indoors or planted outdoors after the last spring frost. Tender annuals require warm soil for germination and a long, warm summer to produce lavish flowers. With our short growing season, it is best to purchase tender annuals as bedding plants, or grow them from seed indoors, to ensure their success. For more information on starting annuals from seed, refer to the chart at the end of this chapter; techniques for transplanting, hardening-off, watering, fertilizing, and maintaining plants are described in chapter nine.

GUIDE TO ICONS

Tender
T

Hardy
H

Half hardy
HH

Full sun
○

Part shade
◉

Shade
●

Cut flower
✄

Dried flower
🌿

Fragrant
❀

Poisonous
✖

Annuals to Choose From

African Daisy *(Dimorphotheca sinuata)* 30 cm (12 in.). Also known as Cape marigold, this plant grows cheerful, up-facing, daisylike flowers in white, yellow, or orange, with dark centres. The blossoms open each morning and close each evening. The bushy light green foliage has slightly hairy, silvery undersides. They prefer well-drained soil and are excellent for dry areas. Although they are drought resistant, they prefer cool temperatures. African daisies look fabulous when planted in broad sweeps as a groundcover or massed in beds. T ○ 🌿

Ageratum *(Ageratum houstonianum)* 25–30 cm (10–12 in.). Also known as floss flower, ageratum grows dense mounds of oval, roundly toothed leaves, crowned with fuzzy blue, pink, or white compact, clustered flowers. It prefers a rich, well-watered soil and is a long-lived bloomer, providing colour from early summer to autumn. Ageratum look particularly lovely massed in beds or edging borders and walks. T ○ ◉

Baby Blue Eyes *(Nemophila menziesii)* 23 cm (9 in.). This is a dwarf, trailing plant with pale green, hairy, fernlike foliage. The bright blue, white, or purple cup-shaped flowers have white centres and bloom early in the season. Baby blue eyes are cool-weather lovers and require sharply drained soil and moderate watering. They are excellent for rock gardens, containers, edging shaded borders, or naturalized as a groundcover. HH ○ ●

Baby's Breath *(Gypsophila elegans)* 60 cm (24 in.). This upright annual consists of a multitude of miniature, dainty white or pink flowers on slender stems that create a frothy appearance above lance-shaped leaves. It thrives in well-drained, alkaline soil but blooms are short-lived so succession sowing is recommended for a continuous supply. Baby's breath makes a perfect companion to showier plants in a border and is a natural for the rock garden or cascading over the side of a wall. H ○ ❧ ⚘

Bachelor's Button *(Centaurea cyanus)* 40–90 cm (16–36 in.). This popular annual forms a bushy plant with greyish, lance-shaped leaves, covered with small, round, ruffled blue, white, or pink flowers in single and double forms. It is extremely adaptable, doing well in poor, sandy, or average soils. A sun-loving plant, it prefers cooler weather but is heat and drought tolerant. It is a favourite for providing early blossoms in the mixed border. H ○ ❧ ⚘

Balsam *(Impatiens balsamina)* 40–90 cm (16–36 in.). Balsam is an old-fashioned plant with double roselike flowers that either hug tall leafy stalks or grow out near the leaf tips. Blossoms come in white; shades of red, pink, orange, and lavender; and bicolour. This plant does best in fertile, sandy soil rich in organic matter. It is equally attractive in beds, borders, and containers. T ○ ●

Begonia *(Begonia semperflorens)* 15–20 cm (6–8 in.). Also known as wax or fibrous-rooted begonias, these popular annuals have green, bronze, mahogany, or variegated leaves. They sport clusters of white, pink, or red flowers, in either single or double form, that bloom from late spring to frost. Compact little plants, they do well in light to medium shade, and prefer rich, well-drained soil. An excellent plant to use as edging for walkways, in shaded borders, or in containers. HH ●

Browallia *(Browallia speciosa major)* 20–30 cm (8–12 in.). Also known as amethyst flower, this plant has star-shaped flowers in shades of blue, lavender, and white that cover mounds of bright green, delicate, roundish leaves. Blue-flowering types often have a contrasting white throat or eye. They bloom from late spring through summer. Plant in evenly moist soil in partial shade. Browallia is very attractive in containers and hanging baskets. T ●

Butterfly Flower *(Schizanthus pinnatus)* 30–60 cm (12–24 in.). The gold-veined, orchidlike blooms of the butterfly flower (also called poor man's orchid) come in a range of colours that includes white, yellow, orange, pink, and purple. The dainty, fernlike foliage is often dwarfed by the showy flowers. The blossoms are short-lived so succession planting is recommended. Butterfly flowers prefer cool weather, moist soil high in organic matter, and filtered shade. They make exquisite container plantings and cut flowers. HH ○ ● ❧

Calendula *(Calendula officinalis)* 25–60 cm (10–24 in.). One of the easiest annuals to grow, these sunny plants are also called pot marigolds. They have a bushy, upright habit; light green, hairy, brittle foliage; and a profusion of single or double daisylike blooms that range in colour from white and cream through yellow, orange, and apricot. The long narrow leaves are slightly sticky to the touch. These plants prefer cool weather and average, well-drained soil. Under the right conditions, the edible blossoms are relatively long-lasting and give warm colour from spring through summer. H ○ 🌱

The cheerful, upturned faces of *Viola* 'Chantreyland' add sparkle to the flower border. JUDITH DOYLE

Large-flowered tuberous begonias brighten shaded garden areas; frost-tender tubers are stored indoors over winter. KEN GIRARD

California Poppy *(Eschscholzia californica)* 30 cm (12 in.). Vivid orange, yellow, scarlet, crimson, salmon, rose, or white saucer-shaped flowers grace vase-shaped mounds of dainty, finely dissected leaves of bluish green. Blooms appear from late spring to fall. The California poppy does well in sandy, alkaline soil with excellent drainage, and should not be fertilized or overwatered. It enjoys full sun but tolerates light shade (flowers close if it is too shady). Particularly attractive in wild or naturalized gardens, it also may be used in borders and containers. H ○ ●

Candytuft *(Iberis umbellata)* 40 cm (16 in.). Flat clusters of fragrant flowers in white, pink, red, purple, or lavender bloom from spring to mid-summer and perch on bushy mounds of narrow, dark green, lance-shaped leaves. These plants tolerate heat when well watered; plant them in moist, well-drained soil. Use candytuft as edging, border plants, and in rock gardens. H ○

China Aster *(Callistephus chinensis)* 15–45 cm (6–18 in.). A member of the daisy family, China asters are branching, erect plants with hairy stems covered with dark green leaves that are serrated or deeply lobed. The double flowers come in many forms: daisy, chrysanthemum, and pincushion are a few examples. Their colours include white, red, pink, blue, or purple, often with yellow centres. Plant China asters in neutral to slightly alkaline, sandy, moist soil. They are excellent for cutting, blooming from mid-July to frost. T ○ 🌱 🐛

China Pink *(Dianthus chinensis)* 10–20 cm (4–8 in.). Fragrant, carnationlike flowers in shades of red, pink, mauve, and white, often marbled or spotted with contrasting colour, are supported on slender grey stems; the grasslike grey blue leaves form compact clumps. China pinks bloom from June to fall and appreciate alkaline, well-drained soil. They look wonderful in borders, rock gardens, containers, or as edging. They are called "pinks" because the flowers look as if they have been trimmed with pinking shears. HH ○ ●

Clarkia *(Clarkia unguiculata)* 22–30 cm (9–12 in.). Also known as Rocky

Mountain garland flower, these plants grow small double flowers on straight, wiry, reddish stems with oval, lance-shaped leaves. The single or double flowers come in white, lavender, red, salmon, and purple; they bloom from July through September. Clarkia are best directly seeded into light, sandy, well-drained soil, as they do not transplant well. Planted in full sun or light shade, they grow best in areas where the nights are cool. This plant was named after Captain William Clark of the Lewis and Clark Expedition. T ○ ◉ ✿

Cockscomb Celosia *(Celosia cristata)* 15–90 cm (6–36 in.). The velvety, crested flowers of this plant resemble the comb of a rooster. They come in white, yellow, orange, red, or pink and bloom all summer. The long, narrow, lance-shaped leaves are often bronze or edged in red. Celosia are sun- and

Annual candytuft has intriguing flowers of layered petals. CALGARY HORTICULTURAL SOCIETY

heat-loving plants that prefer moist, rich soil but tolerate average soil. They may respond to cold temperatures and root disturbance by not blooming. Celosia make attractive specimen plants, but also serve well as edging or in containers. T ○ ◉ ✿ ✿

Coleus *(Coleus blumei)* 30–60 cm (12–24 in.). This is one of the few colourful annuals that grows well in the shade, with brilliant, textured foliage in patterns of red, yellow, purple, bronze, and green. The inconspicuous blue flowers are best removed as they spoil the shape of the plant and detract from its magnificent foliage. Useful for borders or baskets, they do best in moist, well-drained, rich soil and cool, filtered shade. The leaves fade in full sun. T ◉ ●

Richly coloured coleus hybrids revel in moist, shady soil. RUTH STAAL

Cosmos *(Cosmos bipinnatus)* 45–60 cm (18–36 in.). This attractive but sprawling plant grows finely divided, feathery foliage and large, single, daisylike flowers in white, pink, and red with yellow centres. It blooms from early summer to early fall and does best in dry, infertile soil with sharp drainage. It also benefits from staking. Avoid overwatering, overfertilizing, and exposure to the wind. Cosmos are best grown at the back of borders where adjacent plants can lend physical support. HH ○ ◉ ✿

Cup Flower *(Nierembergia hippomanica violacea)* 15–30 cm (6–12 in.). These neat, spreading mounds are covered with fine, needlelike leaves and masses of cuplike, bell-shaped flowers in blue or violet, accented with yellow throats. The blossoms last for summer's duration. Plants grow best in cool climates in average soil; if the summer is hot, provide shade and water well. Nierembergia are particularly attractive as edging and in containers and hanging baskets. T ○

Dusty Miller *(Centaurea cineraria)* 15–20 cm (6–8 in.). The white lacy foliage of this annual is covered with dense, woolly hairs. It is happiest grown in full sun in relatively dry soil. Pinch back growing tips to encourage bushiness. Dusty miller, which is actually a tender shrub, makes a good transition between bright-coloured plants of different types in a mixed border and also looks handsome as edging at the front of the border. HH ○

Evening (Night) Scented Stock *(Matthiola longipetala)* 30 cm (12 in.). The small purplish flowers of this plant cluster along flower spikes amid rough grey green foliage. Inconspicuous during the day, at night they open and release an incredible fragrance. They bloom from spring into early summer and prefer a well-drained soil high in organic matter and cool, moist weather. Plant them in containers near seating areas or along walkways to get maximum enjoyment from the fragrance. H ○ ✿ ❀

Four O'clock *(Mirabilis jalapa)* 90 cm (36 in.). The red, yellow, or white trumpet-shaped flowers are often multicoloured on the same plant. They open in mid-afternoon to bloom all night and emit an enticing fragrance. The dark green leaves are borne on erect, well-branched stems. They bloom from summer to fall, in any well-drained soil, and tolerate humidity, drought, and heat. Plant four o'clocks in masses around the patio or under windows; alternatively, use them as a low hedge or foundation planting. All parts of the plant are poisonous. HH ○ ❀ ✖

Fried Egg Plant *(Limnanthes douglasii)* 10–30 cm (4–12 in.). The small daisy-like flowers with yellow petals have white tips, hence the resemblance to a fried egg. The handsome compound leaves consist of leaflets arranged feather fashion on both sides of a central rib. The plant branches from the base and flowers profusely in early summer. Fried egg plant, or meadowfoam as it is sometimes called, is actually a marsh flower and should be planted in very damp soil. It is worth including in a bog garden or on the perimeter of a water feature. H ○ ❀

Fuchsia *(Fuchsia x hybrida)* 30–60 cm (12–24 in.). The exotic-looking flowers of this plant come in many colours and bicolour combinations; single or double form; small or large size. The plant itself is available in both trailing and upright forms. Fuchsias bloom throughout the summer when supplied with good

Calgary's number of frost-free days is certainly unpredictable, but usually our summer, when annuals provide so much colour, is far too short. We would all like to prolong the season—here are some annuals that are tolerant of a little frost, so add colour to our fall gardens.

- Ageratum *(Ageratum houstonianum)*
- Bachelor's button *(Centaurea cyanus)*
- Dusty miller *(Centaurea cineraria)*
- Godetia *(Clarkia amoena)*
- Lobelia *(Lobelia erinus)*
- Pansy *(Viola* x *wittrockiana)*
- Petunia *(Petunia* hybrids)
- Ornamental kale or cabbage *(Brassica oleracea)*
- Snapdragon *(Antirrhinum majus)*
- Sweet alyssum *(Lobularia maritima)*

drainage, plenty of water, and good soil. It is best to buy bedding plants as seeding is difficult; they are also easy to propagate from cuttings. For those of you willing to make the effort, try lifting them from the garden in the fall with a good rootball and store them in a cool place for the winter, keeping the soil relatively dry. Then repot them in the spring for another season of outdoor enjoyment. Fuchsias are excellent for hanging baskets, window boxes, and other containers. T ◉ ●

Geraniums *(Pelargonium* x *hortorum)* 30–60 cm (12–24 in.). Geraniums are one of the most commonly planted flowers in Calgary. While not true annuals, most are purchased each year for a dependable display of colour. Geraniums like at least half a day of sun and good drainage. They are beautiful in borders and containers, displaying clusters of flowers in white, pink, rose, red, and salmon, often with a dark band on their lobed leaves.

There are also ivy (or wax) geraniums *(P. peltatum),* which are trailing plants covered by succulent glossy green leaves with pointed lobes. The rounded clusters of single or double flowers come in pink, white, rose, red, and lavender, and are usually displayed in hanging baskets. Martha Washington geraniums *(P. domesticum)* are erect and spreading with leaves that have crinkled margins and unequal, sharp teeth. Flowers occur in large clusters, in white and many different shades of pink, red, lavender, and purple, often with dark blotches and markings. Some have smaller leaves and a myriad of tiny flowers—these are wonderful in hanging baskets. Less common are the scented-leaf geraniums, with leaves that emit an identifiable fragrance when rubbed, such as rose, mint, apple, or lemon. The flowers are attractive but smaller than those of other geraniums. These geraniums are often grown by a patio where their perfume is enjoyed when the foliage is brushed; the leaves can be used for sachets.

Geraniums can be brought inside for the winter, but it isn't easy to keep them attractive year after year. Putting them in a bright, sunny window will keep them actively growing, but because our winter days are very short, the plants don't get as many hours of sunlight as they need and become leggy from lack of light. Twelve to fourteen hours a day under fluorescent lights, a few centimetres (an inch or so) above the plants, would be ideal. You could also try keeping them cold (just above freezing, not just a cool basement), dry, and dormant for the winter months. This works well if there is a cold place to store them: a garage heated to just above freezing, or the house wall of an attached but unheated garage can be used, or possibly the crawl space of a split-level house. If the plants remain dormant until the days become longer and are then brought gradually into the warmth and light (about mid-March), they will resume growth and can be grown on or used for cuttings.

Cuttings of geraniums can be taken before the first frost, grown in the sunniest window possible, and pinched back often enough to keep them bushy. Cut a healthy end off the plant just below the third or fourth leaf. After the cut surface dries, dip the cut end into a rooting hormone and then insert it into damp vermiculite. Cuttings will root easily, if kept just slightly damp, in about four to six weeks, and can then be planted in small containers, or several to a larger, shallow one. By spring, they will be ready for planting outdoors. HH ◯

Globe Amaranth *(Gomphrena globosa)* 15–75 cm (6–30 in.). Small, dense, cloverlike flowers in white, pink, orange, or purple are borne on long-stocked stems. The plants themselves are erect and well branched, sporting medium-green oblong leaves. They flower profusely from summer to autumn. Globe amaranths grow in light, sandy, well-drained soil; they tolerate extreme heat, humidity, and drought. They make wonderful dried flowers and the more compact varieties make attractive edging for relatively maintenance-free beds. T ◯ ⚬

Godetia *(Clarkia amoena)* 40 cm (16 in.). Formerly considered a distinct genus, godetia is now recognized as a hybrid belonging to the genus *Clarkia*. The

Godetia has flowers of shimmering satin. MAUREEN IRETON

shimmering petals on the cuplike flowers inspired its common name of satin flower. In cool, sunny conditions, these beautiful blooms provide dazzling carpets of white, pink, salmon, or lilac. Seed them directly into light, well-drained, sandy soil and they will grow quickly and bloom continuously until frost as long

as neither the temperature nor the humidity gets too high. This versatile plant is a must for beds, mixed borders, containers, and rock gardens. H ○ ◉ ✤

Heliotrope *(Heliotropium arborescens)* 45–75 cm (18–30 in.). This old-fashioned favourite is highly valued for its vanilla fragrance. The British often refer to it as the cherry pie plant, likening its fragrance to the smell of a cherry pie fresh from the oven. The round clusters of dark violet, white, or blue flowers contrast

The delicate blooms of impatiens light up shady corners. RUTH STAAL

beautifully with the rough-textured, deeply veined, lance-shaped leaves. If you remove the side branches as the plant grows, the size of the flower cluster increases. For a different effect, pinch back the plants to encourage bushiness and more numerous, smaller flower clusters. Plant in rich, fertile soil with good

drainage and don't overwater; the fragrance intensifies when grown in slightly dry soil. For maximum enjoyment, locate heliotrope in beds, borders, or containers close to seating areas and walkways. T ○ ✤ ✺

Impatiens *(Impatiens wallerana)* 20–25 cm (8–10 in.). Impatiens, or busy Lizzy, forms spreading mounds of glossy dark green or bronze foliage, crowned with many single white, pink, salmon, or red flowers. Double-blossomed varieties are becoming more readily available, as

Elegant lavatera is easily grown from seed. MAUREEN IRETON

are bicoloured ones. Planted in well-drained, sandy soil high in organic matter, impatiens provides dazzling summer-to-autumn bloom under trees, in shady beds, and in containers. T ◉ ●

Kenilworth Ivy *(Cymbalaria muralis)* 10 cm (4 in.). This dainty creeper with lobed leaves has tiny mauve, yellow-throated flowers that look like wee orchids. It is used as edging, in containers, or as a groundcover. It does well in shade with moist, alkaline soil. It self-seeds and can spread quickly. T ◉ ●

Lavatera *(Lavatera trimestris)* 75 cm (30 in.). The beautiful, large hibiscuslike white or pink flowers grow on bushy plants with dark green, maple leaf-shaped foliage and hairy stems. This rapid grower does best when seeded directly into well-drained garden soil of average fertility. In relatively cool temperatures, it provides continuous colour from July to frost. Try planting lavatera, or mallow, at the back of mixed borders, as a low hedge, or clustered to give the effect of a flowering shrub. H ○ ❀

Livingstone Daisy/Iceplant *(Mesembryanthemum)* 15 cm (6 in.). This low-growing, sprawling plant is usually covered with daisylike flowers in white, yellow, orange, pink, or purple that close at night and on cloudy days. The leaves are fleshy and covered with tiny crystals that glisten in the sun, resembling ice. Drought tolerant, it is best suited to dry soils, arid climates, and cool temperatures. Livingstone daisies are attractive as a groundcover or in the front of borders as edging. T ○

Lobelia *(Lobelia erinus)* 10–15 cm (4–6 in.). This ever-popular, reliable annual forms compact or trailing plants with dainty white, light to dark blue, or reddish purple flowers. The small rounded leaves are green or bronze in colour. Lobelia prefers fertile, sandy soil and cool nights. It usually stops blooming in the heat, recovering when it cools down again. This plant is poisonous. Lobelia looks wonderful in containers or hanging baskets, in rock gardens, as edging for beds and borders, or tumbling over a low wall to give the impression of cascading water. HH ○ ◉

Love-in-a-mist *(Nigella damascena)* 60 cm (24 in.). The cornflowerlike blossoms in shades of blue, pink, and white are surrounded by a cloud of dainty, ferny leaves that evoke an impression of mist, hence the name. This plant blooms profusely in early summer but is not long-lived, burning up in late summer heat. The blossoms are followed by pale green, puffed-up seed capsules that

---

CUT FLOWERS

If space permits, a garden with flowers in rows, to permit easy access and not spoil a display garden, is a real luxury for those who enjoy bouquets in the house. Cut flowers can, of course, be worked into any border or flower garden. Try:

- Baby's breath *(Gypsophila elegans)*
- Bachelor's button *(Centaurea cyanus)*
- China aster *(Callistephus chinensis)*
- Clarkia *(Clarkia unguiculata)*
- Godetia *(Clarkia amoena)*
- Marigold *(Tagetes* spp.)
- Nicotiana *(Nicotiana alata)*
- Salpiglossis *(Salpiglossis sinuata)*
- Snapdragon *(Antirrhinum majus)*
- Swan River daisy *(Brachycome iberidifolia)*
- Sweet peas *(Lathyrus odoratus)*
- Zinnia *(Zinnia elegans)*

are excellent for drying. Nigella is happy in average soil, but does not transplant well—it should be sown directly into the ground. It shows to advantage in mixed borders and is also lovely naturalized in a meadow setting. H ○ ◉ ✿ ✿

Marigold *(Tagetes spp.)* 20–60 cm (8–24 in.). Flowers come in a variety of shapes, from single to fully double, and in a range of colours, including yellow, orange, bronze, and white. The plants, which are well branched, are covered with attractive, finely cut foliage. Marigolds are extremely easy to grow: they are heat and drought tolerant, do well in poor or sandy soil, transplant easily, are quick to bloom, and stay in bloom until frost. Use these ever-popular and reliable annuals massed in beds, in mixed borders, or in containers. HH ○ ✿

Nasturtium *(Tropaeolum majus)* 30 cm (12 in.) The flat, round leaves of the nasturtium and its trumpet-shaped flowers of white, yellow, orange, red, or pink make a colourful addition to the garden. Both the leaves and blossoms of this cool-weather plant are edible and are often used to add an exotic touch to salads. They are drought tolerant, thrive in poor but well-drained soil, and must not be fertilized as fertilizer promotes growth of foliage at the expense of flowers. Dwarf varieties are a favourite for rock gardens, containers, and hanging baskets; trailing varieties provide visual impact when trained up a trellis as a living screen. HH ○ ◉

Nemesia *(Nemesia strumosa)* 30–45 cm (12–18 in.). The cheerful multi-coloured flowers have a large lower lip and resemble snapdragons, to which they are related; the leaves are lance shaped and serrated. Nemesia is a cool-weather plant and will not tolerate excessive heat or humidity. When planted in fertile, moist, well-drained soil, it provides vivid colour from spring until frost. HH ○ ◉

Nicotiana *(Nicotiana alata)* up to 90 cm (36 in.). These upright plants with broad, light green leaves are covered by masses of fragrant, tubular, star-shaped flowers. They come in white, green yellow, pink, red, and purple. The old-fashioned varieties bloom in the evening and are the most fragrant, especially the white ones; daytime bloomers are less fragrant. Nicotiana likes fertile, well-drained, moist soil with high organic content. Also known as flowering tobacco, it adds colour to massed flower beds, mixed borders, and containers all summer long. T ◉ ✿ ❀

Ornamental Kale *(Brassica oleracea)* 40 cm (16 in.). This member of the cabbage family grows a profusion of erect, round leaves that may be finely cut or curled, in dramatic shades of white, pink, or purple. Though edible, most are used strictly for their ornamental value. They tolerate light frost and last through September, sometimes fading during mid-summer heat but reviving when the cool weather returns. H ○

Pansy *(Viola x wittrockiana)* 15 cm (6 in.). Pansies are a gardener's delight in spring when their cheerful, fragrant upturned blossoms and heart-shaped foliage make a welcome early appearance. Although pansies are mostly spring-blooming annuals, newer varieties provide bloom well into the summer, until the heat becomes intolerable for them. They come in all colours, bicolour combinations, and with blotched or whiskered markings that give them a saucy facial expression. Mid-summer, trim plants to remove faded flowers and seed pods to ensure renewed bloom and a more compact form as they tend to legginess if left to themselves. Pansies are happy in any good garden soil but appreciate the addition of organic matter. They are pleasing as edging, and in beds, borders, rock gardens, and containers. H ◯ ◉ ᎒

Petunia *(Petunia* x *hybrida)* 30–40 cm (12–15 in.). This old-fashioned, popular addition to the flower bed is likely the most common annual grown here. Look for both upright and cascading varieties. Its fragrant, funnel-shaped flowers come in a wide range of colours, in both single and double forms. Pinch back young plants to encourage bushy growth and deadhead regularly to promote

Dwarf double marigolds are easy and reliable, with nonstop bloom all summer. CALGARY HORTICULTURAL SOCIETY

continuous flowering for a magnificent show of colour all summer long. Petunias are happy in well-drained, sandy soil. They are also drought resistant, but require regular watering during dry spells. Trailing varieties do best in containers and hanging baskets; up-right ones are perfect for massing in beds or edging borders. T ◯ ◉

Phlox *(Phlox drummondii)* 15–50 cm (6–20 in.). The medium green, smooth leaves of this plant form a compact mound that is covered with clusters of single blooms. The name *phlox* originates from a Greek word meaning "flame," which appropriately describes its brilliant colours of white, pink, red, purple, and mauve. They must have well-drained soil, preferably moist, sandy, and high in organic content. Although the plants are heat tolerant, the

A tapestry bedding of lobelia, feverfew, verbena, and viola. MAUREEN IRETON

flowers are not, so they will falter during the warmest part of the summer, reviving again when the temperatures turn cooler. Phlox is a natural for the mixed border. T ◯ ⚘

Poppy *(Papaver* spp.) 60–90 cm (24–36 in.). Two varieties of annual poppy do well in this area—*P. rhoeas,* also variously known as corn or field poppy, and *P. somniferum,* the opium poppy. *P. rhoeas* displays large, single, scarlet flowers; *P. rhoeas* 'Shirley' has semi-double, or double cup-shaped flowers in white, pink, purple, red, or salmon. They grow on wiry, hairy stems above deeply cut green foliage. The flowers of *P. somniferum* are often double and fringed in shades of pink, purple, and white. Its incised leaves are a smooth greyish green. Poppies do not transplant well, so it is wise to seed them directly into the garden in the spring, or take advantage of their ability to self-sow. They are short-lived, blooming only two to three weeks before dying to the ground; for this reason it is best to include them in a mixed border where other plants will fill in after they have disappeared. Plant them in sharply drained, fertile, sandy soil amended with organic matter. H ◯ ⚘

Tall opium ("carnation") poppies add zest to summer gardens. ROSALIE COOKSLEY

Snapdragons provide colour and height to annual borders. MAUREEN IRETON

Portulaca *(Portulaca grandiflora)* 15 cm (6 in.). These dwarf plants add an exotic element to the garden with their shimmering, succulent leaves on brittle reddish stems, and masses of white, yellow, orange, or red roselike flowers that close in the late afternoon and on cloudy days. They spread quickly when planted in hot, dry, perfectly drained, sandy soil, and withstand heat and drought. They make an excellent groundcover for sunny, dry locations and areas of poor soil where few other plants will grow. Portulaca, appropriately called rose moss by some, gives a reliable show of brilliance throughout the summer until frost. T ◯

Salpiglossis *(Salpiglossis sinuata)* 30–90 cm (12–36 in.). The common names painted tongue and velvet flower aptly describe this unusual annual. Its trumpet-shaped flowers have a velvety texture; come in a variety of rich colours including white, yellow, red, pink, purple, and brown; are profusely and richly veined; and bloom throughout the summer months. They are supported by slender, wiry stems on upright, bushy plants with toothed, oblong leaves. For best results, plant these cool-temperature annuals in rich, moist, alkaline, very well-drained soil. Salpiglossis is perfect toward the back of mixed borders. HH ○ ◉ ✤

Salvia *(Salvia splendens)* 15–90 cm (6–36 in.). Otherwise known as scarlet sage, salvias have spikes of bright red, long, tubular flowers, surrounded by equally colourful calyxes that attract hummingbirds. Shades of salmon, lilac, purple, and white are also available. Preferring full sun, they bloom from spring to frost. Plant in well-drained, moist, rich soil; keep well watered; and protect from the sun when the temperatures climb. Salvias add splashes of colour to mixed annual beds or perennial borders. T ○ ✄

Snapdragon *(Antirrhinum majus)* 15–75 cm (6–30 in.). Snapdragons offer large spire-shaped heads of colourful flowers resembling butterflies, on dwarf, medium, or tall stems. They come in many colours and bloom heavily in early summer. If you cut off the faded spikes, they will continue to bloom all summer on smaller flower stalks. The flowers begin to open from the bottom of the stem upward, so snapdragons remain attractive even after the lower blooms have faded. Older varieties have closed, hinged blossoms resembling a dragon's jaw that children like to squeeze and snap open, hence the name snapdragon; some newer varieties have open or double blooms. This cool-weather annual prefers light, moderately rich soil. Avoid overwatering, which can induce soft, weak growth. The varied size and shapes of snapdragons make them very versatile in mixed borders. HH ○ ◉ ✤

Statice *(Limonium sinuatum)* 30–90 cm (12–36 in.). A popular everlasting biennial grown as an annual, statice comprises flat-topped clusters of small, papery flowers on many-branched, winged stems. At the base of the plant, the deeply lobed, lance-shaped leaves form a rosette. The flowers, which bloom in the summer, come in a wide range of vivid colours, including yellow, blue, red, pink, bronze, orange, and white; they are usually available in mixed colours. Statice is happiest in well-drained, light, sandy soil that is low in fertility. It toler-

---

SHADE-TOLERANT ANNUALS

Most of us have some shade in our gardens, and there are not very many annuals that do well there. These will be happy:

✤ Begonia *(Begonia semperflorens)*
✤ Browallia *(Browallia speciosa major)*
✤ Coleus *(Coleus blumei)*
✤ Fuchsia *(Fuchsia x hybrida)*
✤ Impatiens *(Impatiens wallerana)*
✤ Lobelia *(Lobelia erinus)*
✤ Nemesia *(Nemesia strumosa)*
✤ Nicotiana *(Nicotiana alata)*
✤ Pansy *(Viola x wittrockiana)*
✤ Salpiglossis *(Salpiglossis sinuata)*

ates heat, drought, and salt sea spray admirably well (should you ever wish to move to the coast). Its biennial nature gives statice a slightly irregular blooming habit. It is, therefore, best suited for scattering in a mixed border, where its temporary absence will go unnoticed. HH ○ ✿

Strawflower *(Helichrysum bracteatum)* 20–90 cm (8–36 in.). The colourful papery "petals" of this favourite everlasting are actually bracts that gradually unfurl from a tight ball to expose the contrasting florets inside. They are available in a wide assortment of bold and unusual colours, including white, yellow, pink, red, gold, bronze, and purple. As the taller varieties grow leggy very readily, staking is important. They do best in full sun, in light, well-drained, alkaline soil, and thrive in long, hot summers. Strawflowers are a welcome addition to the mixed border. HH ○ ✿

Sunflower *(Helianthus annuus)* 3 m (10 ft). Sunflowers are vigorous, erect, fast-growing plants that bloom throughout the summer. Their giant golden flower heads appeal to gardeners for their sheer size and to birds for their excellent supply of nutritious seeds. The plants themselves are somewhat coarse, with oval, serrated leaves and rough, hairy stems. Plant sunflowers in light, dry, well-drained soil and water only during prolonged dry spells. They make a stunning background to mixed borders. HH ○ ●

Swan River Daisy *(Brachycome iberidifolia)* 25–40 cm (10–16 in.). A favourite among annuals, these bushy, mounded plants are typically smothered with delicately fragrant, daisylike flowers in shades of blue, pink, or white with a dark eye at the centre. The foliage is delicate and lacy. They do well in ordinary garden soil and prefer cool growing conditions, declining and thinning as the temperatures rise. As blooms are relatively short-lived, successive plantings ensure a continuous supply of colour. Try these beauties in containers, massed in beds, as edging, or in a mixed border where neighbouring plants will hide fading blooms and foliage. HH ○ ✸

Sweet Alyssum *(Lobularia maritima)* 15 cm (6 in.). Dainty, hauntingly fragrant, four-petaled flowers in purple, pink, or white virtually conceal the mounded, small green leaves beneath. Planted close together, they create a mass of colour from spring to hard frost. They are perfect for edging beds and rock gardens. As their blooms start to fade, cut them back to encourage continued blossom production. Well-drained soil of average fertility is fine, but alyssum also tolerates poor soil. H ○ ● ✸

Verbena *(Verbena hortensis)* 15–30 cm (6–12 in.). This is an old-fashioned favourite with a stunning display of colour, even in hot, dry weather. The low, upright, or trailing plants are covered in compact, flat clusters of fragrant flowers that come in white, pink, red, blue, and purple. The aromatic foliage is a deep or greyish green. Verbena tolerates poor, sandy soil, drought, and heat, but may stop bloom production during intense summer heat. Otherwise, with regular deadheading, verbena will bloom from summer to fall. A very versatile plant, verbena is equally at home in hanging baskets, containers, rock gardens, or at the front of mixed borders. HH ○ ✸

Viola *(Viola cornuta)* 15 cm (6 in.). Violas resemble pansies, but have smaller

Zinnias are best in mass plantings. MAUREEN IRETON

flowers and are generally longer-lived and more vigorous. They come in all colours, with some sporting black markings that give them their impish facial expressions. Flowers appear over several weeks during the spring. Violas prefer loose, fertile soil and bloom best during cool weather, fading in mid-summer heat. If the tops are sheared at this time, a second blooming usually occurs when the cool weather returns in the fall. Violas are effective as edging or massed in containers. H ○ ●

Zinnia *(Zinnia elegans)* 15–90 cm (6–36 in.). Zinnias are one of the most versatile annuals to be grown—they come in a wide array of sizes, a myriad of colours, and a variety of bloom shapes, including single, quilled, and ruffled. Moreover, they are quick to grow, prolific bloomers, and withstand dry, hot weather, providing continuous colour in late summer when many other annuals have already faded. Zinnias prefer fertile, well-drained soil with added organic matter. They do best in hot, dry climates with long summers and need good air circulation. Plant zinnias in mixed borders where their range of size and shape makes them very versatile. HH ○ ✿

Annual Vines

Annual vines, placed with care and adequately supported, can create a magnificent vertical display of colour as a backdrop for smaller flowers and shrubs in the perennial border. They can camouflage an unattractive wall or fence, cover an arbour, or grow in containers to provide interest on a deck or patio. For maximum impact, they must be grown in rich, well-drained, moist soil under their own preferred growing conditions. Regular fertilizing over the growing season encourages healthy growth, but most often temperature (of the soil and the air) and the amount of sun are what will ensure success. Remember, vines don't have to climb. They can also ramble over the ground to create an easy-care ground-cover, ideal for new gardeners who have spaces to fill until perennials or shrubs mature. Vines can also creep down a slope, dangle over a wall, or cascade beautifully from a container or hanging basket. Experiment with different vines. The advantage of annuals is that if you don't like one, you can always try a different one next year!

Black-eyed Susan *(Thunbergia alata)* 3 m (10 ft). This cool-weather twining vine produces trumpet-shaped flowers in hues of yellow, orange, or white, all with a purple throat. The leaves are ivy shaped. It prefers well-drained, rich, moist soil, high in organic matter. HH ◯ ●

Canarybird Vine *(Tropaeolum peregrinum)* 3 m (10 ft). A member of the nasturtium family, this elegant vine has five-lobed leaves and yellow flowers fringed with a green curved spur. It flowers best in poor, moist soil and should not be fertilized. T ●

Cup-and-saucer Vine *(Cobaea scandens)* 6 m (20 ft). The pendulous, bell-shaped blue flowers of the cup-and-saucer vine are produced from mid-summer through fall and sit on 30-cm-long (12-in.-long) stalks. Tenacious tendrils enable it to climb rough surfaces without support. T ◯

Morning Glory *(Ipomoea tricolor)* 3 m (10 ft). The heart-shaped leaves, vining tendrils, and funnel-shaped flowers in hues of blue, pink, lavender, or white provide a beautiful backdrop for a perennial border. The blossoms open in the morning to reveal their glory and then fold shut again in the afternoon, hence the name. Morning glories need a warm, sunny location and do not tolerate transplanting well, so start in peat pots and plant outside when there is no danger of frost. They require sharply drained soil and plenty of moisture during the

Morning glory, an annual vine, covers fences or trellises with handsome leaves and flowers. MAUREEN IRETON

growing season, producing the best blossoms in the cool, fresh weather of late summer and early autumn. HH ○

Potato Vine *(Solanum jasminoides)* 6 m (20 ft). This is a shrubby, climbing plant with purplish green leaves and white star-shaped flowers that are sometimes tinged with blue. The flowers are borne in large trusses in late summer through fall. This vine is not easily available commercially, but is passed on from gardener to gardener. It is easy to start from a cutting and grows very quickly. T ○

Scarlet Runner Beans *(Phaseolus coccineus)* 3 m (10 ft). This pole bean is widely grown for its clusters of showy, brilliant red flowers and large dark green leaves. As a bonus, the flowers attract hummingbirds and the pods provide good quality beans if picked when young and tender. Sow seeds where they are to grow, in warm soil. T ○

Sweet Peas *(Lathyrus odoratus)* 2.5 m (8 ft). The most popular and beloved of annual vines comes in a wide variety of wonderful colours to mix and match, and with a fragrance that pervades a room with a single bouquet (older varieties are more fragrant). The dainty flowers are held in clusters on long stems that are excellent for cutting. Sweet peas like a well-drained, neutral to slightly alkaline, rich soil and bloom from summer well into fall. They require support and mulch to keep the roots cool and extend the season of bloom. H ○ 🐛 ✺

Tender Bulbs, Tubers, and Corms

Unlike hardy spring- and early summer-flowering bulbs, such as tulips and daffodils, which are planted in the fall and remain in the garden more or less permanently, most summer-flowering bulbs, tubers (short, thick underground stems from which plants grow), and corms (thickened underground stems capable of producing roots, leaves, and flowers during the growing season) are not hardy in the Calgary area. They are often started indoors in pots in the spring to get a head start on flowering and planted outside when there is no danger of frost. As a general rule, plant a bulb at a depth of three times its height and a tuber so that the stem buds are near the surface. Some bulbs, tubers, and corms, such as tuberous begonias, dahlias, and gladiolus, can be dug up and stored indoors over the winter in a cool place. Inexpensive, smaller ones such as *Acidanthera, Anemone,* and *Ranunculus* may also be lifted and stored, but are often difficult to find in the fall and are most often purchased each spring.

To store tender bulbs, corms, or tubers over the winter, dig them in the early fall before they can freeze and allow them to dry in a well-ventilated area. Remove leaves, brush off dirt, dust with bulb dust, and store in a paper bag or cardboard box (not plastic) in vermiculite, peat moss, or sawdust. It is not always easy to find a place with the ideal storage temperature—most basements are too warm. A garage heated to just above freezing is ideal, but an unheated one gets too cold. One prize-winning dahlia grower from Calgary has successfully wintered tuberous roots outside, buried in containers very deep in the ground where they are kept cool and dormant. Some of the most popular plants in the Chinook area grow from tender bulbs, tubers, and corms.

Tuberous Begonias *(Begonia* hybrids). Single or double, large or small, plain or ruffled flowers in white, yellow, pink, salmon, orange, and red add colour to shade gardens. There are also pendula varieties to use in hanging baskets. Tubers may be planted indoors in mid-March, hollow side up, in a mixture containing at least one-third peat moss. Barely cover the tuber with soil. Outside, begonias need moist soil and grow best in shade or early morning sun only, with shelter from the wind.

Callas *(Zantedeschia)* 60 cm (24 in.). Long, lance-shaped leaves and colourful bracts in white, pink, or yellow surround a central spike. Callas need full sun and heavy watering. Plant the rhizomes about 5 cm (2 in.) deep. If they are started indoors at the end of April, or outdoors protected from frost until early June, they should bloom by late July. They make attractive container plants.

Cannas *(Canna)* 90–180 cm (36–72 in.). Tall and dramatic, cannas are ideal for the back of a sunny flower bed. The flowers, which resemble lilies, can be white, red, pink, or yellow. For bloom by late July, plant tubers 12 cm (5 in.) deep in pots indoors in late April or outdoors in an area protected from frost.

Dahlias *(Dahlia)* 30–120 cm (12–48 in.). There are numerous colours and varieties, among them bicoloured, single, pompon, cactus, and peony. Flowers vary with plant size from tiny pompons to huge "dinner plate" blooms. Dahlias like a sunny, sheltered area with good drainage and will bloom from late July to mid-August if started indoors. In February, dahlia tubers can be divided and started in a greenhouse. One root with one eye is necessary for each plant, and a small root will produce just as good a plant as a large one. Place tubers in moist peat for seven to ten days, then transfer them to containers, with holes for drainage, filled with a mixture of one-third each moist peat moss, sand, and loam. Once potted, the tuber should be kept in a well-lit location at a temperature of about 16° C (60° F). Remove all sprouts except one and water when nec-

---

ANNUALS FOR DRIED FLOWERS

For bouquets and arrangements, grow your own! It's much less expensive than buying them, and you can grow the ones you know you will use.

- African daisy *(Dimorphotheca sinuata)*
- Baby's breath *(Gypsophila elegans)*
- Bachelor's button *(Centaurea cyanus)*
- China aster *(Callistephus chinensis)*
- Cockscomb celosia *(Celosia cristata)*
- Globe amaranth *(Gomphrena globosa)*
- Love-in-a-mist *(Nigella damascena)*
- Poppy, Shirley or corn *(Papaver rhoeas)*
- Salvia *(Salvia splendens)*
- Statice *(Limonium sinuatum)*
- Strawflower *(Helichrysum bracteatum)*

essary. Harden-off and plant out when all danger of frost has passed. Dahlias should be planted in holes 12–15 cm (5–6 in.) deep with manure or compost mixed with a little sand in the bottom of the hole. Before covering up the tubers, place a stake behind them, or a marker next to the plant to indicate where the stake should go later so that the tuber is not damaged.

Gladiolus *(Gladiolus)* up to 180 cm (72 in.). Gladiolus have long strap-shaped leaves and florets arranged vertically on thick stems, all facing the same way. They have been widely hybridized, particularly the familiar garden gladiolus *(G. hortulanus)*. They are excellent cut flowers and come in many colours. They prefer a sunny, well-drained area and are particularly appropriate planted with irises as they usually bloom in August after the irises are finished, but the leaves are similar, making a continuous backdrop of foliage in a flower bed. Gladiolus require regular watering and usually need to be staked. Corms may be planted in a 30-cm (12-in.) deep trench and covered with soil to a depth of three to four times the corm height; the trench can then be backfilled as the stems grow.

Many smaller summer-flowering bulbs or tubers are also available. The following are only a few of the many colourful and exotic-looking flowers that grow from tender bulbs, corms, and tubers. If they are treated as annuals, exciting new varieties may be tried every year.

Acidanthera *(Gladiolus callianthus)* 60 cm (24 in.). The fragrant, star-shaped flowers are creamy white with chocolate or purple blotches on lower segments. Plant in a sunny location.

Anemones *(Anemone)*. The daisy-shaped flowers, single or double, in shades of white, lavender, blue, pink, or red, grow from tubers, which should be soaked overnight before they are planted in sun or light shade. The best-known variety is *A. coronaria,* 15–45 cm (6–18 in.) tall; others are the windflowers *A. blanda* and *A. nemorosa,* growing 5–20 cm (2–8 in.) high.

Harlequin Flower *(Sparaxis tricolor)* 30 cm (12 in.). Small funnel-shaped flowers grow in clusters, usually yellow, pink, purple, red, or white, and are splashed with contrasting colours. Plant in full sun.

Oxalis *(Oxalis)* 10–15 cm (4–6 in.) This low-growing bushy plant has clover-type leaves. The most common variety, *O. adenophylla,* has lilac pink flowers and is ideal for sunny rock gardens, pots, or hanging baskets.

Ranunculus *(Ranunculus asiaticus)* 45 cm (18 in.). Ranunculus is a member of the buttercup family. The flowers, in shades of rose, yellow, orange, and white, resemble begonias. Ranunculus likes a sunny location and the tubers should be soaked overnight before planting.

Tiger Flower *(Tigridia pavonia)* to 60 cm (24 in.). The large, showy flowers come in orange, pink, yellow, or white with spotted centres. Plant in sun or partial shade.

NAME, COMMON	NAME, BOTANIC	START DATE	GERMINATION	DIFFICULTY	PLANT OUT DATE	COMMENTS
African daisy	Dimorphotheca sinuata	Mar 15	3–4 wks	easy	Jun 1	
Ageratum	Ageratum houstonianum	Feb 15–30	1–2 wks	easy	Jun 1	Do not cover
Baby blue eyes	Nemophila menziesii	May 1	1–2 wks	easy	May 15	Can be sown outside in May
Baby's breath	Gypsophila elegans	May 1	1–2 wks	easy	May 15	Can be sown outside in May
Bachelor's button	Centaurea cyanus	May 1	1–2 wks	easy	May 15	Needs darkness; can be sown outside in May
Balsam	Impatiens balsamina	Apr 1–15	1–2 wks	moderate	Jun 15	
Begonia	Begonia semperflorens	Jan 15	2–6 wks	difficult	Jun 15	
Browallia	Browallia speciosa	Apr 1–15	2–3 wks	moderate	Jun 1	Do not cover seeds
Butterfly flower	Schizanthus pinnatus	Mar 1	2–3 wks	moderate	Jun 1	Cover flat
Calendula	Calendula officinalis	Mar 15–30	1–2 wks	easy	May 15	Cover flats; may be sown outside in May
California poppy	Eschscholzia californica	sow outside	1–3 wks	easy		Sow outside early in May
Candytuft	Iberis umbellata	Apr 1–15	1–2 wks	moderate	May 15	Can be sown outside in May
China aster	Callistephus chinensis	Apr 1–15	1–2 wks	moderate	Jun 1	
China pink	Dianthus chinensis	Apr 1–15	1–2 wks	easy	Jun 1	
Clarkia	Clarkia unguiculata	sow outside	1–2 wks	easy		Sow outside early in May
Cockscomb	Celosia cristata	Apr 1	1–2 wks	easy	Jun 1	Use peat pots
Coleus	Coleus blumei	Mar 15	1–2 wks	moderate	Jun 1	Do not cover seeds
Cosmos	Cosmos bipinnatus	Apr 7–21	1–2 wks	easy	Jun 1	Can be sown outside in May
Cup flower	Nierembergia hippomanica	Mar 1	2–3 wks	easy	Jun 1	
Dusty miller	Centaurea cineraria	Mar 15–30	1–2 wks	easy	Jun 1	Do not cover seeds
Evening scented stock	Matthiola longipetala	Apr 1 - 15	1 - 2 wks	moderate	Jun 1	Do not cover seeds
Four O'clock	Mirabilis jalapa	Apr 1–15	1–2 wks	easy	Jun 1	Can be sown outside in May
Fried egg plant	Limnanthes douglasii	May 1	1–2 wks	easy	Jun 1	
Fuchsia	Fuchsia x hybrida	Feb 1	2–3 wks	moderate	Jun 15	Tender perennial
Geranium	Pelargonium x hortorum	Feb 1	2–3 wks	moderate	Jun 1	Tender perennial
Globe amaranth	Gomphrena globosa	Apr 1–15	2–3 wks	easy	Jun 1	
Godetia	Clarkia amoena	Apr 1–15	1–2 wks	easy	May 15	Do not cover seeds
Heliotrope	Heliotropium arborescens	Feb 1–15	1–2 wks	easy	Jun 15	
Impatiens	Impatiens wallerana	Mar 1–15	2–3 wks	moderate	Jun 1	Do not cover seeds
Kenilworth ivy	Cymbalaria muralis	Apr 1–15	1–2 wks	easy	Jun 1	Self-seeds; can be invasive
Lavatera	Lavatera trimestris	Apr 1–15	2–3 wks	moderate	May 15	Sow outside in May or use peat pots
Livingstone daisy	Mesembryanthemum	Mar 15	2–3 wks	moderate	Jun 1	Cover flat
Lobelia	Lobelia erinus	Feb 15	2–3 wks	moderate	Jun 1	Do not cover
Love-in-a-mist	Nigella damascena	Apr 1–15	2–3 wks	moderate	May 15	Can be sown outside in May
Marigolds	Tagetes spp.	Apr 1–15	1 wk	easy	May 15	
Nasturtium	Tropaeolum majus	Apr 15	1–2 wks	easy	May 15	Can be sown outside in May
Nemesia	Nemesia strumosa	Mar 15	1–2 wks	moderate	Jun 15	
Nicotiana	Nicotiana alata	Mar 15 - Apr 1	2–3 wks	easy	Jun 1	Do not cover seeds
Ornamental kale	Brassica oleracea acephala	Jan 15– Mar 15	1–2 wks	easy	May 15	
Pansy	Viola x wittrockiana	Mar 1–15	2–3 wks	easy	May 15	Cover flat; refrigerate 4–5 days
Petunia	Petunia x hybrida	Mar 15	1–2 wks	easy	Jun 1	Do not cover seeds
Phlox	Phlox drummondii	Apr 15–30	1–2 wks	easy	Jun 1	Cover flats; can be sown outside in May
Poppy, opium	Papaver somniferum	Mar 15 – Apr 1	1 wk	easy	Jun 1	

NAME, COMMON	NAME, BOTANIC	START DATE	GERMINATION	DIFFICULTY	PLANT OUT DATE	COMMENTS
Poppy, Shirley	*Papaver rhoeas*	Apr 15–30	1–2 wks	moderate	May 15	Use peat pots
Portulaca	*Portulaca grandiflora*	Mar 15	1–2 wks	easy	Jun 1	Use peat pots; can be sown outside in May
Salpiglossis	*Salpiglossis sinuata*	Mar 15	2–3 wks	moderate	Jun 15	Cover flat
Salvia	*Salvia splendens*	Mar 1	1–2 wks	moderate	Jun 1	Do not cover seeds for 48 hrs
Snapdragon	*Antirrhinum majus*	Feb 15–Mar 1	1–2 wks	easy	May 15	
Statice	*Limonium sinuatum*	Mar 15–30	2–3 wks	moderate	Jun 1	
Strawflower	*Helichrysum bracteatum*	Mar 1–15	1–2 wks	easy	Jun 1	Do not cover seeds
Sunflower	*Helianthus annuus*	Apr 15–30	1–2 wks	easy	Jun 1	Usually sown outside in May
Swan River daisy	*Brachycome iberidifolia*	Apr 15–30	2–3 wks	easy	Jun 1	
Sweet alyssum	*Lobularia maritima*	Apr 15	1–2 wks	easy	May 15	Do not cover; can be sown outside in May
Verbena	*Verbena hortensis*	Feb 15–30	2–3 wks	difficult	Jun 1	Cover flat
Viola	*Viola cornuta*	Mar 15–30	1–2 wks	easy	May 15	Cover flat; refrigerate 4–5 days
Zinnia	*Zinnia elegans*	May 1	1–2 wks	easy	May 15	Sow outside in May or use peat pots
Black-eyed Susan vine	*Thunbergia alata*	Apr 1–15	4 wks	moderate	Jun 1	Do not cover
Canarybird vine	*Tropaeolum peregrinum*	May 1	1–2 wks	easy	Jun 1	
Cup-and-saucer vine	*Cobaea scandens*	Feb 1–15	2–3 wks	moderate	Jun 15	
Morning glory	*Ipomoea tricolor*	Apr 15–30	1–2 wks	moderate	Jun 1	Soak or scarify; use peat pots
Potato vine	*Solanum jasminoides*	May 1	1 wk	easy	Jun 1	Worth trying to obtain seeds
Scarlet runner bean	*Phaseolus coccineus*	sow outside	1–2 wks	easy	May 1–15	Edible beans
Sweet pea	*Lathyrus odoratus*	Apr 15–30	2–3 wks	easy	May 15	Scarify; use peat pots; start outside late Apr

EIGHT

Kitchen Gardens:
The Edible Landscape

Planning the Vegetable Garden

Growing vegetables should be fun, so give some thought to the kind of vegetable garden you want to grow—you can plant a large garden plot, grow a mini-garden in pots or planters, or incorporate vegetables into flower beds or borders. As an oversized garden soon becomes overgrown and overrun with weeds, think carefully about the area you can manage. Then, if you are a first-time gardener, cut that by at least one-half. Choose a site that receives at least eight, and preferably ten, hours of sunlight daily. Plenty of sunshine is critical for healthy, tasty vegetables. As winds can desiccate tender seedlings and dry out the soil, look for places sheltered by fences, hedges, trees, or buildings. Vegetables require well-drained soil, so avoid places where water collects, such as at the bottom of a slope. For individual crops, take advantage of microclimates within the plot. Lettuce and spinach like cool growing conditions and need some shade; tomatoes and peppers need all the sun and heat they can get; plant tall vegetables on the north side so they don't shade sun-loving shorter crops.

There are a number of ways you can keep the garden area that is planted to vegetables to a minimum and still get the maximum return on your gardening efforts. In a standard vegetable garden, crops are planted in rows. These are easy to plan and to plant; however, paths between rows take up space so there is less yield per unit area, and water landing on paths is wasted. Consider several small gardens in sunny pockets along the fence, house, or garage instead.

Intensive gardening has been popularized as "square-foot" gardening, where vegetables are grown in raised beds much closer together than is usually recommended. Interplanting is when two or more different vegetables are planted at the same time, in the same area, taking advantage of different growth habits, rooting depths, and nutrient and light requirements. Good combinations are beets, lettuce, onions, and radish planted amongst almost any larger, upright plants; carrots with onions; or pole beans with climbing corn. A continuous harvest is possible with successive plantings of the same vegetable every two weeks, or by planting—on one day—several cultivars of the same vegetable with different maturity dates. These two methods allow more than one crop to be harvested from the same area in one season.

Many space-demanding crops can be grown vertically. The benefits are higher yields from the same garden space, more efficient use of the sun, easier picking, and cleaner produce because there is no splatter from rain or watering. Clingers and climbers include pole or runner beans, tomatoes, snow peas, cucumbers, and squash. Supports can be made from upright poles with a crossboard on top, fences, or an A-frame made from 2 x 2s. Trellis or netting can be used for peas. Tomatoes do not normally climb, but can be staked or caged. Some newly introduced cultivars of tomato, cucumber, pepper, and squash are ideal for growing in containers, which allow gardening on balconies, decks, and patios. Unlike conventional gardens, containers can be moved to shelter whenever weather conditions threaten vulnerable plants.

When you have decided on the position of the garden plot and how much space you need, using graph paper and a convenient scale, mark north and draw in the beds and rows to map out the location of the vegetables you wish to grow. Each will present a different set of considerations. For example, if you vacation in July, avoid crops that mature then. The space requirements for each variety determine how many to plant. Place the sun-lovers so they are not shaded by tall vegetables. Jot down the dates each crop will be sown or transplanted, and when it will mature. During the season, keep a diary of your successes and those things you would do differently next year. You will also find it helpful to record weather data and production levels.

Planting the Vegetable Garden

To produce an edible crop in a relatively short period of time, vegetables require a steady supply of nutrients. Although they can grow in almost any soil, the ideal is deep, well drained, friable (crumbly), and fertile. It should provide structural support for the plants and at the same time be loose enough to allow water and air to penetrate. (See chapter nine for more on soil.) When the soil is ready to be worked, remove weeds and grass roots by spading or rototilling, and rake to smooth the area. Then dig in 8–15 cm (3–6 in.) of compost. If you use a rototiller, till 20–25 cm (8–10 in.) deep and not too finely.

COLD-SEASON AND WARM-SEASON CROPS

Most root and many of the leafy vegetables, peas, and broad beans are native to northern temperate regions. These cold-season crops thrive in our climate and are frost tolerant. They are seeded out as soon as the soil can be worked or are transplanted in May before the last frost date. Warm-season vegetables, such as corn, tomatoes, and peppers, are warm temperate or equatorial in origin and need longer, hotter growing seasons. They must be grown from transplants. (For more information on transplants, see chapter nine.)

The length of the growing season is determined by the number of frost-free days and the heat unit accumulation during those days. In Calgary, the growing season is from about June 1 to September 1. To be on the safe side, crops seeded directly into the garden should have a growing season of 80 days or less. Even though the number of frost-free days is on average 112, the heat unit accumulation in May and September is low, decreasing the effective length of the growing season. Plant growth aids, such as mulches, plastic tunnels, and other devices that modify the environment, are effective in promoting plant maturity and yield increases.

Choose a calm, sunny day to sow seeds directly into the garden; the soil will be warm and the seeds won't blow about. Mark out the rows with string and dig furrows with the corner of a hoe. Sow seeds to a depth of two to three times the width of the seed. Cover them with fine-textured soil, firm the covering, and water lightly. A thin layer of grass clippings or compost helps retain moisture and blocks out intense sunlight. Water the garden plot lightly and frequently until the seedlings are well established.

Thin the seedlings according to the spacing recommended on the seed packets. Rather than pull them up by the roots and risk damaging nearby plants, cut them off at the base of the stem with a knife or a pair of scissors. Beets or lettuce thinnings can be used in salad.

Ideally, a garden needs 2.5 cm (1 in.) of rain or applied water weekly. Water must be available to the feeder roots and not just the top few centimetres (inch or so) of the soil. Vine crops, lettuce, peppers, sweet corn, and tomatoes normally wilt from a strong, hot sun late in the day; plants wilted in the early morning indicate a lack of moisture. Raised beds and intensive gardens will require more water than row plantings.

Keeping the Garden Plot Healthy

A clean garden and robust plants are the best ways to combat pests and disease. Because many pests overwinter in the soil and attack specific families of plants in the spring, crop rotation helps prevent the buildup of harmful organisms. If host plants are absent, the pests starve as they do not feed on plants of another family. Crop rotation also helps avoid the depletion of soil nutrients. Vegetables are grouped into three categories: heavy feeders, light feeders, and soil builders, such as nitrogen-fixing legumes (beans). Divide your plot into three or four sections and in each section group vegetables that belong to the same category. The second year, rotate the plant groupings by one plot. For example, move the heavy feeders into the plot where the light feeders were the year before, and the light feeders to where the soil builders used to be, and so on. Set aside one bed for perennials, such as asparagus and rhubarb. Keep records so you know where to sow the following year's crops.

Vegetables to Choose From

Asparagus. Asparagus is one of the earliest vegetables to appear in the spring. Perennial, it requires a well-fertilized, well-drained permanent spot that allows room for its 150-cm (60-in.) height and 120-cm (48-in.) root spread. It is hardy and easy to grow. It can be expected to stay in production for fifteen to twenty years, so the soil should be properly prepared before planting. A mature patch (at least five years old) may be harvested for as long as ten weeks, yielding 450 g (16 oz.) or more of asparagus for each 30 cm (12 in.) of row. A heavy feeder, it should be fertilized heavily in early spring, with a second lighter application after cutting has stopped. Asparagus prefers full sun but tolerates some shade.

Asparagus is best grown from two- or three-year-old transplants. When purchasing plants, be sure the roots have not dried out. Set them out in a spade-wide trench with the crowns 15 cm (6 in.) below the surface and the roots spread apart. The distance between plants (within rows) is 30–60 cm (12–24 in.). Cover the crowns with not more than 5 cm (2 in.) of soil at the start and fill the trench completely after growth is well under way.

Do not cut spears until the third year, when cutting may be done for two to four weeks depending on the vigour of the growth. In succeeding years, harvesting may continue a little longer, but no later than the middle to end of June. The best time to harvest is about one-half hour before cooking. Judge readiness by width rather than height and cut finger-thick stalks with a sharp knife just below ground level.

Rust can be avoided by planting resistant varieties. Varieties that are successful here include Mary Washington, Viking, and Franklin.

Beans. Beans are excellent crops for the amateur as they are not fussy about soil or climate. All are soil builders. Their roots produce free fertilizer for plant use via bacteria that change nitrogen from the air into nitrates. You can encourage this process by dusting damp bean seeds with legume inoculant, a dry black powder that contains the nitrogen-fixing bacteria. After beans have been rotated through the garden, the powdering can stop because the organisms remain in the soil and attach themselves to the root of any legumes planted in that location. Harvest often to increase yield; an old pod left on the vine sends a message to the plant that the season is over.

Beans are prone to rust (bean anthracnose), which is identified by rusty patches on the leaves. To prevent the fungus from spreading, pull up and destroy infected plants and do not cultivate or pick the remaining beans while the leaves are wet. To reduce the chance of rust, water early in the day so the leaves dry off before nightfall. Discourage black aphids, a problem in broad beans, by pinching back the top of the plant after the first truss of beans has set. Pinching also helps produce better pods.

There is a wide variety of bush beans on the market today, including the more common green snap bean and the yellow wax bean. Broad beans, also called fava beans, are hardy and are the earliest beans to mature. Harvest them like bush beans when immature (5–8 cm/2–3 in. long) and cook them whole, or wait until the insides turn cottony and shell them like peas. There are two types of pole beans: climbing varieties of the bush bean and the scarlet runner. Pole beans are heavy producers that are easily raised in a limited space. The scarlet runner is often planted for its beautiful clusters of red blossoms and large leaves, as well as for its edible pods. Plant around poles or canes 2.5 m (8 ft) long that are placed in the ground about 1 m (3 ft) apart, or fasten three poles together and spread the bottom out to form a tripod. Runner beans can also be grown over a fence or trellis. To help pole beans mature faster, nip off the ends when the vines have reached the top of the support.

Beets. Beets are very hardy and do well here. They are usually seeded directly outdoors. Although a single (mono) seed has been developed, the regular beet seed actually contains five or six seeds, so thinning is required. If the soil is heavy or shallow, the round cultivars do better than the long-rooted ones. Sow twice (see chart at end of this section). Because beets grow slowly, interplant with radishes to mark your rows. Beets do poorly in hot weather and dry soil. The young greens are delicious.

Broccoli, Brussels Sprouts, and Cabbage (Brassicas). In Alberta, broccoli, Brussels sprouts, and cabbage are best started indoors. Transplant seedlings when they are about 10 cm (4 in.) tall (see chart). Transplants are also available at garden centres. All the brassica family are cool-season vegetables and heavy feeders.

Harvest broccoli often, during the coolest part of the day, before the flower buds open, and the plants will yield until fall.

When Brussels sprout plants reach a height of 60 cm (24 in.), pinch the tips to ensure good sprout development and remove the lower leaves to develop sprouts. For the best flavour, harvest when sprouts are 2–4 cm (1–1.5 in.) in diameter. Sprouts mature from the bottom and should therefore be harvested from the bottom up. If sprouts are not firm, it could be a sign of too much nitrogen in the soil.

There are a number of cabbage varieties, green cabbage being the most common. Red cabbage looks like green cabbage except for its deep red colour; Savoy cabbage is green with ruffled, deeply ridged, and veined leaves; Chinese or Napa cabbage has long pearly stalks and rumpled green leaves.

After the heavy-feeding cabbage plants have been in the ground for a month, spread a palmful of blood meal around each plant. Roots are close to the surface, so be careful when cultivating. If the soil is allowed to dry out, subsequent watering may cause heads to split.

Cabbages are ready to harvest when the heads are firm. They continue to grow even after they have reached maturity; restrain their growth to avoid split heads, either by twisting the heads in a circular motion to break loose some of the roots or by using a shovel to slice down one side of the plant to break the roots.

All the cabbage family, including cauliflower and kohlrabi, have troubles in common. Cabbage loopers and worms eat the leaves; cabbage maggots eat the roots. Control loopers and worms by lightly cultivating the soil around the plant to bring them to the surface and then destroy them. Cabbage maggots can be controlled by placing a collar made of cardboard around the plant at planting time. The collar should extend into the ground 2.5 cm (1 in.) and several centimetres (an inch or two) above.

Carrots. Carrots are the most popular of the root vegetables. There are all shapes and sizes; they can be yellow, orange, red, purple, or white. The yellow and orange varieties are the sweetest and most popular. Plant them from early spring to early summer and again in the fall with radish seeds mixed in with the carrot seed. The radishes not only break the ground for the carrots, the fast-growing radish seedlings also mark the rows. Repeat sow at intervals of ten to fourteen days.

When the tops are up about 2.5 cm (1 in.), thin the carrots to approximately 2.5 cm (1 in.). Then, beginning when they reach full colour and are approximately 1 cm (.5 in.) thick, thin them when you want to eat them. Pull them when the ground is moist to avoid breaking the roots or dig them up with a garden fork. Finish harvesting before the ground freezes, or earlier if root crowns appear above the ground.

Keep the soil pulled up around the crowns of carrots to prevent greening from the sun and air. Hairy carrots are caused by too much nitrogen fertilizer or by irregular weather conditions during the formation of the root. Splitting may be caused by heavy rain just as the roots are maturing. Twisted roots indicate inadequate thinning; multiple roots, too heavy a soil or rocks.

Cauliflower. Cauliflower has much in common with cabbage but is fussier. It needs cool weather to mature and it attracts bugs. A good head is pure white and has an even depth of curd. Tie the outer leaves together over the heads as they begin to show buds to prevent them from turning green. The self-wrapping varieties also need to be tied if heat wilts the protective leaves. Purple and green-

A vegetable garden with a unique design. CALGARY HORTICULTURAL SOCIETY

headed varieties do not need to be tied. Pick the heads as soon as they are large, white, and firm. Softness of the head or flowering indicates the plant is too mature. Cauliflower suffers from the same pests as other brassicas.

Corn. The new hybrid varieties of corn are far earlier and sweeter than the traditional ones. Cobs have been improved and can be separated into three categories: standard, sugar-enhanced, and super sweet. The sugar in the standard variety is converted to starch as soon as it is picked. The sugar-enhanced and super sweet hybrids have been modified to increase sweetness and retain tenderness. To harvest, break off cobs when the silk is brown and the juice inside the kernels is milky. Pick corn just before eating to enjoy it at its most sweet and tender.

Plant corn in clumps, or at least in double rows, to ensure pollination. Adequate water is most critical when the corn is in tassel. The roots of corn are very close to the surface, so only the shallowest of cultivation should be practised. Crop rotation is important, especially if there were problems with insects or diseases the previous year. Corn rots if seeded in cool soils (below 13° C/55° F). If planting in a cool soil, use fungicide-treated seed. Using a clear polythene groundcover advances the maturity date of the corn. Try germinating in pots and planting when the soil is warm.

Cucumber. Cucumbers come in every shape imaginable: smooth, warty, crooked, or straight. They are available in either greenhouse or indoor/outdoor varieties. There are pickling and slicing varieties, and many used for both. Cucumbers are heat-loving plants that can be grown on a trellis or fence to save space. They should be grown without check from start to finish. Start plants indoors in peat pots or purchase seedlings from a garden centre. Protect the transplants after setting them out. English cucumbers need more protection than the others and are best grown in a greenhouse or a cold frame.

Cucumbers require plenty of water, especially during hot spells. To increase the yield, pick the first cucumbers when they are approximately 8 cm (3 in.) long. To avoid diseases that are harboured in the soil, avoid splashing dirt onto the leaves. Harvest regularly to keep the vines producing. Cut the cucumber from the stem, taking care not to damage the vines.

Kale. Kale is an extremely hardy, cool-season, nonheading cabbage. It is available in both plain- and curly-leaved varieties, in colours ranging from light green to blue green. Ornamental varieties can be used in flower beds. Harvest kale when the leaves are 15–20 cm (6–8 in.) long. Cut or break off the more tender leaves, as wanted, leaving the plant to continue growing. Kale has few problems, but it doesn't like heat. Growth stops when the temperature is high (27° C/80° F or higher).

Kohlrabi. Treat kohlrabi much like cabbage. You eat the large base of the stem, which looks something like a turnip that has formed on top of the ground. Plant transplants in a cool location as excessive heat makes the plants bolt (go to seed). For successive crops, sow every two weeks until four weeks before the first fall frost. Use thinnings as salad greens. Harvest the entire plant when the stem is about 5 cm (2 in.) in diameter. The best globes are tender enough to be easily pierced by a fingernail. Insect problems are similar to those of broccoli and cabbage.

Lettuce. Lettuce is the most popular of all leafy vegetables. It is easy to grow and prefers cool growing conditions, in a partly shaded spot in the garden or interplanted amongst taller vegetables. There are four main types: head, butterhead, loose leaf, and romaine. Head lettuce, sometimes called crisphead and iceberg, produces fairly solid heads similar to cabbage. Butterhead or bibb lettuce is a semi-heading variety with thick, tender leaves and a buttery flavour. Loose-leaf lettuce is the easiest to grow. It matures earlier than the other types and is tender and sweet. Cos or romaine lettuce is more heat tolerant and does well here.

For spring planting, sow indoors and transplant, or seed directly into the soil. Lettuce is well suited to containers. Plant head lettuce 25 cm (10 in.) apart; butterhead lettuce 10–12 cm (4–5 in.) apart; and romaine and loose-leaf lettuce 10–15 cm (4–6 in.) apart. Make several successive plantings of different varieties every two to three weeks in short rows and consume it at its peak. Pick the outer leaves of leaf lettuce, leaving the plant to continue growing. Slugs can be a problem.

Onions. Choose from scallions or green onions, shallots, pearl onions, yellow onions, red onions, or sweet Bermuda and Spanish onions. Onions are grown either from seeds or from sets. Starting from sets is much easier here. Press sets into the soil so that only the tips show above ground. Plant scallions a bit deeper to get more white stem. Spanish and Bermuda onions require a longer growing season. Either seed them into the garden the previous year or start them indoors and transplant into the garden.

Onions ripen at the same time year after year because the formation and maturity of the bulb is controlled by day length. Therefore, the earlier you plant, the larger the bulbs. Onion tops fall over on their own when they are ready to harvest. If you bend down the tops manually before they are ready, it delays maturity and new shoots will develop. Dry onions outside, protected from moisture and frost, until the roots crumble and you can brush them off.

Parsnip. The parsnip is a very hardy, long-season vegetable. It is well suited to northern gardens because its delicate flavour sweetens with fall frost. Seed the previous fall to get a head start the following spring.

Peas. There are two kinds of peas: the edible-podded snow or sugar pea, and the shelling pea. Plant peas in full sun in a site with good air circulation. Even the low-growing cultivars benefit from some form of vine support—use twiggy sticks or netting supported by stakes. If peas are being sown in new soil, non-treated seed should be inoculated with a nitrifying bacteria (see beans, above). Harvest peas when they are young and tender and snow peas while the pods are small and flat. In dry seasons, peas are susceptible to powdery mildew.

Peppers. There are two types: hot peppers and sweet bell peppers. Bell peppers are crisp and juicy when green, but sweeter when allowed to ripen to red, yellow, or orange. Hot peppers come in many sizes, shapes, and degrees of heat. Peppers are started indoors (see chart). Plant in a sunny (about eight hours a day), sheltered location, preferably in sandy soil. Peppers grow well in contain-

feeders and appreciate feeding with 10–52–10 throughout the growing season to hasten maturity.

In the fall when frost threatens, protect the plants with sheets or harvest the fruit. There are two schools of thought on the best method of ripening green tomatoes. One is to pick the green tomatoes and place them in a box, between layers of newspapers, in a dark, cool place. The other method is to pull up the whole plant and tie it to the ceiling in a cool place and let the fruit ripen.

Tomatoes are susceptible to foot rot, which is caused by the stem being bruised or damaged when transplanting or planting out.

The following chart contains vegetable varieties known to work well here. Don't be afraid to try others, but always choose short-season varieties. The seeding and transplanting times are intended as a guide.

VEGETABLES THAT GROW WELL IN CALGARY					
VEGETABLE	VARIETY	DAYS TO HARVEST	SEEDING INDOORS	TRANSPLANTING OUTDOORS	SEEDING OUTDOORS
Beans, green bush	Blue Lake Stringless	65	1st week May	1st week June	May 24
	Green Crop	48	"	"	"
	Royal Burgundy	51	"	"	"
	Stringless Green Pod	50	"	"	"
	Green Improved	54	"	"	"
Beans, yellow bush	Improved Golden Wax	55	1st week May	1st week June	May 24
	Kidney Wax	52	"	"	"
	Yellow Yard Long	50	"	"	"
	Pencil Pod Black Wax	50	"	"	"
Beans, broad	Broad Windsor	65	no	no	as soon as soil is workable
Beans, pole	Blue Lake Stringless	65	1st week May	1st week June	May 24
	Kentucky Wonder	62	"	"	"
	Romano	60	"	"	"
Beets	Cylindra Formanova	66	no need	no need	late April to late May
	Detroit Dark Red	63	"	"	"
	Early Wonder	63	"	"	"
	Golden Delight	55	"	"	"
	Hybrid Detroit Red	43	"	"	"
	Tonda Chioggia	50	"	"	"
	Ruby Queen	55	"	"	"
Broccoli	Green Sprouting	60–80	1st week April	1st week May	early April, best from transplants
	Hybrid Premium Crop	60–80	"	"	"
Brussels sprouts	Jade Cross Hybrid	110	1st week April	1st week May	best from transplants
	Long Island Improved	90	"	"	"
	Rubine (red)	90	"	"	"
Cabbage	Chieftain Savoy	85	1st week April	1st week May	best from transplants
	Early Copenhagen	68	"	"	"
	Danish Ballhead	100	"	"	"
	Red Acre	68	"	"	"
	Early Golden Acre	100	"	"	"
	Red Rock	68	"	"	"
Carrots	Imperator Long	75	no	no	late April to early June
	Gourmet Parisienne	68	"	"	"
	Little Finger	50	"	"	"

VEGETABLE	VARIETY	DAYS TO HARVEST	SEEDING INDOORS	TRANSPLANTING OUTDOORS	SEEDING OUTDOORS
Carrots continued	Nantes Touchon	60	"	"	"
	Red Cored Chantenay	68	"	"	"
	Red Cored Danvers	65	"	"	"
	Scarlet Nantes	68	"	"	"
	Orbit	50	"	"	"
Cauliflower	Early Snowball	55	1st week April	1st week May	best from transplants
Corn	Golden Bantam	75	end April	late May	mid-May
	Golden Beauty	72	"	"	"
	Honey & Cream	72	"	"	"
	Market Beauty	70	"	"	"
	Northern Extra Sweet	62	"	"	"
Cucumber	Burpless Hybrids	75	3rd week April	mid-May (protect)	best from transplants
	Chinese Long	68	"	"	"
	Earliest Mincu	50	"	"	"
	English Telegraph	75	"	"	"
	Sweet Slice	60	"	"	"
Kale	Green Curled	65	1st week April	1st week May	early April or late fall
Kohlrabi	Grand Duke	50	1st week April	1st week May	mid-May to mid-July
Lettuce	Buttercrunch	70	mid-April	mid-May	early May to mid-July
	Cos	70	"	"	"
	Early Curled Simpson	50	"	"	"
	New York Iceberg	75	"	"	"
	Prizehead Leaf	45	"	"	"
	Red Sails	50	"	"	"
	Slo Bolt	48	"	"	"
Onions	Annual Bunching	70	March 1st	mid-May	use sets, early May
	Early Yellow Globe	90	"	"	"
	Santa Claus	60	"	"	"
	Hybrid White Sweet Spanish	110	"	"	"
	Silverskin Pickling	100	"	"	"
Parsnips	Hollow Crown	130	no	no	late fall or early spring
Peas	Edible Pod Snow	65	no	no	as soon as soil is workable
	Green Arrow	62	"	"	"
	Little Marvel	60	"	"	"
	Wando	66	"	"	"
Peppers	Bell Boy	70	mid-February	early June	no
	Hungarian Yellow	70	"	"	"
	Jalap (hot)	70	"	"	"
Potatoes	Banana	late	no	no	early May
	Caribe	early	"	"	"
	Kennebec	mid	"	"	"
	Pontiac	mid	"	"	"
	Yukon Gold	mid	"	"	"
Radish	Crimson Giant	30	no	no	early spring to mid-July
	Cherry Belle	24	"	"	"
	French Breakfast	25	"	"	"
	White Icicle	30	"	"	"
Rutabaga and Turnip	Early Snowball	40	no	no	as soon as soil is workable

VEGETABLE	VARIETY	DAYS TO HARVEST	SEEDING INDOORS	TRANSPLANTING OUTDOORS	SEEDING OUTDOORS
Rutabaga and Turnip continued	Purple Top	55	"	"	"
	Tokyo Cross	35	"	"	"
	Laurentian	90	"	"	"
Spinach	Longstanding Bloomsdale	45	no	no	early May or in fall
	King of Denmark	58	"	"	"
	New Zealand	55	"	"	mid-May
Squash, summer	Gold Rush (yellow zucchini)	52	late April	late May (protect)	no
	Super Select (dark green zucchini)	48	"	"	"
Squash, winter	Sugar Pie Pumpkin	110	late April	late May	no
	Table Queen Acorn	90	"	"	"
	Vegetable Marrow	90	"	"	"
	Vegetable Spaghetti	90	"	"	"
Swiss Chard	Fordhook Giant	58	no	no	early May
	Ruby Chard	60	"	"	"
Tomatoes	Check with garden centres, varieties change yearly. Choose short-season varieties		Late Feb. to early March; move to larger pots early May	May 24 with protection	no

Herbs

Herbs are plants grown for their flavour or fragrance. They can be enjoyed in the garden, in cooking, and in crafts. Try edging beds with chives, parsley, marjoram, oregano, and sage to add texture and colour to the flower border. Lovage, angelica, tarragon, and fennel are all bold accent plants. Rock gardens are a natural for thymes, which creep and crawl. Shady gardens provide the perfect setting for lemon balm and sweet woodruff. If you trim and clip these herbs all summer, you will encourage compact growth and also have herbs for cooking. Containers are especially appropriate for annual herbs that are started inside and for tender perennials that are taken inside for the winter. If you decide to grow herbs in pots, choose a soilless mix containing peat moss and perlite to provide adequate water retention and drainage. Add compost to improve the soil structure and use half-strength 20–20–20 fertilizer every two weeks. Water as required to prevent wilting, but few herbs like wet feet. Grow them indoors in the winter if you can give them enough light.

Many herbs popular today, such as the parsley, sage, rosemary, and thyme of "Scarborough Fair" fame, originated in the Mediterranean. Their Middle Eastern origins make them sun loving. They tolerate dry heat and thin, well-drained, alkaline soil. Soil that is too rich in organic material or is frequently fertilized results in lush growth at the expense of flavour. Gardeners have their favourite herbs based on appearance, fragrance, or flavour. Sometimes selection is the result of associations with childhood memories, such as the remembrance of fresh chives in home-made cottage cheese or the fall fresh fragrance of dill. Here are some of the more common herbs to choose from.

ANNUAL HERBS

Several popular herbs are annuals. Either purchase them from garden centres in the spring or start them from seed. Specialty herb catalogues offer a wide variety not commonly available locally.

Basil *(Ocimum basilicum)*. At least a dozen varieties of this popular herb are available, in various sizes, with smooth or ruffled leaves of green or purple. A very tender annual, it should be started indoors in late April and not put outside until June. It can then be transplanted into the garden or grown in a pot in full sun. Pinch back to encourage compact growth; remove flowers to prevent it from going to seed.

Borage *(Borago officinalis)*. This 60-cm (24-in.) plant has star-shaped flowers that open pink and turn blue. It adds a cucumberlike flavour to salads. Borage self-seeds freely.

Bronze Fennel *(Foeniculum vulgare* 'Purpureum')*. This handsome, decorative plant, up to 150 cm (60 in.) tall, has richly coloured feathery leaves. Fully hardy to zone 4, it is usually grown as an annual here. Try to overwinter it by mulching.

Cilantro *(Coriandrum sativum)*. Cilantro is a quick-growing annual. When the fresh leaves are used, they are referred to as cilantro; when the dried seeds are used, they are referred to as coriander. Several plantings are needed to ensure a season-long supply.

Dill *(Anethum graveolens)*. This popular annual needs no introduction. The tall feathery plant is a staple in vegetable gardens. It self-seeds freely. A new 'Fernleaf' variety is shorter and slower to bolt.

Parsley *(Petroselinum crispum* or *P. hortense)*. Parsley is a biennial that is usually grown as an annual. The curly-leaved variety *(crispum)* is more familiar than the more flavourful flat-leaved variety *(hortense)*. Both make decorative plants, although *hortense* is less compact. It should be started indoors in March, using individual plastic or peat pots, as it has a tap root and resents being transplanted. Rinsing the seeds several times with hot water to remove the germination inhibitor speeds germination, as does covering the seeds to protect them from light.

Summer Savory *(Satureja hortensis)*. The leaves of this small bushy plant are often used to flavour bean dishes and can be used instead of thyme. Seed in early May in individual pots and plant 30 cm (12 in.) apart in good soil.

TENDER PERENNIAL HERBS

Herbs that originate in far warmer climates than ours and do not tolerate our winters can be grown as pot plants, summering outside and wintering indoors. When putting them out in the spring, acclimatize them slowly and protect them if frost threatens. When bringing them indoors in the fall, wash them carefully to remove any hitchhiking insects. In our short winter days, window light is seldom adequate to maintain good growth. Supplementary light from fluorescent fixtures placed 10–15 cm (4–6 in.) from the plants ensure vigorous, healthy growth.

Lemon Balm *(Melissa officinalis)*. Lemon balm is marginally hardy in the Calgary area—in the right location and well mulched—but to be on the safe side, winter it indoors. Its square stems indicate its membership in the mint family, and its lemon fragrance is slightly minty. It tolerates more sun and less moisture than most mints and benefits from being cut back frequently, as it tends to be untidy.

Lemon Verbena *(Aloysia triphylla)*. Originally a large deciduous shrub in South America, lemon verbena is grown here as a house plant. It requires frequent pruning to maintain a tidy appearance and loses its leaves when stressed and in the fall.

Marjoram *(Origanum majorana)*. Also known as sweet marjoram, it makes a decorative pot plant. Its soft grey leaves are reminiscent of oregano, to which it is related. It can, if well mulched, survive the winter here.

Oregano *(Origanum spp.)*. Oregano comes in numerous forms and, if well mulched, will survive here. They are very ornamental; do try them.

Rosemary *(Rosmarinus officinalis)*. This greyish evergreen shrub has recurrent blue flowers and is native to the Mediterranean coast. Rosemary prefers alkaline soil with good drainage. It is happy in a sunny window when brought indoors for the winter, but does not like to be hot and dry. Mist daily.

PERENNIAL HERBS

These are the herbs that survive our winters with no special care, returning like old friends in the spring.

Chives *(Allium schoenoprasum)*. A member of the onion family, chives can be purchased or obtained from a friend whose clump needs dividing. They do self-seed but grow very slowly. Milder than most onions, chives can be used fresh or cooked. Garlic chives are a larger white-flowered form, most decorative and hardy here.

Lovage *(Levisticum officinale)*. This impressive plant, growing to 180 cm (72 in.), can be propagated by seed or division. Its handsome growth and celerylike flavour earn it a place in good soil in either the flower or the vegetable garden. It prefers full sun but tolerates some shade. The ripe seeds can be used as well as the leaves.

Mints *(Mentha spp.)*. English mint, spearmint, and peppermint are the most common varieties. Gardeners grow them as ornamentals, sometimes reluctantly because of their invasive behaviour. Planting them in bottomless containers sunk into the ground makes them better behaved. They like rich, moist soil and shade. Take a pot full in for the winter and enjoy fresh mint year-round.

Sage *(Salvia officinalis)*. This good-looking ornamental plant offers soft silver contrast in the flower bed. Its silvery colour indicates it tolerates hot, dry areas well. Few of the variegated-leaved or fruit-scented sages are hardy in the Calgary area.

Sorrel *(Rumex acetosa)*. Sorrel is absolutely hardy here. Try it if you like its astringent flavour.

Tarragon *(Artemisia dracunculus sativa)*. This tall plant tolerates some shade.

Some people in Calgary grow French tarragon and find it hardy, but you have to get a root division as it is sterile and bears no seed. Russian tarragon *(A. dracunculoides)* is much less flavourful and comes from seed.

Thyme *(Thymus vulgaris).* There are several varieties available, with one sure to meet your needs. Common thyme is most often used for culinary purposes. Other thymes are grown as ornamentals. Low-growing, matlike types are grown in rock gardens or among paving stones. Like other Mediterranean herbs, it likes warm sun and alkaline soil. Plants can be taken indoors for the winter.

Once you have grown these herbs, further reading and an adventurous nature may lead you to investigate others. There are many books that detail the history of herbs, the myths associated with them, and their uses over the centuries.

Perennial and Shrub Fruit

Many types of perennial and shrub fruit do well in the Calgary area. Some are native to this part of the country and have been hybridized to improve their appearance, ripening time, or the quality of the fruit, while maintaining their hardiness. Others are new types, introduced to our area, that have proven successful.

Currants and Gooseberries *(Ribes* spp.). These prairie natives are completely hardy here. Red and white currants fruit on second- and third-year wood, and older canes are pruned out each spring. Black currants fruit on second-year growth only, so any canes that have fruited are pruned out to allow this year's growth to produce next year. It is important not to prune one-year canes in the spring, as they will only fruit that year. All currants need shaping and thinning regularly, as they become very prickly and tangled. Currants are self-pollinating, which means you don't need two varieties to produce fruit. Gooseberries make good pies and jam. Cultivars of the native gooseberry, such as 'Pixwell', are hardy; European varieties are not. Prune as for red and white currants.

Currants and gooseberries are susceptible to powdery mildew. Growing them in a sunny area with good air circulation helps. Water only in the morning, and water the soil, not the foliage. They can be dusted with sulphur for control. Aphids, indicated by reddish, distorted leaves, are also a problem. Currant worms eat leaves, skeletonizing them. Both pests can be controlled with sprays specifically for fruits and vegetables, but do not spray when the bushes are flowering or pollination will be seriously affected. Currant fly larvae cause "wormy" fruit. To prevent damage, spray the bush with the same type of spray when almost all the blossoms have fallen. It is important to spray well into the centre of the bush and on the underside of the leaves. Repeat after ten days.

Highbush Cranberry *(Viburnum trilobum).* The fruit it produces is not the cranberry we eat with turkey, but is a tart, seedy fruit that makes a delicious red jelly.

Nanking Cherry *(Prunus tomentosa).* These small cherries are tasty fresh, in jelly or marinated in brandy or gin and sugar to make a cherry brandy.

Raspberries *(Rubus* spp.). Purchase raspberries bareroot in the spring or growing in pots during the summer. Plant them facing the sun 60–90 cm (24–

36 in.) apart with 150–200 cm (60–84 in.) between rows and cut back to about 15 cm (6 in.). Support the canes with posts and wire or a fence. A balanced fertilizer such as 15–30–15, 20–20–20, or 18–18–24 is suitable. Raspberries fruit on second-year canes. Remove old canes that have borne fruit, allowing new canes to remain. Summer-bearing varieties are the most reliable. 'Boyne' and 'Chief' are hardy and do well. Yellow raspberries such as 'Honeyqueen' are not quite as hardy, and black and purple ones are not considered hardy here. Fall-bearing types such as 'Heritage' flower later, so are not susceptible to spring frosts, but since the fruit also comes later, it is more likely to be damaged by early fall frosts. Raspberries are susceptible to iron chlorosis (see chapter nine for treatment methods). They also do better if the roots are covered or shaded so that they remain frozen as late as possible, as they tend to break dormancy very readily in the spring.

Rhubarb *(Rheum rhaponticum).* This vegetable is used as a fruit. It is very easy to grow, in a sunny, well-drained spot with room to spread. The leaves are highly toxic and must not be eaten. They are safe for the compost pile, however. Do not pull many stalks the first year of planting as the plant needs the leaves for photosynthesis. From the second year on, rhubarb can be used, but not picked clean.

Saskatoons *(Amelanchier alnifolia).* These large bushes (2.5 m/8 ft high and 2 m/6 ft wide) are native to the Calgary area. They do best with some sun. New cultivars, such as 'Smokey', 'Thiessen', or 'Northline', produce more reliable, juicy, and flavourful fruit than native varieties. The shrubs are pruned in the spring, before they leaf out, in the same way as any large shrub. They produce fruit on the current year's wood. Saskatoons are attractive shrubs with white flowers and fruit that resembles a blueberry. The simple green leaves turn yellow and copper in the fall. They can be used for a tall hedge.

Strawberries *(Fragaria* spp.*).* Strawberries are easy to grow in our area and produce good quality fruit. Small plants are usually purchased from nurseries. They need a sunny location with good drainage. Plant so the crown (where roots and stem meet) is at ground level, about 40 cm (16 in.) apart, with 100 cm (40 in.) between rows. Water well when needed, rather than sprinkling often. A balanced fertilizer, such as 20–20–20, 15–30–15, or 18–18–24, is appropriate; follow directions on the package.

Strawberries produce fruit on second- and third-year plants. It is best to remove blossoms the first year to encourage plant development. Runners (long stems with small plants on the ends) are produced around each crown. Space and plant six to eight of these runners around each plant, anchoring them to the ground with a stone on the stem or a bent wire. Remove the others. Remove the parent plant after two fruiting years and allow the offsets (small plants from runners) to produce. Each year, new plants fill in the spaces left by removing older plants. Pick only ripe fruit, as strawberries do not ripen after picking.

Three types of strawberries grow well in the Calgary area. June-bearing strawberries such as 'Kent' produce large fruit that ripen in June. Flower buds are produced the fall before, so some winter protection, such as a thick covering of straw, is recommended to prevent Chinook damage. These are suitable for canning or jam, as a good crop is available all at one time. Everbearing strawberries such as 'Ft. Laramie' produce one large crop followed by several successively smaller crops over summer and early fall. They are cold hardy, but fruit is a little smaller than June-bearers. They are good for eating fresh. Day-neutral strawberries such as 'Tristar' are not dependent on the length of daylight for fruit production and produce very good quality, larger fruit throughout the summer. Runners from first-year plants can produce fruit. Day-neutral strawberries are not winter hardy in this area and need good winter protection. Cover the bed with dry leaves or straw, and secure with sweet pea net held down with rocks. Strawberries do not survive the winter in a strawberry barrel unless it is brought into an area that is cold but above freezing. Since strawberries produce little fruit the first year, strawberry barrels aren't usually practical. They are best used for annual flowers or herbs. Sweetheart strawberries can be grown from seed, started indoors in February, for small berries that summer. They are often grown in hanging baskets as annuals.

Slugs and squirrels love strawberries. They are susceptible to botrytis and powdery mildew. Preventative measures include watering in the morning, so the soil and foliage can dry before our cool nights, and removing dead leaves and fruit from the soil. Sulphur can be dusted on plants. Strawberries are also very susceptible to iron chlorosis.

NINE

Getting Down to Work: Gardening Skills

This chapter is based on knowledge accumulated collectively over many years by members of the Calgary Horticultural Society. It suggests how to do things and explains why. As part of the fun of gardening is to experiment, we recommend you use these ideas as guidelines only. Gardens are very forgiving so don't get too hung up on the details. Enjoy and learn—maybe you will help us write the next edition of this book.

Soil Characteristics, Improvements, and Digging

Few gardeners think very much about their soil when they begin gardening. They are more interested in planting wonderful flowers and harvesting succulent vegetables. The quality of your soil, however, determines what you can grow and how well it grows. Fortunately, soil can be improved to make a garden where plants thrive. A little information, a few simple tests, and some additions to the soil will pay handsome rewards.

Soil is composed of water and air, mineral particles from rocks, and organic matter from the decomposition of plants and animals. We tend not to think of water and air as parts of the soil, but both are necessary for successful plant growth. Recipes for ideal soil vary but generally call for 65 percent mineral matter, 25 percent air and water, and 10 percent organic matter. Mineral matter in this perfect soil would be 40 percent sand, 40 percent silt, and 20 percent clay.

Although there are some variations within the Calgary region, our soils are rarely ideal. They are generally heavy loam, which is composed of clay, with some silt and some organic matter; a few areas have sandy soil. Clay particles are very small and this is why clay soils compress together like putty when wet and are hard and lumpy when dry. Clay does not drain well and may hold too much water and not enough air. Silt particles are somewhat coarser than clay, but are still very small. Silty soils feel powdery when dry. The largest particles are sand, so sandy soils usually drain quickly; however, they are low in organic matter and not very fertile.

The texture of the soil gives some clues to its composition—lumpy clay, powdery silt, or gritty sand. Water forms puddles on clay, leaves dust-covered spots on silt, and drains quickly through sand. Make a mud pie with a handful of soil; get it so wet that most of it slips off your hands. Rub the thin layer remaining between your thumb and fingers. Clay, and to a lesser degree silt, feels slippery with little texture; you will feel the grit of sand.

Although mineral particles make up the bulk of your soil, organic matter from decomposing plants and animals is also very important. As organic matter breaks down, it releases nutrients that help plants grow. The end result of this decay is called humus. Humus improves the texture of the soil by breaking up the solid clumps of clay so the soil can hold more air. It also increases the water-holding capacity of sandy soils. To test for organic matter, take a few samples of dry soil from different areas in your garden and moisten them with a few drops of water from an eyedropper. If the soil flattens to nothing, you have little organic matter; if the samples stay somewhat intact, you have some organic matter. The colour of the soil also indicates how much organic matter it holds—the darker the better.

Soils around Calgary are grey or brown, with a high clay content. This means that they need to be improved by adding both organic matter and grit or sand. If you are building a new house, try to get the developer to put in 20 cm (8 in.) of good topsoil—30 cm (12 in.) would be even better. Unfortunately, in most new subdivisions, topsoil is only 10–15 cm (4–6 in.) deep and usually lacks sufficient organic matter. Adding compost increases the organic content of the soil tremendously, but gardeners are rarely able to do much more than top dress special areas. Grass clippings or sawdust can be dug in to add organic matter, along with a little extra high-nitrogen fertilizer (high in the first number) to help them decompose.

Many gardening books from other parts of the world suggest that additions, or amendments, to the soil should be dug in to the depth of two shovels—60 cm (24 in.). This time-consuming process, called double digging, is rarely undertaken in Calgary. Our subsoil is usually so poor that it would take tremendous effort to improve it, and it is best left decently buried. "Trenching and turning" might be the better way in Calgary, as you only improve the soil to the depth of one shovel—30 cm (12 in.). Begin by taking out a 30-cm (12-in.) square of earth, mix some peat moss, compost, or other amendments in it, and pile it to one side. Mix amendments into the section beside it, put it into the hole you created, and so on down the line. Finish by putting the first pile of soil into the last hole.

Rototilling adds amendments quickly, but rarely reaches very deeply into the soil. A more serious problem is that a rototiller may pulverize the soil to such a fine fluff that it compacts, excluding needed air and water. This is particularly a problem in clay soils like Calgary's.

Some gardeners work a mixture of peat moss and vermiculite into their soil. It is sometimes difficult to find ideal peat moss. The best choice is coarse sphagnum peat moss, which is more acidic than the sedge peat moss commonly used for house plants. Its pH helps counteract the alkalinity of the soil in Calgary, and its coarseness means it lasts longer in the soil before it fully breaks down and needs to be replaced. It also does not blow around as much as finer peat moss. Try mixing together a large bale (113 L/4 cu. ft) of coarse peat moss and a large bag (80 L/70 qt) each of perlite and vermiculite. The peat moss and vermiculite increase the soil's water-holding capacity; perlite provides aeration. Wear a dust mask as these materials can be dusty. Get everything damp—but not wet—and dig 8 cm (3 in.) of this mixture into your soil to the depth of your shovel. This may need to be done every few years as perlite and vermiculite lose their texture with alternate freezing and thawing. The improved soil is easier to dig, does not crack in the heat, and has a good balance of water and air. With deep, rich soil, plants can be grown closer together as the roots will go down into the soil rather than along the surface to seek nutrients. Deeper roots make for healthier plants.

Some Calgary gardeners also add coarse sand or grit to heavy clay soil. Make sure it is very coarse or you will end up with something like cement. Silica sand, grades 5 to 7, is recommended for most plants except those that need exceptional drainage.

Gypsum, or calcium sulphate, lightens clay soils by causing the soil to form larger particles. The recommended rate of application is 1–4.5 kg/9 m² (2–10 lb per 100 sq. ft). The sulphur in the compound does not acidify the soil as much as agricultural sulphur, but it does combat alkalinity. Calgarians are a little hesitant to use gypsum because it looks like lime, which we all know we should never use! However, gypsum is beneficial and should be used more than it is.

Sandy soils are found in some areas around Calgary. They contain enough grit, but need organic additions such as coarse peat moss, mushroom compost, sawdust, compost, or grass clippings to bind them together and increase their water-holding capacity. In this part of the world, it is almost impossible to add too much organic matter to your soil. A good supply of organic matter also feeds an increasing worm population, whose tunnels aerate the soil and whose castings add nutrients.

Another theory suggests you should not add any amendments to the soil—or only to the depth of 2.5 cm (1 in.)—because digging destroys the delicate structure that nature has developed to support plant life. This approach is possible if you are growing native plants in a natural landscape, but most gardens do benefit from soil improvement.

Whether your soil is acidic (sour) or alkaline (sweet) also affects how plants grow. Acidity and alkalinity are measured on a pH scale from 1 to 14, where 1 is very acidic and 14 is very alkaline. Seven is neutral and most plants prefer to grow in the 6–7 range. At either end of the scale, the nutrients in the soil are less available to the plants. Soils in Calgary usually have a pH of 8 or higher; water, flowing over these alkaline soils, also raises the pH.

You can have your soil professionally tested for pH or use an inexpensive home soil-testing kit to get a general idea of the pH. Check with the Calgary Horticultural Society or the Yellow Pages in the telephone book for testing laboratories. Plants with yellowing leaves and green veins or plants that seem to be drying out even though the soil is wet can indicate soil that is too alkaline or an accumulation of salts. These problems are more noticeable on plants such as bleeding hearts and mountain ash trees that prefer more acidic soil.

Lowering the pH of the soil is a little more difficult than changing the soil texture, but it is possible. Organic matter adds acidity as it decomposes. Because it improves both texture and pH, it should be your first choice for treatment. Aluminum sulphate and iron sulphate are faster acting but can become toxic if concentrations are too high. Follow instructions very carefully when using any of these products. High-nitrogen fertilizers also help lower the pH of the soil, as do fertilizers for acid-loving evergreens and other fertilizers that are acid based. (Ask a knowledgeable salesperson where you buy your fertilizer or look for words such as sulphur on the back of the bag.) You can also spread pure agricultural sulphur over the soil at the rate of 2 kg/90 m² (5 lb per 1000 sq. ft). The sulphur pellets will slowly oxidize over several years, increasing the acidity. Finer particles break down more quickly, but all types need to be replenished from time to time. Lowering the pH of the soil in the Calgary area needs to be done regularly, as salts are constantly leaching into the soil from alkaline water and the underlying alkaline clay subsoil.

It is best to improve your soil slowly over several years. Perhaps tackle one bed a year or put in a little extra effort when you are redoing a bed. Digging in amendments during the fall is a great idea because gardeners generally have more time then. Not quite "finished" compost, sulphur, or gypsum can be used; it will break down further by next spring. Over time, you will find that, if you look after the soil, it will look after your plants.

Watering the Garden

Garden plants cannot live without water, which carries nutrients up from the soil to the leaves, where plants manufacture the food they need to survive. Water then carries the food throughout the plant and cools it by releasing water vapour through transpiration.

Calgary receives, on average, less than 40 cm (16 in.) of precipitation per year and is classified as semi-desert. Most of the trees and gardens we see here are not native to dry sites and are therefore dependent on supplemental watering. Experienced gardeners know it is not just the amount of water but its distribution during the season that is critical to a garden. Some years seem so wet that extra watering is not necessary, but drought usually occurs some time during the growing season. Additional water is necessary from early spring until just before freeze-up in the fall—and even during extended winter Chinooks.

Since soils vary considerably in their capacity to hold water, it is important to determine what kind of soil you have in your garden. Sandy soil drains rapidly; soils rich in humus from decayed organic matter hold an appropriate amount of water better than either sand or clay. Calgary generally has heavy clay soil, which holds a lot of water. For this reason, it is best not to water more than once a week, even in the most severe drought conditions. The general rule is to apply

2.5 cm (1 in.) of water to fill the root zone and soak down to a good depth. This will ensure that a dry zone of soil is not left to separate the moist upper soil from the moisture deep in the subsoil. Some gardeners suggest providing 5 cm (2 in.) of water out to beyond the drip-line around large trees. The drip-line is the distance out from the tree to the end of the longest branches. The best way to determine how much water the garden is receiving is to use a water gauge marked up the side in centimetres and inches. You can buy one or make one from a margarine container permanently marked with the measurements. Time how long it takes to apply 2.5 cm (1 in.) of water and then use this time to plan your watering schedule. Verify the measurement occasionally, as water pressure can vary.

Allow the soil to dry out somewhat before watering again. Too frequent and thorough watering can cut off the supply of air in the soil by filling every space between the soil particles with water. Root growth then stops. The longer the air is cut off, the greater the damage. Frequent, light watering never gives the water a chance to move very far into the soil. This results in shallow-rooted plants that do not tap into the reserves of water found deeper in the soil. Consequently, the plants cannot survive even brief periods of drought or high heat. A once-a-week deep soak is much better than little and often. Be on your guard in periods of frequent, light rainfalls. You may still need to water to achieve 2.5 cm (1 in.) per week. Of course, young seedlings and newly transplanted trees and shrubs need additional water until they are established. Bare soil in flower beds and vegetable gardens may also need more water than soils protected by mulches and grass.

Tap water in Calgary is very cold, even in the summer, so watering the garden lowers the temperature of the soil and the air above it somewhat. Many plants are not bothered by cool soil; others do not perform well unless the soil temperature remains fairly high. The growth of warm-season plants such as tomatoes is slowed down by constantly cool soil. Such choice plants may be watered with water stored in a rain barrel or a watering can warmed by the sun. You can use tepid tap water if the hot water system in your home is not softened by a salt-based water softener—softened water contains salts that can draw moisture from the plant cells.

Calgary's water is alkaline, just like the soil over which it flows. Watering leads to a slow increase in the soil pH over a period of years, and irrigation research has shown that watering over many years can also bring salts to the surface from deep in the subsoil. (Refer to the section on soils in this chapter for suggestions for lowering soil pH.)

In periods of extended heat, many plants wilt around the middle of the day. The leaf surface becomes hot enough that the plant sends a signal to the leaves to shut down transpiration, their natural cooling mechanism. Soaking dry soil around the roots without wetting the leaves helps, but plants can wilt even if the soil is damp. These plants recover as the day cools down.

Watering in the morning avoids the excessive evaporation that happens when gardens are watered in the heat of the day and allows the plant to dry before nightfall. Leaves dry very slowly in the cool night temperatures in Calgary and wet leaves invite attack by disease-causing organisms. The evening, probably the most popular watering time for home-owners who are at work all day, is without a doubt the worst possible time to water.

The best watering systems do not waste water, either through evaporation or by watering driveways, sidewalks, and streets. Hoses that "weep" water at soil level are popular. They can be buried, but you need to check periodically that they are working. Drip irrigation uses tubes to deliver water to specific places rather than all along the hose. Soaker hoses have holes that emit a fine spray along their length; they can be placed face down so all the moisture goes into the ground. Oscillating sprinklers cover large areas; some can be programmed to shut off after they have delivered a set amount of water. Other sprinklers deliver water in a variety of shapes. Rubber hoses, although more expensive, are more flexible and easier to handle in cool weather than plastic ones. Organized gardeners remember to bring in their sprinklers before frost—those who don't, lose the sprinkler when the water in it freezes and breaks it.

Automated sprinkler systems can be set to water at optimum times, even during the workday or holidays. Some systems can be programmed to deliver different amounts of water to different parts of the property so each area is receiving the requisite amount. These systems should provide water in the same manner as hoses—a deep soak rather than little and often. The usual method is to bury the pipes below the ground, but there are also computers that attach to your tap to control above-ground hoses. In cold climates like ours, underground pipes must be drained and blown out each year so they don't break when the water freezes. Before going to the expense of installing an underground system, be sure you are fully aware of the seasonal maintenance the system requires.

Calgary gardeners are beginning to take more advantage of rainfall. A rain barrel is an old idea whose time has come again. Set a garbage can, or a more attractive wooden barrel, under the downspout to collect run-off from the roof. Use a gravel base to deflect violent flows that may come with heavy rain storms. During the working season, the barrel can be camouflaged with moisture-loving plants and vines in the overflow area. The collected water is warmer and less alkaline than Calgary tap water. A lid or screen cover is a good idea to keep leaves out and prevent mosquitoes from laying eggs on it. A lid also keeps the cat from falling in! Drain the barrel in the winter so it does not crack. Alternatively, you can consider connecting the downspout from the roof to perforated pipes laid on beds of gravel and buried 45–90 cm (18–36 in.) below ground. These systems carry and spread water considerable distances; the gravel base and depth below the ground mean puddling and freezing are not problems.

Chinook conditions and little or no snow cover both lead to a significant drop in the moisture level in the soil over the winter months. The wisdom used to be that watering throughout the fall encouraged continued growth when plants should be slowing down and hardening-off. Now it is felt that a well-watered plant is a well-nourished plant, one that is better prepared to withstand winter. A heavy watering in late October to mid-November, before the ground freezes, will fill the soil with adequate moisture before winter really arrives.

South-facing foundation areas benefit from periodic watering to maintain soil moisture if the soil thaws during extended Chinooks. Plants such as evergreens, which seem to survive the winter well, may die just before the onset of spring because they are unable to maintain the necessary water levels in their tissues. Watering at this time may save them. Winter mulches can also help reduce moisture loss by preventing thawing and the resulting evaporation.

You can substantially reduce the need for watering if you work with nature instead of against it. Xeriscaping, a term for using plants and procedures to minimize water requirements, allows you to reduce the supplemental water needed. (See the section on xeriscaping in chapter three for details.) Alternatively, adding amendments to the soil can increase its water-holding capacity and so reduce watering frequency.

Composting

Composting is the decomposition, or breakdown, of plant materials into a nutrient-rich soil known as humus. Bacteria, fungi, and worms do all the work; gardeners just speed the process up a bit. Composting is a great way to dispose of waste from your garden and kitchen. Somehow you feel better about that vegetable or piece of fruit that went mouldy at the back of the refrigerator if you can add it to the compost pile and get some use out of it. And you feel environmentally responsible when you reduce the amount of garden waste you put in the garbage. Composting is important in Calgary because our heavy clay soil contains little natural plant material. Compost lightens the soil, helps it hold more oxygen and water, modifies the pH by making it slightly less alkaline, and adds valuable nutrients to the soil.

Don't be frightened by detailed books that make composting sound like something you do in a chemistry lab. It is really not that difficult. Making compost is like following a recipe for stew. Some of us follow the instructions exactly, others are more casual. If you understand a bit about how the process works, you can be as creative as you want within the broad guidelines. There are two types of composting actions: aerobic, which requires oxygen for decomposition, and anaerobic, which requires very little oxygen. Aerobic composting is much faster, producing compost in months rather than the years anaerobic composting may take. Anaerobic composting also is more likely to produce nasty odours.

In aerobic composting, the organisms responsible for decomposition vary, depending on the stage of decay and the amount of oxygen available. Earthworms, sowbugs, millipedes, centipedes, beetles, ants, and snails munch and dig through the cooler outer portions of the pile. Certain bacteria and fungi break material down into carbohydrates, proteins, and amino acids. This process releases carbon dioxide and heat and sets the stage for the heat-loving bacteria. If enough water and oxygen are available, these bacteria multiply and consume all available food and oxygen. This can happen very quickly and can produce temperatures in excess of 80° C (170° F). If the pile is left undisturbed, it cools down when oxygen is no longer available and the process slows down. That is why composting is speeded up if the pile is turned.

There are a number of composting methods that a gardener can use.

Never Turn Method. Garden waste and kitchen scraps are piled in an out-of-the-way corner or container and forgotten for a year or two. The outer edge decomposes aerobically; the inner part, anaerobically. The material eventually becomes humus, although it may not be totally decomposed until the second year. It will likely not get hot enough to kill weed seeds. The pile needs watering occasionally but little other effort is required.

Sheet Composting. A thin layer of garden waste is spread over the garden as a mulch. By the end of the season, the bottom layer will have begun decomposing, adding nutrition to the soil. A little extra nitrogen fertilizer must be spread over the mulch so the nitrogen needed for decomposition is not drawn from the soil.

Green Manures. This method is not as common in Calgary, with its short growing season, as it is in some other parts of the world. It is done by planting a quick-growing plant such as annual rye grass, buckwheat, alfalfa, or clover in either the early spring or the fall. When the plants are still young, they are turned under, into the soil, to decompose.

Sealed Container Composting. Commercially available compost barrels placed over a pit in the ground are an example of this anaerobic method. Because the action takes place in the ground, odours are controlled. The same principle works using a sealed plastic bag or garbage can. A double layer, heavy plastic bag is filled with one-third soil, one-third kitchen scraps or grass, and one-third brown, dry plant materials. It is watered until it is damp but not soggy. The bag or garbage can is then sealed, rolled around to mix the material, and placed in a sunny spot. If it is rolled once a week, finished compost can be ready in a couple of months. There is no odour—until you open the bag!

Compost Piles. Compost piles are the most common method of composting in Calgary. There are a few factors to consider when selecting a site. First, consider convenience. If the pile is too far from the door, it may be easier to toss kitchen scraps in the garbage. If the pile is placed in the main garden, finished compost will not have to be transported as far and any nutrients that drain from the pile can be used by plantings around its edge. Next, consider wind and sun. A sheltered location reduces the need for watering, as wind can dry the pile and drain heat from it. A pile located in full sun heats somewhat faster in the spring and works a bit longer in the fall, but loses more moisture in the summer. The opposite is true of a pile in the shade. An ideal location has part sun, part shade.

A good size for a compost pile is at least 1 m³ (1.3 cu. yd). If it is too small, it will not get hot enough to kill weed seeds and will take longer to "cook." If it is too large, it can pack down, which reduces the amount of oxygen available. You can add oxygen to a larger pile by inserting an air pipe into the middle of the pile. Weeping tile, a perforated plastic pipe, or a bundle of branches are all possibilities.

You can buy commercial containers for composting or make your own. Commercial containers are usually plastic with holes to supply air and a door to remove the finished compost. Some, called "tumbler types," rotate on a stationary bar so they can be turned to speed up the composting process. A home-made

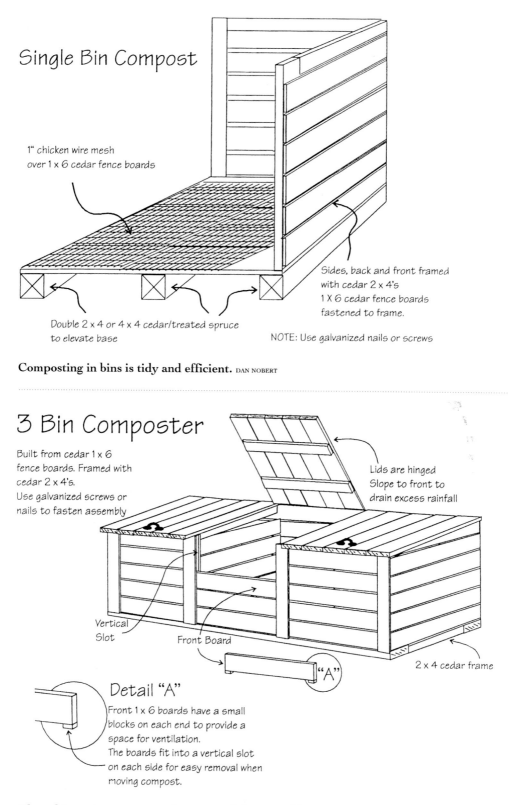

Single Bin Compost

1" chicken wire mesh
over 1 x 6 cedar fence boards

Double 2 x 4 or 4 x 4 cedar/treated spruce
to elevate base

Sides, back and front framed
with cedar 2 x 4's
1 X 6 cedar fence boards
fastened to frame.

NOTE: Use galvanized nails or screws

Composting in bins is tidy and efficient. DAN NOBERT

3 Bin Composter

Built from cedar 1 x 6
fence boards. Framed with
cedar 2 x 4's.
Use galvanized screws or
nails to fasten assembly

Lids are hinged
Slope to front to
drain excess rainfall

Vertical
Slot

Front Board

"A"

2 x 4 cedar frame

Detail "A"

Front 1 x 6 boards have a small
blocks on each end to provide a
space for ventilation.
The boards fit into a vertical slot
on each side for easy removal when
moving compost.

Three-bin systems separate the stages of decomposition. DAN NOBERT container, which can be enlarged, might be a better idea. Each year as you see the benefits of compost, you will want to create more. The container can be built with wooden slats, chicken wire and stakes, cinder blocks, bales of straw, or anything else that will keep the pile together. Because the process of composting requires oxygen, the wooden slats should have space between them; a raised floor with air holes or a bottom layer of branches lets air into the bottom layer; a cover keeps the pile tidy and prevents it from getting too soggy when it rains.

Some composting set-ups use a three-part system in which material is moved from one container to another. New material is in the first section, "decomposing" in the second, and "nearly ready" in the third. There needs to be an easy way to move material from one section to another and to take out the finished compost—perhaps with removable dividers or hinged doors. Another method is to enclose a large area (2 x 4 m/6 x 13 ft) with chicken wire held in place by stakes. Leave an opening to walk in as an entrance. Start the pile in one corner, toss it to the other side after a week or two, add more material as it becomes available, and toss it back again. Keep doing this until the pile is ready. This kind of work is great for relieving tension! Pile the nearly finished compost in a corner near the entrance. A pile this size is not pretty, but it certainly makes a good deal of wonderful compost.

There are two types of material in a compost recipe—"green" and "brown." Green materials are high in nitrogen. They include kitchen food wastes such as vegetable and fruit peels, trimmings, and leftovers; coffee grounds, including filters; tea bags; and bread. Bread is sometimes not recommended because it can attract pests but it decomposes quite easily. Also "green" are green garden plants and fresh grass clippings, if they have not been treated with pesticides within the last month; green leaves and hedge trimmings; dead plants, as long as they are not diseased; grass sod; and weeds, if they have not gone to seed or been sprayed with pesticides. Lawn weed killers are said to break down in thirty days but many people still do not put dead weeds in their piles. Some gardeners are also hesitant to put weeds with seed heads or fat little grass roots in the compost. They are not confident the pile will get hot enough to kill all the weed seeds and the invasive roots. Dry, brown materials are high in carbon. They include dry leaves, dried plants, dried grass clippings, small twigs and prunings, brush, straw, wood chips, sawdust, evergreen needles, cardboard, paper, paper towels, newsprint, lint from dryers, and vacuum fluff.

If you talk to three people about what the mix of greens and browns should be, you'll get three different answers. Don't worry about exact proportions—recommendations range from 20 parts brown material to 1 part green material all the way to 50 percent of each. Greens help heat things up, but they need the browns to work with. Remember, a mixture decomposes faster than just one type of material.

Certain things should not be put in the compost pile. On this list are meat, fish, dairy products, fatty or oily foods (these can smell and attract animals to your pile); diseased plants and weeds that have gone to seed; peony foliage, which can spread botrytis; plants treated with pesticides; thickish branches, pieces of wood, peach pits, and hard nut shells, which take too long to decompose; and cat manure. The latter sometimes contains parasites that can be passed on to humans and cause serious diseases in young children and pregnant women. Manure from a healthy dog is considered acceptable.

Some folks who compost save their green and brown materials in separate closed containers until they have enough to make a pile. A covered pail under the sink is a practical method to collect useable kitchen wastes. It can be taken out to the compost pile even in the winter. Keep an extra bale of straw or a bag of leaves by the pile to cover the additions decently until spring. Other people just add materials to the pile as they become available and let nature take its course.

Once the ingredients are assembled, organisms are needed to do the decomposition work. Commercial starters can be purchased, but the best source is good garden soil or compost—it is teeming with bacteria, fungi, earthworms, and other helpful beasties. A few shovelfuls of dirt mixed into the compost, or even just the soil clinging to the roots of plants going into the pile, do the trick. A sprinkle of high-nitrogen fertilizers provides an extra source of the nutrients the organisms need to get the process off to a good start; manures can also be used. A handful or two of agricultural sulphur reduces the alkalinity of the finished compost.

If you want to keep the pile hot and working faster, there are a few thing you can do. Make sure materials are finely chopped to expose more surface area to the micro-organisms. Because the organisms need oxygen and water to work, mix the materials so they don't pack down and squeeze out the oxygen. Water the pile from time to time so it is as wet as a damp sponge but not soggy. Try to keep a lower spot in the top of the pile to collect moisture. Turn the pile to aerate it and bring material from the outside into the centre. In theory, you should turn your pile every time it cools down, which could be once a week. Few Calgary gardeners have time in our short summer season for such efforts. From time to time, check the pile to see if it is damp enough, mix in the latest batch of grass clippings, and, maybe, turn it once or twice a season. Encouragement is provided: a few days after you have built your pile, put your hand into it and feel the heat!

A well-maintained pile should not smell. Unpleasant odours usually mean the pile is too wet and decomposing anaerobically; add more air by turning it and increase the ratio of brown material. A pile that is damp and sweet-smelling—but cold—needs more greens to supply nitrogen and heat it up.

A compost pile started in the spring will usually be ready for use the next spring. Spring is an ideal time to work the wonderful humus into flower beds and vegetable gardens or to add it as top-dressing to the lawn. A new batch of compost can be started with the clean-up material from your yard and the first grass clippings of summer. Compost started in the fall can be worked into beds the next fall and put around perennials as a winter mulch.

Composting is the single most important thing you can do to improve your soil, and really it is so easy. If you can find a corner, do try it. Soon you will be out with the rest of us in the fall—begging bags of leaves for your compost pile from the neighbours.

Plant Nutrition

Just like people, plants need nutrients to grow and flourish. In nature, the process of plant decay makes nutrients for other plants. Where there are sufficient nutrients, plants succeed; where nutrients are lacking, they grow poorly or die. As gardeners we need to know when and how to enhance plant nutrition by adding fertilizers. The nutrients plants need can be supplied organically from plants and animals, through compost, manures, and organic fertilizers, or inorganically through chemical fertilizers.

Knowledge of fertilizing techniques is particularly important in Calgary. Many of the plants we grow come from other parts of the world where the nutrients they need are available naturally. With proper fertilization, their overall health is better and they are more likely to succeed here. Gardeners here also use their growing areas very intensively; many trees, shrubs, vegetables, and flowers are competing for nutrients in the soil. Although different plants may use different nutrients, and crop rotation is possible with vegetables, flowers are generally grown in the same place year after year and lawns remain in place for decades. Extra nutrition also encourages faster growth and earlier maturity, so tomatoes ripen before the frost and the most vegetables and flowers are produced.

The three main elements that plants need for nutrition are nitrogen (N), phosphorus (P), and potassium (K). Fertilizer packages show the percentage of each element as 10–20–15, which means 10 percent nitrogen, 20 percent phosphorus, and 15 percent potassium. The remaining ingredients are the inert carriers of the elements. The elements are always listed in the same order, which is easy to remember because it is alphabetical—nitrogen, phosphorus, potassium.

Nitrogen is necessary for the rich, dark green growth of the leaves and stems. It promotes fast growth and also provides food for beneficial soil bacteria, which turn organic material into desirable humus. Growing plants need a steady supply of nitrogen as it can be lost quickly by leaching, or washing out, of the soil. A lack of nitrogen is shown by pale green or yellow leaves. Too much nitrogen results in weak, spindly growth at the expense of flowers and fruits, increased susceptibility to insect and disease damage, and delayed maturity.

Phosphorus encourages root growth and hastens plant maturity. It is necessary for the production of flowers, fruit, and seeds. Adequate phosphorus also increases winter hardiness and resistance to disease. It is a particularly important element in our short growing season as it hastens maturity. Lack of phosphorus means slow growth, thick or purplish leaves, poor flowers and fruit, and late maturation. It is not plentiful in our soils so there is no danger of applying too much.

Potassium is the third major element in fertilizer. It is necessary for cell strength, root system growth, fruit formation, and the overall health of the plant.

It helps plants withstand the stress of winter and is an important part of fertilizers recommended for winterizing the lawn.

In general, Calgary soils are adequately supplied with the minor, or trace, elements such as calcium, magnesium, sulphur, and iron, all of which are needed for good growth. However, highly alkaline clay soil can lock up these nutrients so they are unavailable to plants. Suspect iron chlorosis, caused by a lack of available iron, when you see yellow leaves with green veins. It can be quickly, but expensively, treated with chelated iron. Reducing the pH of the soil is a better solution. Therefore, Calgary gardeners should look for fertilizers that use sulphur or other acid-based compounds to deliver nutrients. Ask a knowledgeable salesperson for assistance, as it is sometimes hard to tell what the fertilizer carrier is from the package. Acidic fertilizers for evergreens can be used to supply nitrogen to many other plants and counteract the effect of Calgary's alkaline soil and water. Be aware, however, that some plants, such as dianthus and baby's breath, prefer alkaline soil. Gardening books from other parts of the world regularly state you must add lime to your soil to "sweeten" it; that is, make it more alkaline. Do not do this in Calgary!

Some chemical fertilizers are dissolved in water and applied as a liquid. This is the fastest-acting method as it makes the nutrients quickly available to the plants. The chemicals are either dissolved in a watering can, held in an upper chamber of a root-feeding probe where they are mixed with water being delivered at the end of the pipe, or siphoned from a pail to be mixed with water coming through the hose. If you write the capacity on the container you are going to use for mixed liquid fertilizers and then write how much concentrate you need for this container on the bottle, you don't have to recalculate the required mixture each time. Granular fertilizers are applied as tiny pellets that need to be broken down by water and bacteria to make the nutrients available.

Whether you use organic or chemical fertilizers is a personal choice, as the source of the nutrients is immaterial to plants. The nutrients supplied by each are much the same, but organic fertilizers generally have more trace elements; inorganic fertilizers are more concentrated. Organic fertilizers work more slowly than chemical ones and larger quantities are needed before they approach the nutrient level of chemical fertilizers. Some organic fertilizers are manures, bone meal, blood meal, and fish fertilizer. Bone meal increases the alkalinity of the soil, which is generally not desirable in Calgary; blood meal is acid forming, which is preferable. Fresh manures can burn just as chemical fertilizers can. As well, nitrogen is lost very rapidly from all fresh manures. Manures and compost do add bacteria and fungi that help break down chemical fertilizers into forms plants can use. In general, chemical fertilizers are more convenient and concentrated than organic fertilizers, but overuse can burn delicate plant tissues. Signs of overfertilization are lush and rank growth, and brown edges on leaves and grass. A good safety precaution for all chemical fertilizers is to apply them at half the recommended strength, repeating the application if necessary. The best decision may be to take advantage of the benefits of both organic and inorganic fertilizers by using a combination of the two.

Successful fertilizing means applying the right kind of fertilizer at the right time to the right plants. Manufacturers are constantly developing new fertilizer mixtures, so don't be concerned if you can't find the exact compositions recommended in this book. Just choose something with a similar ratio between the three main elements. Remember that fertilizers cannot make plants grow. Soil, with a little assistance from fertilizers, provides the materials that plants use when the soil is warm enough and the sunlight is sufficient for growth. Fertilize little and often to avoid encouraging excessive growth or burning your plants. Ask a knowledgeable salesperson to help you choose the right fertilizer for your purpose, ask questions if you don't understand, read the instructions on each package carefully, and follow instructions precisely.

SPRING

Lawns. Apply a time-release, high-nitrogen fertilizer in mid-May to encourage leaf growth. Do not use a weed-and-feed combination until the lawn is growing vigorously and weeds are evident.

New Plants. Use a starter or transplant fertilizer with a high middle number, such as 10–52–10 or 5–15–5, to get annuals, perennials, and vegetables over the shock of transplanting and to give them a boost for the short growing season. The ratio should be 1–2–1 or 1–2–2 for flowers. You want to keep the nitrogen (the first number) low or you will encourage leaves at the expense of roots and flowers. Continue to use the fertilizer every few weeks for any plants that are heavy feeders, such as sweet peas and tomatoes.

Perennials. A little fertilizer spread around these plants just as they are beginning to grow is beneficial. It is important that the fertilizer does not come in direct contact with roots or tender new foliage. Choose 5–10–10, 11–48–0, or another low-nitrogen mix. Compost spread around and carefully scratched in also provides long-term benefits for these long-term plants.

Bulbs. Spring bulbs appreciate a little fertilizer just as their shoots appear above the ground and again after they have finished blooming. Scratch a small amount of something like 11–48–0, 15–30–15, or 16–20–0 into the soil around them to help them replenish themselves for next year's flowers.

Trees and Shrubs. With their wide-ranging roots, these plants usually benefit from fertilizers provided for other plants. They rarely need extra fertilizer, which might encourage rapid and weak growth. New trees and shrubs are watered in like other transplants with high middle number (phosphorus) fertilizers such as 10–52–10 to encourage root development. Evergreens benefit from special fertilizers that acidify the soil.

Vegetables. A good starter fertilizer (10–52–10) is beneficial at an early stage of growth, especially for heavy feeders such as tomatoes. Leaf and root crop vegetables welcome something like 16–20–0 or 20–10–5 applied at a rate of 2–3 kg/90 m² (4–6 lb per 1000 sq. ft).

SUMMER

Lawns. Reapply a time-release, high-nitrogen fertilizer in early to mid-July. Don't fertilize so much that the grass must be cut every three days or your enthusiasm will diminish rapidly!

Annuals. Some annuals may need a light treatment of flower fertilizer (1–2–1 or 1–3–1 ratio) during the summer, just as their first flush of bloom is over. If they are planted in good soil, they may not even require this.

Perennials. Some perennials benefit from flower fertilizer (1–2–1 or 1–3–1 ratio) just as their buds are forming. They rarely need more after that.

Vegetables. Apply a mid-summer fertilizer, rich in phosphorus but low in nitrogen, to encourage bigger and better fruit and root crop yields. Leafy vegetables can benefit from additional nitrogen.

FALL

Lawns. Apply a winterizing fertilizer or weed-and-feed combination early in the fall to prepare the plants for winter and get them off to a good start in the spring.

Bulbs. Quite a difference of opinion exists about how helpful bone meal really is, given its tendency to increase soil alkalinity. However, many people put a little bone meal in the bottom of holes for newly planted bulbs. It should be separated from the bulb by some sand. Bone meal releases its nutrients very slowly and is quite expensive for the amount of nutrients it provides (1–2–1 is common). If bulbs are planted with a little sand for drainage and a little compost for nourishment they will be stronger and healthier.

Starting Seeds Indoors

There are a number of practical reasons to start plants from seeds. Many seed packages can be bought for the price of a box of annuals, and a seed saver has no cost for seeds after the initial investment. Uncommon annuals and perennials have to be started from seed if they are not available from local garden centres. Many plants need a long growing season to reach the flowering and fruiting stage; starting them inside gives them the head start they need in Calgary's short growing season.

Seeds may be obtained from your own or other people's gardens, garden centres, mail-order seed houses, or botanical gardens. Store them properly to ensure maximum viability; the internal activity of seeds is accelerated by increases in temperature, humidity, and sometimes light. Keep them in an airtight container at low temperature and humidity. Refrigeration is ideal. With proper storage, most remain viable for several years.

Seeds must be started early enough to ensure good growth before planting out, but late enough that they are not too overgrown or rootbound to transplant successfully. Many catalogues and other seed sources suggest planting dates based on a longer growing season and an earlier planting-out date than we have in Calgary. A general rule in Calgary is to start annuals in early to mid-April, six to eight weeks prior to our planting-out date at the beginning of June. Tender perennials grown as annuals, such as heliotrope, geraniums, pansies, snapdragons, impatiens, and begonias, need to be started much earlier to develop and bloom at the proper time. Generally allow two to four weeks for germination and twelve weeks to grow. This pushes the start date for these plants back to late January or early February. (Refer to chart at the end of chapter seven for recommended seed-starting dates.)

Perennials, which do not need to reproduce annually by seed, also usually need an early start as many of them have developed elaborate and complicated strategies to prevent or delay germination until success would be assured in their natural environments. First-time seed starters are better to begin with annuals, which reproduce yearly by seed and so have not developed as many tricks. Once you know a few techniques to satisfy perennials' germination requirements, many of them can also be grown without too much difficulty.

Special germination needs are generally listed on the seed packages and fall into four categories:

Light or Dark? Some seeds need to be exposed to light to germinate. Just sprinkle them on the soil and mist them with water to make sure they have made contact with the soil. For seeds that need darkness, shield the container from the light with a sheet of cardboard. Be sure to take it off as soon as the seedlings appear or they will grow lank and leggy.

Stratification. Some seeds need to be exposed to low temperatures and moisture before sowing to soften their outer coating. These seeds can be mixed with a bit of damp peat moss, sand, or vermiculite, or planted directly in their container, and then slipped into a plastic bag. Place this bag in a refrigerator for the time required, which can vary from a few weeks to several months. Return them to room temperature to germinate or plant them directly in the garden. Alternatively, layer the seeds with damp sand in a pot and leave it outdoors for the winter in an exposed position where the seeds will alternately thaw and freeze. The sand/seed combination can be planted directly into the garden in early spring, as soon as the soil can be worked.

Scarification. Some seeds have such tough coats that they must be nicked to allow moisture to penetrate. Purchased seeds may have had this done already. To do it yourself, rub the seeds over sand paper or use the point of a sharp knife to pierce the seed coat.

Soaking and Washing. Soaking seeds can also soften tough coats. As well, rinsing the seeds two or three times removes germination-inhibiting chemicals that prevent some seeds from germinating until there is enough moisture for the seed to have a good chance of growing.

Germinating and raising seedlings are easier if a dedicated place, with water nearby and control over light, temperature, humidity, and air circulation, is available. Barring that, make the best use of what you have. Many flats of annual flowers and vegetables were successfully raised before artificial lights were readily available. South-facing windows provide the best light, but the short hours of daylight in the winter, especially before the end of March, reduce the light available. Plants stretch toward the light, so turn the flats frequently. Since seedlings near a window can be subject to night chills, they may need to be moved away or covered at night.

If you are using artificial light, an area in the basement works best as it is out of the way and not subject to the hazards of high traffic. Arrange the space to accommodate the desired number of 4-foot two-tube fluorescent fixtures, each of which will provide 40 watts of light for the seedlings. A cool white and a warm white fluorescent tube provide light from both ends of the colour spectrum, which is needed to support good growth. Growlights are available at much greater cost and do not provide significantly better results. Ideally, the tubes should be replaced yearly or, at the very least, as soon as a dark deposit appears at the end of the tubes. This indicates the amount of light delivered is declining, although the light still works.

You can use a variety of planting containers to start seeds. Styrofoam cups, plastic dairy containers, and many other items are suitable as long as they hold the planting medium and seeds securely, have adequate drainage, and provide enough room for the roots to develop. Always punch holes in the bottom and be aware that round containers can waste space. Peat containers are almost essential for plants that do not like to have their roots disturbed. Mini-greenhouse trays are popular; they hold 72 potential seedlings and the clear top maintains the humidity needed for germination and small seedlings. A considerable number of other cell packs and tray combinations are possible. Choose a larger size cell or a box that holds six or nine seedlings if you do not plan to "pot on" your seedlings into larger containers. The small cells restrict the root growth of all but

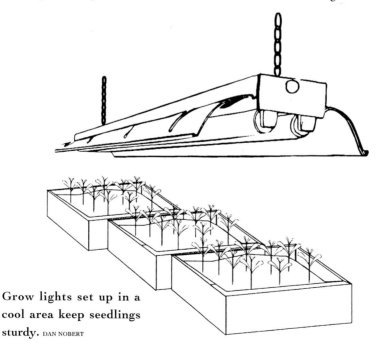

Grow lights set up in a cool area keep seedlings sturdy. DAN NOBERT

the slowest-growing seedlings before spring arrives. Covers are not absolutely essential for the trays, especially if you are growing a large number of plants together. The plants themselves will create a microclimate and keep the humidity high enough. Look for unperforated trays with grooved bottoms so flats do not sit in water. With reasonable care, trays and flats can be reused for several years. Whatever you use must be scrupulously clean; if not new, wash away all traces of soil and soak in a mild bleach solution (1 part bleach to 10 parts water) to sanitize them.

Seedlings need sterile soil that their roots can penetrate easily. This is one time when it is worthwhile to pay for good seed-starter and potting-on soils. Some gardeners use one mix for germination and another for growing the seedlings. If seedlings are going to grow in the same container until they go out in the garden, use the richer potting-on mix. Do not use garden soil as it can contain weed seeds and disease organisms. Even if sterilized, garden soil does not create a suitable environment for seedlings unless it is mixed with vermiculite or perlite to lighten it up and improve drainage. Compost could be used, but it too may have weed seeds and carry diseases.

Fill the containers with the planting medium, water them from below until the surface glistens with water, and allow them to drain—that way you don't have to water them from the top and risk washing the seeds around. Large seeds are easy to place; small seeds are harder to manage and even with great care are usually overseeded. Some gardeners mix a few seeds in a small amount of vermiculite or sand to spread them more thinly. Label all your flats to prevent errors and confusion. Use a waterproof marker on a plastic label to ensure the label is still readable when you are putting plants out. You may think you will remember which is which—but don't bet on it! Sticks used for labelling must be short enough to allow the newly seeded flats to get close enough to the lights. Seeding time is a good time to start keeping notes. Record what was seeded when, noting germination times and success rates. You can adjust your timetable for next year based on this year's experience.

For germination, maintain an air temperature of 20–25° C (70–80° F). Some seeds need bottom heat to increase soil temperature and benefit from being placed on top of the fluorescent light fixture, a warming tray, or even the refrigerator. A soil-heating cable can also be put in the bottom of the tray. Bottom heat speeds up germination, even for seeds that are said to need cooler temperatures to germinate. When seeds have germinated, maintain temperatures at 15–20° C (60–70° F) with temperatures 5° C (10° F) cooler at night. You can achieve good plant growth at basement temperatures as cool temperatures reduce the seedlings' light requirements and help ensure stocky growth. If your basement is warm, try to reduce the heat in one area.

When seedlings have germinated, supply twelve to sixteen hours of light a day. The seedlings need rest periods to utilize the food produced during "day" time under the light. There is some evidence that giving two eight-hour "days" with four-hour "nights" increases growth faster than a single sixteen-hour "day." A reliable timer to establish days and nights is a must with artificial lights.

It will save many trips up and down the stairs and provide a consistency that is hard to match. A timer designed for outside use will accommodate the grounded three-prong plug most growlight units have.

The light source should be as close as possible to the top of the seedlings without touching them and never more than 8 cm (3 in.) away; insufficient light results in weak and spindly growth. As seedlings grow, a system for raising and lowering the lights, the seedlings, or both is needed. Lights can be suspended from chains; flats can be elevated on blocks of wood, empty flats, or whatever raises them to the necessary height.

Ensure the seedlings don't get too crowded. Leaves that overlap lead to spindly growth as plants compete for available light and nutrients. Overcrowding reduces air circulation around the plants and promotes fungus and disease. Damping-off is one such fatal fungal disease in which plants that seem perfectly healthy suddenly rot off and fall over at soil level. There are several chemical treatments available at garden centres, but your best defences are sterile soil that is not too wet and good air circulation. Use a small fan to move the air around and keep the soil damp but not saturated. Bottom watering helps prevent overwatering, but the excess water must be poured out when the surface of the soil becomes damp. Fungus gnats, tiny dark insects that fly around in a cloud when disturbed, do no harm but do indicate that the soil is too wet. Be aware, however, that peat pots and small flats dry out quickly. Check your seedlings daily to prevent potentially fatal wilting. Too little water is as bad as too much.

Seedlings require transplanting into larger containers with a richer soil mix at the two-leaf stage. If the starter soil mix was rich enough, seedlings can also be thinned by cutting off the excess ones and leaving the rest to grow. Transplanting or "pricking out" allows you to select the best specimens and provide them with more room to grow. Some roots are broken in the process and this stimulates the growth of feeder roots. Moisten the germination mix well and let it drain for a few hours. Prepare containers with the richer "growing on" mix. Make sure there is enough food for them. Sterile compost or a time-release fertilizer added to the potting soil ensures adequate nutrition. Poke holes in the new soil for the baby seedlings and gently pry them out, using any small pointy object. Lift the seedlings by their seed leaves, not their stems, as they can survive a torn leaf better than a pinched or broken stem. Place them a bit deeper in the prepared hole and carefully firm the soil around the stem. Start feeding the seedlings using half- or quarter-strength 20–20–20 fertilizer every other watering. If you misjudged your timetable and plants show signs of outgrowing their space, you can save them by planting them into larger containers. This is important, as seedlings with tightly packed roots will never flourish in the garden.

An alternative to starting seeds indoors is to let your plants self-sow in the garden and move around the seedlings that appear in the spring. This is a good excuse for not deadheading in the late summer. A surprising number of garden plants self-sow, even those that are challenging to germinate indoors. Some examples are monkshood, poppy, primrose, sweet alyssum, snapdragon, bleeding heart, and many members of the daisy family.

Cold Frames, Hot Beds, and Other Tricks

Cold frames and hot beds are really just boxes with transparent lids. A cold frame is heated by the sun; a hot bed has some additional heat provided. They are used to create a microclimate for hardening-off annuals before they are planted out in the garden, to grow early salad greens, to create the warmth needed by hot-weather plants such as tomatoes and peppers, and to protect fragile plants during the winter. The short growing season in Calgary, our cool nights, and variable spring weather mean these devices are useful throughout the growing season. There are different units with aluminum frames, polycarbonate double-wall glazing, and automatic opening devices that respond to the inside temperature of the unit. Home-made units are also possible at a fraction of the cost.

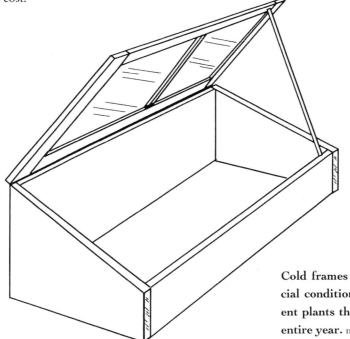

Cold frames provide special conditions for different plants throughout the entire year. DAN NOBERT

Permanent cold frames should face directly south to get as much sun as possible. Choose a location near a ready source of water and close enough to the house to make it easy to use. Protection from the wind is important. Earth can be piled around the box to further insulate it. If it comes into contact with soil, treat the wood with a preservative safe for plants. The back wall is usually higher than the front. The lid is glass or, more safely, plastic. Old storm windows can be used, but they must fit well as a cold frame should be reasonably airtight. The lid can be hinged or slide on runners. A practical design has a lid hinged in two places, both along the back and halfway down. The lid then folds to the back like a bifold door. During the heat of the day, the lid is propped open. At night and on cool, cloudy days, it is closed. You must watch the weather if you don't have a box equipped to open automatically when the heat rises. The unit can heat up very quickly, resulting in a drop in soil moisture and plant stress.

If all you need is a temporary shelter to harden off annuals in the spring, you can set up open boxes on your patio using 4 x 4 or 6 x 6 plywood boards. Even picnic benches turned on their sides or bales of straw can be pressed into service. Our grandparents leaned old storm windows against the house. Flexible or rigid plastic sheets, lightweight, almost transparent fabric designed to provide protection from insects and frost, or old sheets can be spread over the structure at night. If it snows, leave the blanket over the plants until it warms up again. Fabric "frost blankets" are available under various brand names and protect against 1–2° C (3–4° F) of frost. They are made of a spun polyester fabric, don't get wet like ordinary blankets, and are easy to store.

In the spring, put annuals and seedlings started indoors in the cold frame to harden off before planting out. Lettuce and spinach seeded in pots in the house and put in the cold frame in mid-April produce very early salad greens by mid-May. Leave little perennial seedlings, too small to be planted in the garden, in the cold frame until they are planted out in late summer. Germinate seeds in pots in the shady area at the front of the frame in the summer. In the fall, place borderline alpines and other small perennials still in pots in the cold frame, water them well, and cover with dry leaves. To prevent moisture buildup that might rot the plants, don't close the lowered lid tightly until freeze-up. During the winter, cover a cold frame in a sunny location with light-coloured material to reflect the heat and keep the contents cold.

A hot bed has much the same design as a cold frame, but the base is usually set 30 cm (12 in.) into the ground. In the past, hot beds were heated by rotting fresh manure; now heating cables are laid under a layer of soil or the box is heated by incandescent light bulbs or in-car warmers. Cover the heat cable with 2.5 cm (1 in.) of soil and a screen to prevent roots from penetrating too deeply, and then add a final 15–20 cm (6–8 in.) of soil. A 2 x 1 m (6 x 3 ft) hot bed needs 200 watts of power if light bulbs are used. Take care to keep the bulbs at least 50 cm (20 in.) above the plants so leaves are not burned.

It is also possible to make a hybrid unit. Set it on top of the soil like a cold frame and add heat with a heating cable or a 60-watt bulb hung on a nail inside the unit. You can trap heat in the unit by covering the frame at night as with a cold frame. As in many other gardening matters, experimenting is the best way to find out what works for you.

If you are interested in growing tomatoes or peppers, you will find a taller variation of a cold frame very useful. It needs to be tall enough to contain the mature plants and must have a removable side or lid. It is also better if it can be moved to a different site each year so viruses or pests do not build up because of growing one crop in the same place each year. It must be firmly anchored as wind is an ever-present danger in Calgary and can topple anything not tied down. The advantage of such a crop shelter is the night warmth it gives such subtropical plants and the enhanced heat during the day. A crop shelter 4 m long x 1 m wide x 1.5 m high (15 ft x 4 ft x 5 ft) holds six large-growing tomato plants. Keep the frame open during the day as the temperature can build up to 60° C (130° F) and kill your plants. If you use lights bulbs to keep out the cold, you can usually set plants out in the shelter during the first week of May. A few large stones or gallon jugs of water placed in the shelter will act as passive solar heaters, collecting heat from the sun during the day and releasing it at night. Short of a greenhouse, these structures are probably the most reliable way to grow tomatoes and peppers in Calgary. They also can extend the tomato season until well into the fall.

Cold frames and hot beds are more or less permanent additions to your garden. There are a variety of other less permanent methods that you can use to stretch your growing season. An easy one is to cut the bottoms from clean 4-L (1 gal.) milk jugs or other plastic bottles of the same size. The bottomless jugs are placed over transplants and pushed about 2.5 cm (1 in.) into the ground to secure them. The top of the jug is left off during the day for ventilation. If it is put back on toward the end of the afternoon, the air in the jugs will remain slightly warmer than the outside air during the night.

You can also buy wax paper hot caps and other small glass or plastic covers. They all give approximately 2–3° C (4–6° F) of frost protection and let light in for the plants during the day. Even newspaper gives protection, but needs to be removed every day to allow light to reach the plants. The problem with all these little covers is that they are too small to trap enough solar radiation to insulate plants if the temperature really drops.

Another technique introduced in the last few years is the double-walled plant protector. Water poured between the walls collects heat during the day and radiates it back into the containers during the night. It can protect to -8° C (18° F) and can be drained and reused for a number of years.

Larger protectors are available in the form of tunnels or row covers. These are particularly useful in the vegetable garden, where plants can be set in rows under wire hoops that support plastic covers. The plastic has slits for ventilation and is firmly tied to the wires and held in place with soil along the sides. You take it off when the season warms up and the plants begin to press against it, usually in late June. If plants must be pollinated before then, open the ends during the day to allow insects to enter and pollinate the plants.

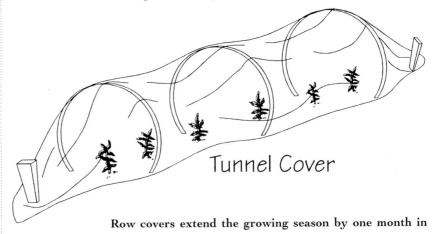

Tunnel Cover

Row covers extend the growing season by one month in spring and fall. DAN NOBERT

With our short growing season in Calgary, some of these season stretchers can really help get our gardens off to a good start. Be aware, however, that you will be tending them in the busy spring season. Opening and closing lids, covering and uncovering plants takes time. Start small and see if you enjoy getting the jump on the season!

Creating Microclimates

Although you can't do anything about the weather, you can modify the effects of the climate by identifying or creating microclimates in your garden. As a neighbourhood matures, with more houses and trees to block the wind and moderate the climate, plants that might not have survived in the past find the conditions they require are slowly being created. Vines with large leaves might now be decorative; previously they would have been battered and ragged.

Each location in your yard has its particular and changing advantages and disadvantages. The specific microclimates along a south-facing wall, close to the foundation, sheltered from the prevailing west winds, or in the shade of a hedge may be just right to protect and encourage plants that are normally too tender for prairie living. Shade-loving plants can be grown under trees; behind fences, screens, or hedges; or on the north side of buildings. Light can be increased in dark areas with white fences and houses and large windows that reflect the light. Reflected light also produces heat that is desirable for warm-season crops. Strong sunlight stored by stone, brick, and cement walls during the day is radiated back at night to mitigate the cool night air. Soil heat can be increased by using plastic mulches and temporary covers. Prairie farmers have long used shelterbelts to break the velocity of the wind; the same principle can be used to a lesser degree in the city. Even the house next door can provide some protection from the wind. However, two houses close together can also create a tunnel that the wind rushes through, destroying all but the hardiest plants in its path.

Conditions will change in your garden over the years as perennials, shrubs, and trees mature. Sunny beds will become shaded by trees, a fountain and pond may increase the humidity beside them. Careful observation will identify these special microclimates in your garden. For each plant, try to identify and create a climate similar to the one it came from. Plant it in several likely locations and wait and see which suits it best.

Planting Out

When to plant? is one of the first questions gardeners new to Calgary face. Gardening books from other locations speak of the advantages of planting perennials, trees, and shrubs in the fall so they can "settle in with the rains of autumn." Here it is just as likely to be a snow storm! In general, plants in Calgary benefit from spring planting, which allows them the whole summer to get established before facing the stress of winter. Plants in pots, growing well and not crowded or rootbound, can be successfully planted throughout the growing season, although they will have less time to become established. Early fall planting is possible, especially for perennials that bloom in the spring. Public parks, and gardeners with very large yards, may plant in the fall because they simply do not have enough time to plant in the busy spring. As well, plants are sold at reduced prices in the late summer so taking a chance may be worthwhile. Buy them as soon as they go on sale so they will have as long as possible to get established—and mulch them well to protect them over their first winter.

There are exceptions to the rule, however. Iris (early August), oriental poppies (mid-August), and peonies (early September) are all better planted in late summer after they have bloomed, but they should be mulched their first winter. Hardy bulbs should be planted as soon as they become available in the fall so they can establish roots before the winter. Daffodils are planted the earliest, at the beginning of September; tulips can be planted the latest, up until the end of October. Some lilies, especially the Asiatic varieties, can be planted in the fall, but there are local gardeners who feel they have a better survival rate if planted in the spring.

Spring planting begins with "hardening-off." About two weeks before they are to be planted in the garden, move the young plants outside into a cold frame or to a sheltered, shady spot such as on a porch or under a tree. Bring them back inside at night or cover them up. In a few days, move them into the sun for half the day. Gradually increase the exposure until the sun-lovers spend the whole day in the sun and they all stay out at night if there is no risk of frost. This coolness is beneficial for most plants, but some, such as cucumbers, tomatoes, melons, and celosia, do not benefit from it and should be kept warm and hardened off by being kept on the dry side for ten days or so.

Many hardy perennials can be planted out before the Victoria Day weekend. Except for frost-tolerant annuals like pansies, snapdragons, and sweet peas, most annuals should not be planted out until June 1. Late May frosts are not unusual. Gardeners may get impatient waiting for this day but the time can be well spent. Because perennials stay in one spot for a number of years, it makes sense to spend a little extra time preparing the ground for them; even annuals have soil preferences. Check to see whether they need lean or enriched soil, improved drainage, or extra nourishment.

To reduce plant stress and dehydration, wait for an overcast day or transplant in the late afternoon or evening. Soil in the planting beds should be moistened a day in advance. Water the plants well several hours before planting and let them drain so they are not soggy. If you must plant on a sunny day, cover newly planted transplants with pots or tents of newspaper to protect them from the sun and wind. If the roots of plants in pots or cell packs have matted together, pull or tease them apart with a kitchen fork to preserve as much root as possible and encourage new root growth. The suggested spacing is usually provided with seed packages or plants from the garden centre. Time will teach the new gardener which plants make a better show planted a bit closer together and which need more space to grow to perfection.

Dig a hole slightly deeper than the root ball, put the transplant in carefully, and firm the soil so there is a slight depression around the stem. All transplants but those needing lean soil benefit if the planting hole is enriched with compost. Most plants are set just a bit deeper than they were in the container. Tomatoes benefit from being planted considerably deeper, or on an angle, so more roots can form along the buried stem. Water the transplant immediately with diluted 10–52–10 transplant fertilizer, or use 5–15–5 with its rooting hormones, 125 mL (1/2 cup) for a small plant and 250 mL (1 cup) or more for a larger one. The high phosphorus content in these fertilizers encourages root growth and helps the plant recover from the shock of transplanting. Tear off the top collar from peat pots so it does not draw water away from the plant once it is in the soil. The complete peat pot is planted, but is sometimes slow to disintegrate in our climate. Slitting the pot to the base in two or three places makes it easier for the roots to penetrate the surrounding soil. Carefully done, this disturbs the roots very little. Pots may also be completely removed unless the roots have grown through them.

Trees and shrubs are most often planted in the spring, giving them a summer and fall to form a good root system before winter. Loosen the soil and add amendments such as peat moss and compost. The additional nutrients nourish the plant and make it easier for the roots to grow out to seek nutrients over a wider area. Be sure the hole you dig is large enough to give the roots ample room to spread, anywhere from two to five times the width of the root ball. Remove all trees and shrubs from their containers before planting. Fibre pots do not rot in this climate, plastic lasts forever, and wire baskets can constrict the roots and eventually kill the tree. Even burlap should be removed or cut away. Untangle roots that were tightly coiled inside the container and cut the damaged ones off. Pour some 10–52–10 fertilizer in the hole and let it soak into the loosened soil at the bottom. Position the plant in the hole and spread out the roots as broadly as possible. Make sure the stem is at the same depth in the soil as it would grow naturally, with the slight flare of the trunk just at the soil line. This may or may not be the depth it was in the container. Firmly pack a mixture of good soil, peat moss, and compost back into the hole, leaving a shallow depression to hold water. Pour more 10–52–10 fertilizer in the depression, fill it with organic mulch, and water it slowly to thoroughly soak the root ball. A newly planted tree needs regular, deep watering all summer, especially when the weather is hot and dry. Trees vary as to the amount of moisture they need. Consult knowledgeable people for help if you are not certain—your local horticultural society, city information phone lines, garden centres, or television and radio programs.

In windy areas particularly, newly planted trees may need to be staked. Do not make the tree immovable as that hinders trunk development. If several ropes are tied to stakes in the ground, be sure they are equally snug but don't restrict all movement. Cushion ropes with pieces of hose or plastic and leave them in place for at least the first winter. Be sure the ropes are removed by the second year or they will eventually cut into the bark of the growing tree.

Transplanting, Dividing, and Other Propagation Techniques

There are many reasons why perennial plants and trees and shrubs are transplanted or moved. A plant may have grown so large that it has outgrown its space, or a once sunny spot may have become too shady. Gardeners learn from experience and frequently decide something would look better or be healthier in another location. They may decide really aggressive spreaders are better behind the back fence rather than in the main flower beds or they may need to make space for new additions. Finally, every few years it is a good idea to dig up a small section of a flower bed and enrich the soil before resettling the plants. Few of us do this very often, but it pays handsome rewards when we do. Be aware, however, that certain plants, especially those with long tap roots such as baby's breath or sea holly, may be impossible to move successfully.

As with planting new plants in this part of the world, transplanting or moving plants is usually done in the spring. Any disturbance of roots stresses the plants and they do better if they have the summer to recover and tie back into the earth before the onset of winter. Early blooming perennials are transplanted in late spring after they finish blooming. Many gardeners have transplanted and divided plants with some success in the early fall. The exceptions to the general rule are iris, which are best transplanted in early August; oriental poppies, about mid-August; and peonies, early September. Large trees and shrubs, which need some preparation for the move, may need to be prepared in the early spring and actually moved in early summer.

If plants are simply going to be moved without being divided, take as big a root ball as possible so the roots receive minimal disturbance. If they are moved in the spring, the foliage will still be low enough that you can see what you are doing and will not make excessive demands on the reduced roots. Prepare the soil as needed, position and plant them as you would a new plant, and give them some transplant fertilizer (10–52–10). The crowns, or growth points, of many perennials have a way of growing higher than the surrounding ground over time. Set them back at ground level so the crowns are just below the soil surface.

If trees and shrubs are to be moved, they survive much better if they are moved when they are young and their roots have not spread too far. If you need to move a shrub, advance preparations are helpful. A month before the move, use a sharp spade to cut the roots to at least the depth of the spade in two opposite quarter-circles around the plant. Make the cut as far out from the shrub as the root ball you eventually move will be. Severing the roots encourages the growth of new roots within the root ball. Pour some transplant fertilizer within the potential root ball to encourage the new roots. After a few weeks, cut the other two quarter-circles and use more transplant fertilizer. Allow some time for those roots to grow and then move the shrub, planting it in a similar manner to a new plant. The top growth should be pruned back slightly so there are fewer demands on the reduced roots

For really large trees, the process should start the year before the move. In this case, the quarter-circle cuts should be trenches so that all the roots can be found and severed. After cutting the roots, repack the trenches with enriched soil and compost to encourage new roots to form in the root ball. Large trees are usually moved professionally, but can benefit from this preparation.

Gardeners also divide perennial plants for a number of reasons. The plant may grow too large for its position in the flower bed; the centre may become so overgrown with roots that it dies out, leaving a ring of healthy growth around the empty "donut hole"; more plants may be needed for elsewhere in the garden, to give to friends, or to share at a horticultural society's plant exchange. Like planting and transplanting, division is usually done in the spring—with the exceptions noted in the preceding section on transplanting.

If the purpose of the division is simply to obtain more plants, rather than to revitalize the plant, a small section can simply be cut from the edge of the plant with a sharp spade or butcher knife. The size of the section that can be safely removed depends on the size of the parent plant. Just be sure two or three growth points or crowns are taken, as well as a good piece of root.

Plants with dead centres should be dug up, the centres discarded, and the healthy outer edge cut into sections with at least two or three growth points and a good piece of root. Dig the plant out first, so you can see what you are doing. Some large plants may split into divisions naturally. Most can be divided with a sharp spade or heavy butcher knife, but some roots are so tough and intertwined that two spades or garden forks, back to back, are needed to pry them apart. Big daylily clumps may even need to be split with an axe. Replant the new divisions in the same manner as transplants—in properly prepared soil, with the crowns just covered with soil and a slight saucer in the soil with some transplant fertilizer poured around it.

Although dividing plants is the most common way to get new plants from existing ones, there are other techniques. Terminal stem cuttings of about 8–10 cm (3–4 in.) can be taken from the tips of the new growth when they are about 15 cm (6 in.) long. They are cut at, or just below, the node with a sharp knife or shears. The lower leaves are removed, leaving at least two or three at the top, and the bottom of the stem is dipped in rooting hormone, which can be purchased at a garden centre or hardware store. Use something like a pencil to make a hole in a damp mixture of vermiculite and peat moss and insert the stem. Keep the rooting medium damp at all times; humidity around the cutting can be raised by placing the container in a plastic bag, held away from the leaves with toothpicks or straws stuck into the soil. After a couple of weeks, tug the plant very gently. When it firmly resists, the roots have formed and the plant can be transplanted into a pot of good soil to grow on before being planted out. Cuttings are usually taken in the spring or early summer to allow the new plants to establish themselves over the summer. They can be planted into the ground in late summer or kept in a cold frame over the winter and planted out next spring. Plants such as chrysanthemums, dianthus, cotoneaster, caragana, and lilacs can be readily increased by cuttings.

Root cuttings are also possible, particularly with the thick and vigorous roots of plants such as oriental poppies, bleeding hearts, or perennial cornflowers. Anyone who has tried to remove these plants from a flower bed understands the principle—leave even one piece of the root behind and a new plant appears! A piece of healthy root, about 0.5 cm (.20 in.) in diameter and 3–5 cm (1–2 in.) long, is cut from the parent plant in the early spring. The cutting is laid on the surface of the rooting medium, or inserted at a slight angle, and covered with 1–2 cm (0.5–1 in.) of soil. Keep the rooting medium damp. Both stems and roots will grow from the buds on the root. The new plant can be transplanted into potting soil when the stems are 8–10 cm (3–4 in.) tall.

Another propagation technique is layering. The principle is demonstrated by groundcovers that root as they creep along the ground. New plants are created when you sever the stem between the parent plant and a growing tip that has established roots near the end of the stem. Many plants can be induced to root in the same manner by bending a stem over, pinning it to the ground, and covering the spot with a mound of soil. Make a slight cut in the part of the stem where it will be buried to hasten rooting; the new plant can be severed from the parent when it is firmly rooted.

Mulching

Mulching or covering the soil with a layer of organic or inorganic material has become increasingly popular in the past decade. Many organic materials previously sent to the landfill make very good mulches. Most popular are bark chips, wood chips, sawdust, pine cones, leaves, and grass clippings. Inorganic mulches of various gravels, crushed rock, and shale are also used.

Gardeners in Calgary reap unique benefits from mulches, which can be used successfully—but differently—in both winter and summer. The main purpose of winter mulches is to keep the soil constantly frozen, not to keep it warm. During the winter, soil under a cover of mulch remains frozen longer during Chinooks; if the soil does not thaw, it retains the moisture plants need in the spring. Frozen soil also reduces the likelihood of premature breaking, and subsequent freezing, of buds on trees and shrubs; perennials and bulbs are less likely to come up too early and be nipped by lingering frosts.

Winter mulches are usually, but not always, organic. Some gardening books suggest peat moss as a mulch, but in Calgary it tends to wick water away from the soil and dry out. It then blows away or forms a surface that water cannot penetrate. Coarse peat moss, if it is mixed with other materials, can be used in moderation. Straw bales can be purchased at garden centres in the fall and spread over the beds. The straw can be raked up in the spring and mixed with fresh grass clippings to make excellent compost. Be warned—there seems to be a far greater volume to pick up in the spring than was distributed in the fall! Hay should not be used as it contains too many seeds to drop in the garden and sprout next spring.

Some knowledgeable Calgary gardeners visit tree lots close to Christmas day and offer to take away unsold trees. The lot owner must clear the space and usually welcomes the assistance. Christmas trees are acidic so their needles lower the pH of our alkaline soils a bit. It is quite easy to lay whole trees over the bed at Christmas time. The hard work comes in the spring when the small branches and the needles need to be stripped off, either for a summer mulch or for the compost pile. The trunks can be cut up for firewood.

Dry leaves make good mulches, especially if you run over them with the lawn mower so they are too fine to form a solid, impenetrable mat. Burlap, or nets such as those used for sweet peas, can be pegged down over leaf mulches to keep them in place. You can also use discarded annuals and the tops of perennials if they are healthy.

Apply organic mulches to a depth of at least 10 cm (4 in.). You will be surprised how much material it takes to mulch a flower bed!

One inorganic winter mulching method used by several Calgary gardeners is the mulch blanket. These are made of insulating microfoam sown between two large pieces of burlap. They can be made to any size, although 1 x 2 m (3 x 6 ft) is suitable for most gardens. They last for years and can easily be rolled up for storage. The blankets need to be pegged down to keep them from blowing off. If there is snow covering, so much the better. You can use old carpets in the same way. These methods are tidier than organic mulches, but organic mulches enrich the soil beneath them as they rot down or provide great material for the compost heap. As in so many other gardening matters, the choice is yours.

Whatever form of winter mulch you use, conventional wisdom suggests you apply it after there has been a really good frost and the ground is frozen, usually about mid-October to mid-November. This is to ensure that mice and other creatures do not settle in for the winter. However, a lot of successful gardeners in this area rake leaves into their flower beds as they fall, thereby beginning winter mulching earlier. There is merit in this approach as freeze-up comes in fits and starts in Calgary and no one enjoys gardening in a blizzard.

Mulches also play a role in the summer. Soil covered by mulch loses less water through evaporation and therefore requires less watering than uncovered soils. Weed seeds, blocked from the light, germinate with difficulty; the few that struggle through the mulch are easily removed. Mulch helps prevent the soil from compacting, especially in areas of heavy foot traffic. On slopes, mulching prevents soil from washing away and increases the amount of rain that percolates into the soil rather than running off. Mulches placed over the garden in the summer, after the soil has warmed up in the spring, insulate the soil and mitigate the effects of our typically cool evenings. Stone, pea gravel, and shale mulches pick up heat during the day and release it at night, further protecting plants from falling night temperatures. Some of the plant material in organic mulches decomposes over the summer, starting with the material closest to the soil. This creates a very thin layer of compost that adds nutrients but uses up nitrogen, so it is a good idea to sprinkle a small amount of a high-nitrogen fertilizer over the mulch to avoid this problem.

Different organic mulches affect the soil differently. Coniferous bark, wood chips, and cones are somewhat acidic. They take longer to decompose but add a little bit of beneficial acidity to our soil. Sawdust and wood chips from poplars break down more quickly. They are not acidic but do increase the organic material in the soil. As well, all decomposition has a slightly acidifying effect. Grass clippings can be used as a mulch in moderation. Don't put them on too thickly as they tend to pack down and create a barrier to air and water. Mixing them with some coarse peat moss may help. If you spread them thinly (5–8 cm/2–3 in., lightly packed) and allow them to dry completely before the next layer is added, they can be very effective. Apply extra nitrogen as grass breaks down quickly and may pull nitrogen from the soil for the decomposition process. Grass treated with weed killer or weed-and-feed should not be used as the weed killers are designed to kill plants other than grasses. Although groundcovers are not usually thought of as mulches, they serve the same purpose, shading the soil and choking out weeds.

Mulches in vegetable gardens do not need to be as attractive as those in display beds. The old method of laying a board between rows to reduce soil compaction still works. Straw has long been used around strawberries. Newspapers can be folded and laid down to a depth of a few centimetres (an inch or so) between rows. Hold them in place with pegs or a bit of soil on the edges. It used to be said that coloured ink dyes contained harmful chemicals so only black and white newsprint should be used. Today's inks are vegetable based and do not pose a problem.

A dust mulch is another possibility. Soil is cultivated frequently to no deeper than 2.5 cm (1 in.). Loosening this layer of soil kills weeds, allows water to run into the soil, and provides an easily maintained covering over the soil where plant roots are.

GETTING THE MOST FROM YOUR MULCHES IN CALGARY

- Remove mulches gradually in the spring. Pull them aside to leave space for emerging plants, but be ready to push them back if frost threatens.
- If winter mulches are well on their way to decomposing and will not overwhelm your plants, do not take them off in the spring, just scuffle them into the soil. Only remove the really large bits—such as the Christmas trees!
- Do not add new mulch in the spring until the ground has warmed up.
- Leave a bit of space around the stems of the plants to allow water to penetrate more easily.
- Check under your mulch from time to time to make sure you have not created a breeding ground for pests such as slugs. This can be a problem, especially with organic mulches in a wet summer.
- Styles in mulches change over time—red shale is much less popular than it used to be; pea gravel is being seen more. Also, choose mulches that match your style of home and garden. Grass clippings and bark chips do not fit a desert-style garden; red shale does not go with a woodland border.

Stone, gravel, and bark chip mulches are usually laid over garden fabric to further reduce the chance of weeds coming through the mulch. Garden fabrics can be purchased in rolls in garden and hardware stores. They are porous enough to allow air and water through them, but too finely woven for most weeds to penetrate. Plants are placed into the soil through holes made in the fabric by cutting a cross and folding back the flaps. Eventually, however, stray seeds begin to grow in soil that has blown in and settled in the mulch itself. A few tough ones may even penetrate the fabric from below. Therefore, these types of mulches reduce, but do not eliminate, garden maintenance.

Lawns

For most home-owners, a lush green lawn is desirable as an attractive frame for their garden and home. Lawns are not the only answer to landscaping, however, so consider how much grass is needed for strolling, games, and play spaces for children. Lawns demand time, resources, and considerable effort to plant, water, cut, rake, weed, and fertilize. Other landscaping alternatives, such as perennial groundcovers, mulches, flower and shrub beds, decks and patios, could be combined with a smaller area of grass with pleasing and less demanding results.

Establishing a lawn takes planning. Begin by deciding where decks, paths, and other permanent features will be located. Then plan how flower beds and lawns would best set off these features. If an existing grassed area is very compacted, weed infested, or otherwise unsuitable for refurbishing, complete replacement may be the best answer. Remove the old sod and soil and proceed as for a new lawn.

Prepare the subgrade for a lawn by removing all debris such as rocks, branches, or construction material. Establish a grade sloped away from the house to prevent water from seeping into the basement. Fill in the hollows and remove the high spots. Then use a large landscape rake to level and smooth the surface. You could also use a 2 x 4 or 2 x 6, approximately 2.5 m (8 ft) long, as a levelling tool. Spread topsoil or loam evenly over the subgrade to a minimum depth of 12 cm (5 in.)— 20 cm (8 in.) is even better. Mix peat moss with the topsoil, either by hand or with a rototiller, to improve its texture and moisture-holding capacity. A lawn fertilizer (10–30–10) to encourage root growth could be worked into the soil mixture at this point or it could be applied later. If the fertilizer is not sulphur based, some agricultural sulphur can also be added to lower the pH of the soil. Use a water-filled roller to pack the soil lightly. Use a garden hose or rope to outline the area to be grassed. Industrial-grade plastic lawn edging, bricks, stone, or wood will keep the lawn edge clean and easy to mow—the lawn mower wheels can be run along it to cut cleanly and avoid hand cutting.

The choice whether to seed or sod depends on several factors. Sod is considerably more expensive than seed, but it is quick and relatively easy to install. The biggest benefit is an instant lawn. It is also more effective than seeding on a slope, where seed could be washed away. A disadvantage to sod is the limited selection of grass available. The main advantage to seeding a lawn is that it is much less expensive. The disadvantages are the time and effort involved in maintaining the correct moisture level in a newly seeded lawn, and keeping pets and people from walking on it for several weeks.

SEEDING A LAWN

Several brands of grass seed mixtures are appropriate for our climate. They generally contain combinations of several grasses, with more of particular grasses in mixtures for sunny or shady areas. Kentucky bluegrass, which spreads rapidly by creeping roots, is winter-hardy and needs sun; creeping red fescue, which is best used in shady areas, tolerates drought. Sometimes a "nurse" grass that grows quickly to protect the emerging seedlings of the chosen lawn grass is added. It is an annual that does not survive the first winter.

Lawns can be seeded in the spring or fall. Mid-summer is usually too hot and dry. If seeds are sown in the spring, the plants have all summer to develop. Spring and early summer rains make watering easier; however, the grass seedlings will need constant care if the first summer is hot and dry. Lawns seeded in the early fall (mid-August to mid-September) have cooler weather to begin growth and still have long enough to develop sufficiently to survive their first winter.

The coverage is listed on packages of lawn seed so you can determine how many packages are needed. To find the area of the lawn in square metres or square feet, multiply the length by the width and subtract space taken up by trees, flower beds, sidewalks, and other landscape features. Don't be tempted to skimp on seed to save a few dollars or your lawn will be sparse and disappointing. Overseeding will not improve the lawn as each plant needs its own space for roots. Drop spreaders and broadcast spreaders, carried or designed to be hung around the neck, work very well. It is best to set the spreader at half the recommended rate and apply the seed in two right-angled passes to ensure a complete coverage. A light raking will give the seed little valleys to settle into. In areas where wind is a problem, or on a slope where seed may wash downhill, use burlap to cover the area just until the seed sprouts, then remove it immediately. The emerging seedlings will be pulled out with the burlap if you leave it on too long.

Keep newly seeded lawns damp until the seedlings have germinated and are growing well. Depending on soil temperature, most lawn seed takes between fourteen and twenty-one days to germinate. Water with a sprinkler or a hose nozzle with a soft spray rather than with an oscillating sprinkler, which may create puddles. Be careful not to drag a hose across the area as the tiny plants can be easily uprooted. As the lawn grows and the roots develop, water the lawn for a longer time and less often. An oscillating sprinkler can now be used to cover a wide area.

As the new lawn begins to grow, there may be many weeds growing even faster. They are not all bad. Weeds can shade and protect the emerging seedlings. Once the grass can be mowed, most weeds will be cut off and will not survive. Pull any remaining weeds by hand; do not use chemical herbicides on new grass. When the grass reaches a height of about 5 cm (2 in.), cut it cut back to 2.5 cm (1 in.). In dry, windy areas, allow the grass to grow a little longer before cutting.

SODDING A LAWN

Sod can be laid from spring well into fall, although laying sod in hot weather requires considerably more care and water. Sod is sold by the square metre in 2 x 0.5 m rolls. Determine the number of rolls required by using the same mathematical formula used for seeding. Arrange delivery so the sod can be laid within two days of arrival; it will dry out or decompose if it is left rolled too long. Prepare the soil as for seeding. Lay sod in a pattern like bricks with the seams staggered. It is best to begin at a straight edge, such as a sidewalk or patio. Butt edges snugly; if the sod needs to be trimmed to fit, do it cleanly with a sharp knife. Kneel on a board when laying the next row to prevent messing up the laid sod. Your weight on the board will also tamp down the sod to ensure good root contact. When the job is finished, check the area for high spots that need to be tamped down and low places that need filling. Water the area thoroughly, soaking through to the topsoil under the sod. Keep the new lawn moist until new growth is established. Gradually change the frequency to fewer and longer waterings.

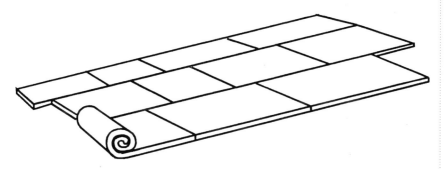

Stagger the seams when laying sod. DAN NOBERT

CARING FOR A LAWN

Wait until the lawn is dry in the spring before you begin to work on it to avoid compacting the damp turf. Rake the grass to remove any debris and to help it stand upright. Check your lawn mower for mechanical condition and sharpen the blade. Lawns are often fertilized to keep them green, but healthy, deep-rooted grass needs far less fertilizing. Wait until you can see weeds before using weed-and-feed fertilizers. Apply a time-release, high nitrogen fertilizer such as 27–14–0, 21–3–4, or 21–7–7 in mid-May. It will release its nutrients slowly over about six weeks. Do not apply fertilizer on wet grass as it may stick and cause chemical burns. Spread evenly, perhaps using a mechanical spreader, and water in well. Set the spreader at half the recommended rate and make two right-angled passes for more even coverage. If you spill granular fertilizer, scrape up as much as possible and then water the area copiously to dilute and distribute it. A second application of a time-release fertilizer in early July means you can relax for the rest of the summer. Fertilizers that are not time-released can leach out of the soil very quickly; excessive use results in a rush of growth that requires cutting two or three times a week.

Apply a winterizing fertilizer in mid- to late-September, while the lawn is still growing. Some nutrients are released immediately and help the plants withstand the stress of winter. While the lawn is still growing, winterizing weed-and-feed fertilizers work well; the weed killer is carried rapidly to the roots, which are gathering stores for winter. Most of the nutrients in the winterizing fertilizer will be activated when the weather becomes warm enough in the spring, so you don't need to watch our fitful spring weather to determine when to fertilize. There is little danger of the nutrients becoming active during a Chinook; although the air feels wonderfully warm, the soil remains cool, particularly when it is protected by a layer of turf.

Established lawns require water for good health and growth—approximately 2.5 cm (1 in.) every seven to ten days or when the soil has dried down to the root zone. If your grass has a slightly bluish tint or shows footprints, it is beginning to wilt and needs watering. Water should penetrate to a depth of 15–20 cm (6–8 in.) to encourage deep root growth. Healthy lawns that grow 8–10 cm (3–4 in.) high with deep root systems require less frequent watering. Such lawns also choke out weeds and are more resistant to pests. (See further information on watering, pests and diseases, and weeds in this chapter.)

Lawns that are not well cared for may develop thatch, which is a tightly interwoven mat of grass leaves and stems that repels water, prevents air circulation, provides a breeding ground for insects and disease, holds fertilizer, and encourages root growth in it instead of in the soil underneath. Common causes are using a quick-release nitrogen fertilizer that promotes excessive top growth, cutting grass very short, which causes shallow roots, leaving on excessive grass clippings, and watering often and lightly. Treating a serious case of thatch can be a long process, so prevention is preferable. Each spring, rake the lawn vigorously or use a power rake to break up the thatch; gather it up and add it to the compost pile. Every two or three years, use a core aerator to remove plugs of soil 5–8 cm (2–3 in.) deep. This aerates the lawn and allows penetration of water, fertilizer, and roots. Follow aeration by evenly spreading and watering in compost or organic fertilizer, such as well-aged manure, to add bacteria to help decompose grass clippings that can cause thatch buildup. Water deeply and less frequently and catch grass clippings if thatch appears.

Lawns can be disfigured by dog droppings and urine that cause excessive growth and then dead spots. Removing the manure and flooding the urine spots copiously to dilute and distribute the acidic matter helps.

There are many types of lawn mowers available; the one you choose depends on your personal preference. Just make sure it is mechanically sound and has a very sharp blade. Dull blades tear and bruise grass, causing damage that must be repaired before the grass can begin to grow. Sharp blades cut through thick grass easily, resulting in less wear and tear on the lawn and the mower.

Before cutting the grass, walk over the area and remove bones, rocks, sticks, and other debris that might cause damage to the mower or yourself. In the spring, cut grass to a height of 5–8 cm (2–3 in.) to encourage thicker growth. During the summer, when it starts to grow faster, you can let it grow to 8–10 cm (3–4 in.). The extra height encourages deeper roots and gives the plants more leaf area for food development. Longer grass also chokes out weeds and provides shade to help prevent the soil drying out. Cutting more than one-third of the height at any time drives the plants into shock. If the grass is cut frequently or with a mulching mower, the light grass clippings can be left on the lawn to decompose. Heavier clippings do not decompose well in our dry climate; rake them up or use a bag on the lawn mower to collect them for the compost pile. If the grass grows too high between mowings, cut it down to size gradually. Remove 5 cm (2 in.) on the first mowing. Let the lawn recover for several days, then cut another third, and so on until it is back to approximately 8 cm (3 in.). Gradually reduce the mowing height in the fall—no shorter than 5 cm (2 in.)— to help prevent matting during the winter. If possible, remove all debris and leaves before the first snowfall.

Weeding

A weed is, by broad definition, anything growing where it ought not to—the "lonely little petunia in an onion patch." A more specific definition of weeds is provided by the Alberta Department of Agriculture. If you are new to Alberta and unsure about a plant's status, check with the local Alberta Agriculture District Office, the Calgary Horticultural Society, or the City Parks Department.

"Know your enemy" holds true with weeds. How you approach weed control depends on how long the weeds live and how they propagate. Annual weeds, such as chickweed, are most easily eliminated if they are removed before they go to seed. Some annuals germinate late in the year, overwintering to flower and produce seed as early as mid-April, so diligence is needed to get these before copious amounts of seeds are released. Other annuals start out in the spring, giving you more time to deal with them. Biennial weeds allow you two seasons to eliminate them. Perennials, such as dandelions or thistles, persist until removed, establishing large communities if allowed to grow unchecked. Removal of enough root to ensure the plants die is as important as preventing seed production when dealing with perennial weeds. In all instances, it is easier to remove small weeds, or small numbers of weeds, than it is to deal with a large community of well-established weeds.

The first step in weed control is prevention. Obtain well-screened compost or loam, with few weed seeds or roots of perennial weeds. Use straw for winter mulch instead of hay, which contains weed seeds. Do not compost weeds that have set seed. Do not cut grass so short that lots of sunlight reaches the surface of the soil to encourage weed growth. Repair and reseed patches in the lawn where open soil invites weeds to grow. Mulch perennial and shrub beds with organic or inorganic mulches—this does not eliminate weeds, but it does make it harder for them to become established and easier to remove them.

If some weeds get by your early defence system—and some always will—get them while they are small. Weed patrol is a good reason to walk about and see everything that is going on in your garden. Frequent observation of what is happening helps detect not only weeds but also other pests and diseases, and keeps you on top of deadheading and other tasks.

If you decide to use herbicides, it is very important to know what kind of herbicide is appropriate, when is the best time to apply it, and how to use it safely. Try to select the weed-control approach with the lowest environmental impact. Read and follow all directions. Wear protective clothing. Do not use in windy conditions, as the wind will extend the area of application far beyond the intended area.

Herbicides fall into four types:

Pre-emergent herbicides contain germination inhibitors. They are useful for preventing annual weed growth among established perennials or trees and shrubs. They do not kill weeds that are already growing, but they do prevent most new ones from sprouting. Our relatively short growing season means one application in the spring is usually sufficient. Read the instructions on the package carefully. These products cannot be used around pansies or other members of the viola family, nor within two weeks of setting out new transplants. Obviously, they also cannot be used where desirable plants are being grown from seed.

Contact herbicides are absorbed through leaves and carried throughout the plant. They may be nonselective, killing anything they come into contact with, or selective, like broad-leaf herbicides, which kill many broad-leaved weeds but not grasses. They may be sprayed on large areas, sprayed selectively on individual plants, or brushed or painted on. Be careful that the spray does not drift onto desirable plants.

Soil sterilants are designed to prevent all plant growth in an area and remain active in the soil for two years or more. Use them with caution as watering and rain may leach them far beyond where they were originally applied. As well, it is impossible to determine the extent to which roots from trees and other plants, yours or your neighbour's, may extend into the area being treated.

Home remedy herbicides should be considered carefully. Salt and boiling water is sometimes recommended for eliminating grass encroaching into sidewalks or patio areas. Although this is effective in the short term, excessive amounts of salt leaching into the nearby soil, where plants grow, is detrimental.

If you decide to battle weeds with tools rather than herbicides, there are many varieties to consider. The dandelion digger will pry out a single weed very effectively. There are hoes to push and hoes to pull; there are hand cultivators and full-sized cultivators. The price usually reflects the quality of the tool, which suggests how long it will last. Look for something that feels comfortable, meets your needs, and fits your budget. When weeds appear in large enough numbers for you to take tools in hand and declare all-out war, proceed with caution. Use good body mechanics, exercising the larger muscles of your legs and arms instead of smaller back muscles. Remember, you are weeding, not cultivating. The idea is to remove the weeds, not to move large amounts of soil. Clean, sharp tools make the job easier. Like the common cold and mosquitoes, weeds will always be with us. But, with the right information and the right tools, we can keep them in check in our gardens.

Pest and Disease Control

Plants, diseases, and bugs have survived together for millions of years. The difficulty of pest control lies in deciding how to balance our need to protect our plants with our obligation to protect our surroundings and our health. Most of the time, it is a matter of learning what is causing the problem, what treatments are possible, and what will happen if nothing is done.

Most plants can easily survive a few holes in their leaves, as long as there is still enough leaf surface for photosynthesis. Some holes aren't caused by bugs. Shothole disease is common on 'Schubert' chokecherries in June, making the leaves look as if they have been peppered with a shotgun. The fungus that causes this is self-limiting and usually no longer active by the time the holes are noticed. There is no point in spraying an insecticide. Similarly, each insect has a different life cycle. If we recognize these cycles, we can apply controls at the most effective times; spraying to prevent bugs is ineffective before the bugs arrive or if it rains after we spray.

If you decide a plant needs help to survive or to maintain its health, there are several choices to eliminate or control the problem. A hard spraying with water from the garden hose is quite effective in keeping many pests under control, but it must be done regularly. You can hand pick some insects, such as potato beetles, off plants. Naturally existing controls, such as ladybugs to kill aphids, are

---

QUESTIONS TO ASK WHEN ASSESSING DAMAGE

- What caused the holes in the leaves? An insect, a fungus, or was it physical damage such as hail or wind?
- Is there evidence of a pest? masses of insects? a slimy slug trail? spider mites' webbing?
- Is the discolouration of a leaf the result of a disease or the leaf's reaction to a chemical applied to it or to the soil near it?
- Is the loss of needles or leaves a natural occurrence that happens to all trees at this stage of their maturity?
- Is what caused the damage still happening or did it happen at a particular time and won't likely happen again?
- Is the damage on a part of the tree that it really needs for survival, such as the main trunk, or a part that will be replaced, such as the end of a young branch?

another safe option. The only responsibility we have is to protect the ladybugs by not spraying with anything that harms them. Most people know that ladybugs are wonderful little aphid eaters and can easily recognize them. Few, however, recognize their larvae, which look like little royal blue armadillos with orange spots. They are even hungrier than their parents, so should not be destroyed. Unfortunately, natural controls are not always as successful as we would like. Ladybugs don't always choose our plants; purchasing them can be frustrating if the first thing they do is "fly away home" to someone else's garden.

There are many other beneficial insects. The big shiny black beetle that disappears quickly when disturbed in dark places eats cutworms, slugs, and small caterpillars. Spiders, of course, should not be harmed, as they are insect eaters. The striped, wasplike syrphid flies lay their eggs on plants badly infested with aphids so their larvae can eat them. Identifying insects is not always easy, but with practice and some help, you will gain more confidence in deciding whether to "kill the little beasts," to allow them to stay, or perhaps even to welcome them. A pocket lens can help with identification and a little research will open up a whole new world.

Next in line is using the safest chemical control that will do the job. Be aware of dangers to wildlife, pets, and humans. Some home-made remedies may actually be more toxic than commercially available ones. Because trade names change continuously as new products are developed and older ones are removed from the market or renamed, the suggestions that follow only recommend types of pesticides based on how they work, not brand names. Even chemical compounds change from time to time; few of us are very good at remembering complex chemical names anyway. Ask knowledgeable staff where you purchase your garden products for recommendations based on the suggested type of treatments for each pest. Read the label of the product thoroughly before you buy it. This gives you the opportunity to be sure it will do what you want and to ask any further questions.

The importance of reading and understanding labels cannot be overemphasized. The general principles are: follow the manufacturer's directions precisely; do not bring your hands to your mouth to eat or drink when using pesticides; wear protective clothing; wash exposed skin afterward.

Contact pesticides kill by coming in direct contact with a pest. They generally, but not always, have a short residual life (the length of time the chemical remains effective). Some pesticides, such as vegetable sprays, break down after one day. "Days to harvest" is the number of days, excluding the day of spraying, that must pass before it is safe to eat sprayed food. It is wise to explore any possible alternatives before using chemical controls on plants used as food. Many other pesticides have a sixty- to ninety-day residue; these should never be used on edible plants, although they are safe for flowers.

Systemic pesticides are absorbed by the plant and carried by the sap to make the plant poisonous to pests. Even the fumes can be very toxic, and because these chemicals are absorbed through a membrane, they can also be absorbed through a person's skin.

INSECT PESTS

Ants. Ants are neither necessary nor harmful to peonies; they are simply attracted to the sweet nectar. However, ants do "farm" aphids for the honeydew they provide, so should be somewhat controlled in the garden. Ants in ant hills can also cut through the roots of plants with their tunnelling. They can be eliminated with boiling water if there are no plants close by. A powdered insecticide can be used around flowers, but check for safety before using it near vegetables. Ant poison, which the ants take back as food to the whole hill, is available in tins with very small holes. Put the tin under a bit of board or an upturned flower pot if children are around.

Aphids. Aphids, which can be almost any colour and large or tiny, attack many different plants. Leaves, particularly new ones, are curled and distorted. Stem tips can be totally hidden from sight by a mass of aphids. The sticky honeydew they excrete attracts ants. The honeydew can be covered with a sooty mould, further disfiguring the leaves. Hosing down affected plants with a steady stream of water cleans up plants temporarily. A small infestation can be wiped off and squished between your gloved fingers. Aphids are difficult to eradicate totally, as they produce live, female, pregnant young. Be selective and chemically spray only those plants that really need it.

Birch Leaf Miners. The damage caused by birch leaf miners is first noticed as light green spots on the leaves of birch trees. These spots become larger and brown as the season progresses. The larvae are feeding between the upper and lower surfaces of the leaves and can only be reached by a systemic insecticide applied as a soil drench around the tree. This is done just as the leaf buds are opening. This chemical treatment does not kill the insects in the soil; the chemical is drawn up the tree as the sap flows upward, making the leaves poisonous to the larvae. A tree that is well watered and healthy will be more resistant to this pest.

Caterpillars. Caterpillars are the larvae of a number of insects. They munch on tender vegetables and the leaves of flowers and trees. Watch to see how much damage is being done. Sometimes you can pick caterpillars off by hand or hose them off with a strong spray of water and then collect them for disposal. There are insecticides that are safe to use on vegetables, often up to one day before harvest. Row covers can prevent cabbage butterflies from laying eggs on the plants. You must put these on before the little white butterflies start hovering over the cabbage plants. There is also a biological control, *Bacillus thuringiensis,* that infects and kills the caterpillar. These bacteria can be destroyed by chlorine in water or by sunlight, so mix the solution with water drawn from the tap the day before to allow the chlorine to dissipate, and apply it at dusk.

The tiny caterpillar that damages the flower heads of delphinium and monkshood in May is the larva of the delphinium moth (golden plusia). You can control it by dusting the developing tips with rose or flower dust at regular intervals in early spring. Because these pests have only one life cycle a year, another approach is to cut the plants back to the ground when they are 30 cm (12 in.) high. Dispose of the foliage and the caterpillars in the garbage. New growth quickly replaces the parts you have removed. Alternatively, just snap off damaged stems and dispose of them.

Cutworms. Suspect cutworms if a plant suddenly wilts, and upon inspection, you see it has been chewed off at ground level. Damage is commonly seen in June. Prevention is the best control. Sink collars made from cardboard milk cartons, or cans with the ends removed, into the soil around the stems to prevent cutworms from getting near seedlings. There are also chemical controls that are relatively safe to use; apply them at night, which is when the dull grey cutworm is active.

Lilac Leaf Miner. The larvae of lilac leaf miners feed between the upper and lower surfaces of lilac leaves, eventually creating brown patches. After they emerge, they roll the leaves up and continue feeding. You can dislodge the eggs by spraying the underside of the leaves in late May, you can pick off damaged leaves, or you can use a systemic insecticide.

Maggots. Maggots can make root vegetables inedible. Where you have had problems with maggots in previous years, spread a granular maggot insecticide along the rows at planting time and reapply it a couple of times during the growing season. You can also rotate vegetables each year so that foliage-type vegetables are in the soil that root vegetables were in the year before.

Sod Web-worms. Sod web-worms spin silken webs at the base of grass. Their larvae chew off the grass near the roots, causing irregularly shaped dead patches in the lawn. A lawn insecticide is the only control.

Thrips. Thrips are tiny so the whitish streaks they produce where they have sucked the juices from the plant are usually the first indication of their presence. The gladiolus thrip also attacks iris and is best controlled by treating the corms while they are in storage. Foliar insecticidal sprays can be used in the garden.

Yellowheaded Spruce Sawfly. Spruce sawfly larvae are likely the first pests you will notice in the spring. They look like little green caterpillars with yellow heads, and they chew new needles on spruce trees, leaving bare tips on the branches and distorted brown needles. Watch for them in early June; the larvae look just like the needles on the tree, so are often not noticed until the damage is done. A strong spray of water dislodges them temporarily. Contact insecticide is effective.

OTHER GARDEN PESTS

Dew Worms. Dew worms are huge earthworms that create mounds of heavy clay soil, or castings, brought up from a metre or so (3 ft) below the ground. The castings make a lawn look and feel very bumpy. The worms are brought in with new plants or a load of soil. You can reduce their numbers by limiting their food. Rake up dead grass and remove grass clippings to the compost heap. Alternatively, water deeply to encourage the worms to go deeper into the soil, where their castings will be less noticeable. There are contact chemicals that kill the worms, but they break down fairly quickly in the soil. More worms will soon move in from places where the chemical has not been applied, such as flower beds, where lumps don't matter, under driveways, or from the neighbour's yard.

If chemicals are continually added to the soil, beneficial earthworms will not survive. It is not advisable to roll the lawn to eliminate the lumps, as that compacts the soil. A better approach is to give the lawn a good stiff raking regularly to eliminate the lumps and, possibly, to fill in the hollows with topsoil.

Slugs. Slugs thrive in damp, cool weather. If leaves of flowers and vegetables develop jagged holes, watch for the slimy, silvery trails of slugs and check under leaves regularly. They are said not to be as active in hot, dry weather, as they cannot easily crawl across dry soil. However, warm weather encourages lush growth, meaning slugs do not need to travel as far to find food; plants stressed by heat seem more susceptible too. A cover of sharp sand, or a product called diatomaceous earth, spread on the soil around their favourite plants, such as pansies, hostas, marigolds, and strawberries, slows them down. Keep soil free of debris where slugs can hide and check under organic mulches from time to time. If you have the stomach for it, go out in the early morning or in the evening with a flashlight and hand pick them. Drop them into a jar of salty water. Or place a board or half an eaten grapefruit in an area where slugs abound and scrape off the slugs you collect into your water jar. Don't put a board down unless you are prepared to remove slugs daily or you will simply create a slug hotel. An empty tin filled with beer and buried to the lip in the soil can attract and drown up to two hundred slugs per tin. If you must use slug bait, remember it is very attractive—and poisonous—to dogs and cats. There is no antidote. Some baits are said to be bitter and less attractive to pets, but they are still poisonous. A safer method is to use small margarine containers with slug-sized holes punched in the sides near the bottom. Put the slug bait in the containers and replace the lids. If these are placed under plants where slugs are, you can empty them, or simply throw them away when they are full. Around vegetables, only use slug bait as a barrier, well removed from the vegetables themselves.

Spider Mites. Spider mites attack spruce, junipers, and roses in hot, dry weather, but are less likely to be a problem during rainy weather. When the weather turns warm and dry, watch carefully for fine webs that look like angel hair on a Christmas tree, with tiny white specks, finer than pepper grains, in the webs. A regular hosing down with water helps prevent them from taking hold. If a pesticide is necessary, choose a mite killer rather than an insecticide as these little pests are related to spiders and are not true insects.

ANIMAL PESTS

Cats. Cats can be a real irritant when they choose your flower beds for their toilet, especially if they aren't your cats. The problem is usually noticed in a warm and dry south-facing bed in the winter. An easy solution is to cover the bed with chicken wire in the fall so the cats cannot dig in it. During the summer, use the chicken wire to support peas or other vines and re-use it in the fall. The soil is moist in the summer and more places are available, so the cats probably won't be as much of a problem. Fences and gates can also be designed to keep out all but the most agile cat. If you are around to provide control, a spray with a water gun will encourage cats to go somewhere else. Another solution is to create a

"Japanese garden" for them. Dig a hole about 15 cm (6 in.) deep and 30 cm (12 in.) square. Fill it with sand and put some rocks and plants around it to give the cats privacy. They will love it and leave your other flower beds alone. Don't forget to clean it out from time to time. Calgary's cat by-law restricts cats to their own property; the Calgary Horticultural Society has plans for a cat run that can be copied.

Deer. Deer have become a real problem in neighbourhoods close to natural areas. They eat evergreens and the bark of ornamental trees, particularly in the winter, when food in their natural habitat is scarce. They often disappear in the summer, but if they visit, they eat almost anything in the garden, even plants reputed to be deer resistant. They show a preference for tender new growth; new shrubs in deer-prone areas may need to be protected with chicken wire for a few years. A variety of deterrents can be tried; new methods are needed as the deer become accustomed to older ones. Bars of strongly scented soap, hung like Christmas ornaments at deer-nose height from trees, may keep them away; some people swear by human hair hung the same way. Chips of the same soap often keep them away from flower beds. Metallic ribbons and sheets or motion-detector lights may have some effect. Deer like to be able to see where they will land before jumping; planting shrubs inside your fence may deter them. There are also chemicals that make the bark of trees taste unpleasant but do not hurt either the tree or the deer. They are painted or sprayed on, but can only be applied to bark not to foliage. This will also deter rabbits, as will wrapping the trunk to make nibbling more difficult.

Squirrels. Squirrels may look cute and many people like to feed them, but they can be very destructive in the garden. Black and grey squirrels are not native to this area. They escaped from the Calgary Zoo in the 1930s and have been spreading out from Saint George's Island ever since. Few areas in the city are free of them now, and they have been reported in Okotoks and Strathmore. The black colour is actually a recessive gene, so in time we will see more of the grey colour. Squirrels love to eat bulbs and will also eat flowers and the new growth on shrubs. Blood meal is said to discourage but not harm them. Sprinkle it around bulb and flower beds. It is useful in supplying nitrogen to the soil as well, but has to be replenished regularly after rain. Plants and bulbs can be covered with chicken wire to keep squirrels away. Various homemade repellents, such as cayenne pepper, can be tried, but a better solution might be to offer them an alternate food, such as sunflower seeds.

DISEASES

Cytospora Canker. Cytospora canker is a fungus that commonly affects fruit trees, saskatoons, mountain ash, and cotoneaster shrubs and hedges. It is often mistaken for fireblight but it has a very different appearance. Cracks along the branches, with the bark peeled back from the crack, are often the first indications that it is present. Leaves and branches beyond this point die slowly from lack of water and nutrients. Later, little orange dots appear on the dead wood. This is nectria canker, another fungus that lives on dead wood and indicates

DUTCH ELM DISEASE

Dutch elm disease is a fungus disease that clogs the water-conducting vessels of trees and eventually kills them. It only affects elms and has wiped out many magnificent trees in the eastern parts of the country. The disease is spread by elm bark beetles, a few of which were collected in monitoring traps in Calgary in 1994. The presence of these beetles does not necessarily mean our trees have the disease, but it does mean they are at risk. If you have elm trees, keeping them well watered and healthy will increase their resistance. Watch for drooping, curling, and yellow or brown leaves early in the season. Call Calgary Parks and Recreation for more information.

areas that have been killed by the cytospora canker or other diseases. Cytospora canker is particularly prevalent in cotoneaster hedges in wet weather, where the interior has little light or air circulation. It cannot be cured because the fungus is in the sap of the plant. Keeping the plant well fertilized will help, as will pruning out a lot of the interior dead wood and shortening the hedge to enable light to encourage new growth to fill in the centre. Pruning branches well below the affected part on fruit trees improves the appearance of a tree, but if new infections occur, or it appears in the trunk, the tree may not survive. There is no fungicide that has any affect on cytospora canker. Sanitize pruning tools before using them on other plants to avoid spreading the disease.

Fairy Ring. Fairy ring is a lawn disease in which rings of deeper green grass appear, often with mushrooms in them. Eventually the grass dies and turns brown in the ring. The cause is a fungus that forms an impenetrable mass of fungal mycelium, like roots, below the surface that moisture cannot penetrate. Flood the area with water, perhaps adding a little dish soap, and puncture the whole area repeatedly with a garden fork. Apply a high-nitrogen fertilizer and keep the area very well watered and fertilized. The sooner the treatment is begun, the less effort it will take to cure the problem.

Fireblight. Fireblight is a bacterial infection. It affects the same plants as cytospora canker, so confusion is common. The first symptom of fireblight occurs as a tree flowers. Typically, blossoms and leaves on affected branches suddenly turn brown and hang on the tree. The farther down the branch, the darker brown they are, so that at the tip they look scorched, hence the name. The tip of the branch curls over like a shepherd's crook. Cankers exude bacterial ooze that is spread by rain, wind, insects, and pruning tools. If fruit forms, it turns leathery and dark and remains on the tree. Preventative treatment should be applied if there are infected trees in your immediate area. Blossoms, the most susceptible part, can be sprayed with copper spray when they first open and every four to five days until they have finished blooming. Read labels and follow instructions for safe application. There is no chemical control for fireblight once it occurs. Prune out affected branches well below the diseased part, sanitizing the pruning tools after each cut. Seal pruned branches in plastic bags and put them in the garbage. If a tree is severely affected for several years, or large cankers form in the trunk, it cannot be saved and should be removed to avoid spreading the infection to other trees.

Powdery Mildew. Powdery mildew, or *Spaerotheca pannosa,* is a fungus that makes plants look as if they have been dusted with dirty icing sugar. The disease can cover most of the foliage. New growth is misshapen and eventually dies. Some plants, such as perennial phlox, delphinium, bee balm, and begonias, are particularly susceptible, so it is a good idea to look for resistant varieties. Controls include keeping plants healthy to be more resistant, improving air circulation by keeping them well spaced, and watering in the morning, rather than in the evening, so foliage is dry before nightfall. Using too much high-nitrogen fertilizer on lawns also may encourage mildew. There are systemic fungicides, but they are quite expensive. Contact fungicides, such as powdered sulphur, may be less effective as rain, which encourages powdery mildew, also washes off the fungicide. Home remedies, such as baking soda or baby powder, may work but bear in mind they may add unwanted elements to your soil.

There are, of course, many more pests and diseases than these. Check your plants daily to learn how they develop and to notice problems before they become too serious. By learning what to expect, you will have more confidence in your own judgement and a garden that is in balance with nature. If in doubt, ask someone you trust—a good gardener, a horticultural help line, or a knowledgeable person at a garden centre. Avoid having your yard sprayed routinely. It is ineffective, expensive, and environmentally wrong.

Pruning

Each tree and shrub has a natural shape. It should be pruned to encourage that natural shape and never sheared—unless it is in a hedge. A tree that has been pruned to a pleasing and appropriate shape when it is young requires very little pruning as it matures. Stand back from the tree to visualize its future shape and prune to create space for each branch. Tying bright ribbons on the branches you intend to remove will help you visualize the end result and avoid cutting the wrong branches. Never remove more than one-third of the branches in one year as heavy pruning may cause excessive and weak growth.

Pruning is also important for a tree's health. Remove diseased wood to prevent the spread of infection, and cut away excess branches to allow light to penetrate into the centre of trees, such as fruit trees, for good fruit production. Pruning can correct poor placement of branches, weak growth that will never develop properly, and crossed branches that rub and provide a place for pests and disease to enter. Pruning can also rejuvenate plants by stimulating new growth; often a third or a quarter of the old growth is removed each year to encourage a plant to produce new, more colourful stems. Many shrubs benefit from having all the litter in the middle thinned out every few years. Finally, some forms of pruning are done to train a tree or shrub in a specific style, such as an espalier with branches trained flat against a wall.

Sanitize pruning tools after each cut where disease is suspected with a mixture of 50 mL (1/4 cup) disinfectant such as Lysol or Dettol mixed with 1 L (4 cups) water, or 100 mL (1/2 cup) bleach to 1 L (4 cups) water.

There are a few simple pruning rules that are important—and easy to remember. Size can be controlled by pruning within certain limits but it is far better to choose the right-sized plant in the first place; heavy pruning to maintain size can result in some very unnatural and ugly specimens. Too sharply angled joins or "crotches," which are weak and may break, should have the less important branch removed, preferably leaving the branch with a crotch closest to an 80- or 90-degree angle from the trunk. Prune away branches growing against the natural shape of the tree. If the tree has a spreading shape, remove the little branches, or water sprouts, that grow straight up. This type of growth is usually too soft and spindly to amount to much. Suckers, which are unwanted shoots coming from the roots of the plant, can be ripped off in the late summer each year. If they are left to persist, they will have to be excavated and cut off flush against the trunk below the surface of the soil.

Use sharp tools when pruning and make as clean a cut as possible. Shredded bark around a wound invites insects and disease to enter. In general, there is no need to seal the cut with chemical sealers or paints. Trees heal themselves by sealing off the cut areas with calluses that close off the soft, living tissues from the cut.

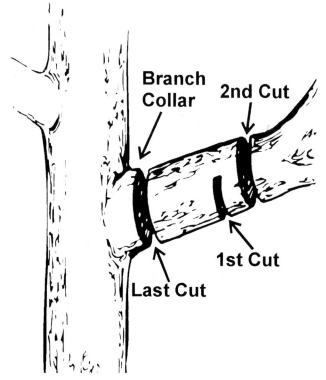

Branch Collar

2nd Cut

1st Cut

Last Cut

Healing is better if the "collar" or ridge of bark is not damaged. DAN NOBERT

Cut a branch just beyond the slight swelling or collar where it joins the tree; injuring the collar makes it difficult for the tree to callus over the wound. Leaving a stump makes this healing more difficult and may result in a branch that dies back to the main trunk. Any cuts to shorten a branch are made just above or beyond an outward- or upward-facing, smaller branch or bud, cutting at a 45-degree angle with the higher point above the bud in the direction you want the growth to go.

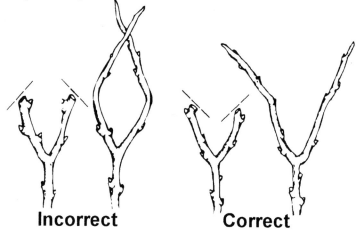

Incorrect **Correct**

Prune at a 45-degree angle just above an out-facing bud. DAN NOBERT

Most deciduous trees, with the exception of maple and birch, are pruned in early spring before they start to leaf out but after severe frosts are over—late March or early April. The wounds callus over quickly as the trees start to grow and are well healed by winter. Pruning in the fall (after mid-August) is not necessarily harmful, but the wounds have less chance of healing well with our dry air and cold temperatures. Fall pruning that does not heal bleeds the following spring and weakens the tree. Birch and maples bleed copiously if they are pruned when the sap is moving quickly up the tree in the spring. By late June or July, the sap is no longer under such pressure and they can be safely pruned.

Trees and shrubs that bloom in the spring or early summer are best pruned just after flowering is finished. This is because they are blooming on last year's wood from flower buds that formed in the fall. If you cut the branch ends of trees such as lilacs in the fall or early spring, they will not bloom. Trees that bear flowers along their branches, such as Nanking cherry or bridal wreath spirea, will bloom on what remains of the branch but will produce fewer flowers. Pruning these plants after flowering has the added benefit that they will likely replace the one branch cut off with two or three branches, meaning there will be more space for flower buds to form for next year. Pruning before blooming does not harm these plants. You might sacrifice flowers for a season and prune in the early spring or fall for other reasons—to shorten long branches that have been broken by a heavy snowfall or to take advantage of bare branches to see into an overcrowded centre.

Summer-blooming shrubs, such as potentilla, shrub roses, or the pink-flowering spireas, have flowers that are formed on the new growth of the present season. They are pruned in the very early spring, before this new growth, with its flower buds, begins. No further pruning is done, unless it is important enough to sacrifice flowers.

Evergreens present special pruning problems and are rarely pruned as much as deciduous trees and shrubs. The leaders, or spires, should never be removed. Do not cut off the lower limbs of spruce trees as the tree needs them to shade the roots and reduce evaporation. Mugho pines benefit from having their new growth, or candles, reduced to one-half or one-third each June, after they have elongated but before the needles have developed. This keeps the trees bushy and compact. Similar pruning can occasionally be done with spruce, but if it is done on a regular basis, it creates such a dense outside surface that the needles on the inside of the tree die from lack of light. Junipers and cedars can be lightly shaped to remove winterkill and encourage denser growth in the early summer, but should be allowed to develop in a natural manner and not artificially sheared.

Hedges may be trimmed several times in a season. Some gardeners think that pruning later in the season has a dwarfing effect as the plant has less energy to put out replacement growth. After leaf drop in the fall or before new growth in the spring are good times to thin out dead wood in the centre of hedges. Flowering hedge plants are pruned in the same way as individual shrubs; they are often left as untrimmed hedges so blossoms are not sacrificed. Prune all hedges so that they are slightly wider at the bottom than at the top, to allow light to reach the bottom branches.

If you are going to hire someone to prune for you, be sure you hire a competent professional. Ask to see credentials, which should indicate a licensed arbourist. Get price quotes from several companies and go and look at work they have done. If you are not sure, ask the opinion of someone you trust before letting your tree "go under the knife."

Afterword

Gardens evolve as gardeners' skills and confidence grow. For many new garden-ers, their earliest attempts at choosing plants focus on annuals, which represent a smaller initial investment than perennials or shrubs. For example, to a new gar-dener, petunias often look like a safe bet. With masses to choose from at the local garden centre, they seem to give quite a "colour bang for the buck." Beginning gardeners search for the baskets with the most plants, buy the tallest ones (in full bloom), set them out in smart rows, hope for instant flower beds, and are happy if the plants survive.

Soon, with a little more experience and the sharing of new-found knowledge with neighbours and friends, gardeners start to make choices. They realize they do not have to grow the orange marigolds of their youth and there are alterna-tives to cotoneaster for creating attractive hedges. Gardening became a passion for one Calgarian when she abandoned the once-obligatory vegetable garden and left behind years of guilt from chickweed-infested peas and un-thinned rows of carrots fighting for space. Her vegetable patch was transformed into a beauti-ful trellis-enclosed garden room alive with pink shrub roses, clematis, veronicas, and catmint (the raspberries were allowed to stay.)

Novice gardeners often limit their use of gardening books to quickly checking the height, colour, or soil requirements of a particular plant before hurrying back to their flower beds. However, as their enthusiasm grows, many people find themselves enjoying gardening books for their own sakes, often acquiring new ones for their libraries and becoming much more knowledgeable on matters horticultural along the way.

As gardeners read more gardening books and magazines, participate in gar-den tours, or join horticultural societies, they are introduced to new plants and start to look a little farther afield for them, searching out less common or novel species that appeal. They take weekend drives to country nurseries in search of unusual trees or shrubs. For them, the idea of trying perennial plants that return year after year is appealing, and when they buy annuals to fill in the blank spots in their newly created perennial border, they now know that smaller, more com-pact plants transplant better than the taller ones in full flower, their blooms already half-spent. Moreover they notice that groups of five or seven plants make a greater colour impact than plants placed singly in rows. They may also have the courage and confidence to spend a small fortune ordering bulbs from an enticing looking mail-order catalogue—a previously inconceivable notion!

Eventually, committed gardeners decide to get really serious and grow some coveted species of perennials from seed under growlights. A whole new world of opportunity opens up to fill those frustrating days early in the year before it is possible to get outside to dig in the dirt again. Botanical plant names begin to drift around in their heads—although it will be a while yet before they trip off their tongues. For those who have been hooked, gardening is a joy instead of a chore; more often than not they find themselves thinking in terms of vistas in the landscape, shape, form, seasons, and winter colour. At the same time their gardens show evidence of maturing, much like someone making a successful transition to graceful middle age. In the end, the dedicated gardeners know that much of the pleasure of gardening lies in envisioning how their gardens will evolve in the future. Although their visions may never quite be achieved, they know they can always try again next year!

Further Reading

These books are all in print at press time, and have been chosen to be either useful local guides or to provide you with plenty of colour pictures, mostly both. Many of them can be borrowed from local libraries. We greatly regret that we cannot, for lack of space, provide a complete annotated bibliography, but one is available from the Calgary Horticultural Society office.

Bartholomew, Mel. *Square Foot Gardening.* Emmaus, PA: Rodale Press, 1981.

Bennet, J., and T. Forsyth. *The Harrowsmith Annual Garden.* Camden East, ON: Camden House, 1990.

Black & Decker. *Building Decks: Black & Decker Home Improvement Library.* Minnetonka, MN: Cy DeCosse, 1991.

Brickell, Christopher, ed. *The Gardener's Encyclopedia of Plants and Flowers.* London, UK: Dorling Kindersley, 1989.

Chaflin, E. B. *Garden Pools and Fountains.* San Ramon, CA: Ortho Books, 1988.

Chatto, Beth. *The Dry Garden.* London, UK: J. M. Dent & Sons, 1978.

Editors of Sunset Books and Sunset Magazine. *Waterwise Gardening, Beautiful Gardens With Less Water.* Menlo Park, CA: Lane Publishing, 1989.

Fair, Keith, and Carol Fair. *Clematis for Colour and Versatility.* Swindon, UK: The Crowood Press, 1990.

Harper, Pamela, and Frederick McGourty. *Perennials — How to Select, Grow & Enjoy.* Tucson, AZ: HP Books, 1985.

Harris, Marjorie. *The Canadian Gardener's Guide to Foliage & Garden Design.* Toronto: Random House, 1993.

Hayword, Gordon. *Garden Paths: Inspiring Designs and Practical Projects.* Charlotte, VT: Camden House, 1993.

Hessayon, D. G. *The Flower Expert.* London, UK: Expert Books, 1993.

Hill, Lewis. *Pruning Simplified.* Rev. ed. Pownal, VT: Storey Communications, 1986.

Hole, Lois. *Lois Hole's Northern Flower Gardening, Bedding Plants: A Guide for Cooler Climates.* Edmonton, AB: Lone Pine, 1994.

Hole, Lois. *Lois Hole's Northern Vegetable Gardening: A Guide for Cooler Climates.* Edmonton, AB: Lone Pine, 1993.

Ireland-Gannon Associated, Inc. *The Backyard Landscaper: 40 Professional Designs for Do-it-Yourselfers.* Wixom, MI: Home Planners, 1989.

Knowles, Hugh. *Woody Ornamentals for the Prairies.* Edmonton, AB: University of Alberta Press, 1989.

Kublick, Lyn. *The Prairie Herb Garden.* Saskatoon, SK: Western Producer Prairie Books, 1990.

Mather, Jan. *Designing Alberta Gardens: The Complete Guide to Beautiful Gardens.* Red Deer, AB: Red Deer College Press, 1994.

Millarville Horticultural Club. *Gardening Under the Arch.* Millarville, AB: Millarville Horticultural Club, 1982.

Neal, Bill. *Gardener's Latin: A Lexicon*. Chapel Hill, NC: Algonquin Books, 1992.

Ortho Books. *Easy Composting*. San Ramon, CA: Ortho Books, Chevron Chemical Company, 1992.

Osborne, Robert. *Roses for Canadian Gardens*. Toronto: Key Porter, 1991.

Pearman, Myrna. *Winter Bird Feeding: An Alberta Guide*. Lacombe, AB: Ellis Bird Farm, 1991.

Philips, Sue, and Neil Sutherland. *A Creative Step-by-Step Guide to Container Gardening*. North Vancouver, BC: Whitecap, 1994.

Reader's Digest Association Limited. *Reader's Digest Encyclopaedia of Garden Plants and Flowers*. London, UK: Reader's Digest, 1993 (reprinted with amendments).

Robinson, Mary A. *Alpines: Step-by-Step to Growing Success*. Marlborough, UK: The Crowood Press, 1991.

Scott, George Harmon. *Bulbs: How to Select, Grow, and Enjoy*. Tucson, AZ: HP Books, 1985.

Shewchuk, George W. *Rose Gardening on the Prairies*. Edmonton, AB: University of Alberta Faculty of Extension, 1988.

Toop, Edgar, and Sarah Williams, eds. *Perennials for the Prairies*. Edmonton, AB: University of Alberta and University of Saskatchewan Faculty of Extension, 1991.

Vick, Roger. *Gardening on the Prairies*. Vancouver, BC: Douglas & McIntyre, 1992

Vladicka, Betty. Alberta Tree Nursery and Horticultural Centre. *Alberta Horticultural Guide*. Edmonton, AB: Alberta Agriculture, Food and Rural Development, 1994.

Yakimovich-Parenteau, Virginia. *The Prairie Landscape Design Guide*. Streamstown, AB: Virginia Yakimovich-Parenteau, 1990.

Resource List

Plants

PERENNIALS, BULBS, ETC.

Aimers Seeds and Bulbs
81 Temperance Street
Aurora, ON L4G 2R1

Cruickshanks, Inc.
1015 Mount Pleasant Road
Toronto, ON M4P 2M1

Ferncliff Gardens
8394 McTaggart Street
S.S.1, Mission, BC V2V 5V6

Garden Import
P.O. Box 760
Thornhill, ON L3T 4A5

Prism Perennials
C 45, S 25, RR#1
Castlegar, BC V1N 3H7

Rainforest Gardens
13139 224th Street, RR#2
Maple Ridge, BC V2X 7E7

Stirling Perennials
RR#1, Dept. T
Morpeth, ON N0P 1X0

Wrightman Alpines
RR#3
Kerwood, ON N0M 2B0

ROSES

Corn Hill Nursery Ltd.
RR#5, Route 890
Petitcodiac, NB E0A 2H0

Hardy Roses for the North
Box 2048
Grand Forks, BC V0H 1H0

Pickering Nurseries
670 Kingston Road
Pickering, ON L1V 1A6

TREES, SHRUBS, ETC.

Boughen Nurseries
Valley River, MB R0L 2B0

Morden Nurseries
P.O. Box 1270
Morden, MB R0G 1J0

Saskatoon Farm
RR#1
DeWinton, AB T0L 0X0

Sprout Farms
(fruit tree nursery)
P.O. Box 538
Bon Accord, AB T0A 0K0

MISCELLANEOUS PLANT SOURCES

Eagle Lake Nurseries
P.O. Box 2340
Strathmore, AB T1P 1K3

Edwards Garden Centre
7948 Bowness Road NW
Calgary, AB T3B 0H2

Golden Acre Garden
Sentres Ltd.
620 Goddard Avenue NE
Calgary, AB T2K 5X3

Golden Acre Garden
Sentres Ltd.
14111 Macleod Trail SW
Calgary, AB T2Y 1M6

Holes Greenhouses
101 Belrose Drive
St. Albert, AB T8N 1M9

Sunnyside Greenhouses
3439 69 Street NW
Calgary, AB T3B 2J8

Vale's Greenhouse
& Landscape Design
3rd Street NW
Black Diamond, AB T0L 0H0

Seed Sources

VEGETABLES AND FLOWERS

Alberta Nurseries and
Seed Company
P.O. Box 20
Bowden, AB T0M 0K0

Dominion Seed Company
115 Guelph Street
Guelph Street and Maple Ave
Georgetown, ON L7G 4A2

McKenzie Seeds
Brandon, MB R7A 4A4

Stokes Seed Company
39 St. James Street
St. Catharines, ON L2R 6R6

Vesey's Seeds Ltd.
York, PEI C0A 1P0

HERBS

Richters Herb Catalogue
Goodwood, ON L0C 1A0

WILDFLOWERS

ALCLA Native Plant
Restorations Inc.
3208 Bearspaw Drive NW
Calgary, AB T2L 1T2

The Canadian
Wildflower Society
4981 Highway 7 East,
Unit 12A
Markham, ON L3R 1N1
(membership required)

Friends of the Devonian
Botanic Garden
University of Alberta
Edmonton, AB T6G 2E1
(membership required)

Living Prairie Museum
2795 Ness Avenue
Winnipeg, MB R3J 1S4

Prairie Habitats
P.O. Box 1
Argyle, MB R0C 0B0
(catalogue $2.00)

HERITAGE SEEDS

Heritage Seed Program
RR#3
Uxbridge, ON L9P 1R3

Water Garden Supplies and Plants

Bearberry Creek
Greenhouses and Nursery
RR#2
Sundre, AB T0M 1X0

Moore Water Gardens
P.O. Box 340
Port Stanley, ON N0L 2A0

Books

Capability's Books
2379 Highway 46
Deer Park, WI 54007

Harrowsmith
Camden House Publishing
7 Queen Victoria Road
Camden East, ON K0K 1J0

Timber Press
9999 SW Wilshire, Suite 124
Portland, OR 97225

Botanic Gardens

Calgary Zoo,
Botanical Gardens,
and Prehistoric Park
P.O. Box 3036, Stn. B
Calgary, AB T2M 4R8

Devonian Botanic Garden
University of Alberta
Edmonton, AB T6G 2E1

Royal Botanic Garden
P.O. Box 399
Hamilton, ON L8N 3H8

UBC Botanic Garden
6804 SW Marine Drive
Vancouver, BC V6T 1Z4

Van Dusen Botanic Garden
5251 Oak Street
Vancouver, BC V6M 4H1

Societies

*(The officers in societies
change yearly. Contact the
CHS office to receive the
current membership person's
name of the society in which
you are interested.)*

Calgary African Violet
Society

Calgary Bonsai Society

Calgary Horticultural
Society

Calgary Rock and Alpine
Garden Society (CRAGS)

Calgary Rose Society

Foothills Orchid Society

Stampede City African
Violet Society

The Canadian
Wildflower Society
4981 Highway 7 East,
Unit 12A
Markham, ON L3R 1N1

Index

In this index, numbers appearing in bold indicate the main reference to a plant or topic; italic type indicates photographs or illustrations.

Iron chlorosis 179, 193
Irrigation. *See* Watering
Ivy 27, **78** (perennial), **149** (annual). *See also*
    Engelmann ivy; Kenilworth ivy
Ixiolirion (ixiolirion) **134**

J

Jacob's ladder (*Polemonium*) 46, 47, **117–18**, 138
Japanese painted fern (*Athyrium niponicum pictum*
    syn *A. goeringianum*) **129**
Japanese spurge (*Pachysandra terminalis*) 47, 103, **114**
Japanese tree lilac (*Syringea reticulata*) 44, 50, **69**
Johnny jump-ups (*Viola tricolor*) **126**, 137
Journal, keeping a 9–11
June drop (in apples) 71
Juniperus spp. (juniper) *14, 23, 30,* 32, 33, 34, 35, 43,
    44, 46, 61, 65

K

Kale, edible **169**, 174
Kale, ornamental (*Brassica oleracea*) 147, **151**, 161
Kenilworth ivy (*Cymbalaria muralis*) 27, 59, **149**, 161
King cup. *See* Marsh marigold
Kinnikinnick (*Arctostaphylos uva-ursi*) 34, 35, 47,
    92, 103
Knapweed. *See* Cornflower
Kohlrabi **169–70**, 174

L

Lady fern (*Athyrium filix-femina*) **128–29**
Lady's mantle (*Alchemilla mollis*) **91**, 137
Ladybugs **217–18**
Lambs' ears (*Stachys byzantina*) 24, 26, 31, 32, 43, 55,
    123
Lamiastrum galeobdolon (archangel) 47, 103, **108**
Lamium maculatum (dead nettle, lamium) 47,
    103, **108–09**
Landscaping, hard 20–22
Large gardens, planning 28–30
Larix spp. (larch) **63**
Larkspur. *See* Delphinium
Lathyrus latifolius (everlasting pea) **109**
Lathyrus odoratus (sweet pea) 26, 27, 30, 33, 41, *42,*
    52, 150, 158, 162, 204
Lavandula angustifolia (lavender) 33, 34, 53, **109**
Lavatera trimestris (lavatera) *10,* 53, **149–50**, *149,* 161
Lawn mowers **214–15**
Lawns **211–15**; and xeriscaping 44; cutting 215;
    fertilizing 194, 195, 213–14; maintaining 36;
    preparing for winter 13; seeding 212–13; sodding
    213; spring care of 5
Layering (to propagate) **208**
Lemna minor (duckweed) **60**
Lemon balm (*Melissa officinalis*) 33, **177**
Lemon verbena (*Aloysia triphylla*) **177**
Leontopodium spp. (edelweiss) 57, 106, **109**, 138
Leopard's bane (*Doronicum caucasicum*) *97,* **98**, 137
Lettuce 25, 27, 38, 52, **170**, 174
Levisticum officinale (lovage) **177**
Lewisia spp. (bitterroot, lewisia) 56, 106, **109**

Liatris spp. (blazing star, gayfeather) 23, 48, 49,
    109, 140
Lighting 39
Ligularia spp. (golden groundsel, ligularia) 47, *109,*
    109–10, 140
Lilac (*Syringa*) 25, 28, 33, 41, 43, 51, 75. *See also*
    Japanese tree lilac
Lilac leaf miner 220
Lilium spp. (lily) 26, 33, 41, 48, *53,* 54, **110–11**, *112,*
    139, 204. *See also* Daylily
Lily-of-the-valley (*Convallaria majalis*) 24, 26, 33,
    46, **96**, 103, 137
Limnanthes douglasii (fried egg plant, meadowfoam)
    146, 161
Limonium spp. (statice, sea lavender) 54, **111**
    (perennial), **154–55** (biennial), 159, 162
Linden, little-leaf (*Tillia cordata*) **69**
Linum spp. (flax) 32, 48, *57,* **111**, 139
Liverwort. *See* Hepatica
Livingstone daisy (*Mesembryanthemum*) **150**, 161
Lobelia erinus (lobelia) 27, 41, 47, 52, 147, **150**, *152,*
    154, 161
Lobularia maritima (sweet alyssum) 27, 33, 147,
    155, 162
Locoweed (*Oxytropis* spp.) 49
Lonicera spp. (honeysuckle) 24, 25, 33, 34, 35, 41, 47,
    51, **74–75** (shrub), **77–78** (vine), 138
Loosestrife, yellow (*Lysimachia punctata*) **112**
Loosestrife, purple (*Lythrum salicaria*) **125**, *125*
Lotus vine 27
Lovage (*Levisticum officinale*) **177**
Love-in-a-mist (*Nigella damascena*) 41, **150–51**,
    159, 161
Low-maintenance gardening 36–37, 38–39
Lungwort (*Pulmonaria* spp.) 45, **119**, 137
Lungwort, tall (*Mertensia paniculata*) **45**, 47
Lupinus spp. (lupins) 49, **111**
Lychnis spp. (campion, catchfly, lychnis, Maltese
    cross) *53,* **111–12**, 139
Lysimachia spp. (creeping Jenny, moneywort,
    loosestrife) *31,* 103, **112**, 139
Lythrum salicaria (lythrum, purple loosestrife)
    125, *125*

M

Macleaya cordata (macleaya, plume poppy) **112–13**
Maggots 220
Maidenhair fern (*Adiantum pedatum*) **128**
Male fern (*Dryopteris filix-mas*) **128**
Mallow. *See* Musk mallow; Prairie mallow; Scarlet
    mallow
Maltese cross (*Lychnis* spp.) *53,* **111–12**, 139
Malus spp. (apple, apple-crabs) 23, 25, 50, **53–54**, 71
Malus spp. (crabapple) 23, 25, 31, 33, 34, 35, 41, 50,
    53, 62, **67**, 68
Malva moschata (musk mallow) **113**, 139
Maple (*Acer* spp.) 25, 34, 35, 41, **66**, 69
Marigold (*Tagetes* spp.) *23,* 27, 41, 52, *53,* 150, 151,
    152, 161
Marjoram (*Origanum majorana*) **177**